CLASSICS
OF
SEA POWER

The Classics of Sea Power series makes key works of professional naval thought readily available in uniform, authoritative editions. Each book is chosen for its eloquence, incisiveness, and pertinence to the great ideas of naval theory, strategy, tactics, operations, and logistics. The series is a companion to histories, anthologies, and other interpretative writings, providing a depth of understanding that cannot be had from reading secondary sources alone.

Rear Admiral Bradley Allen Fiske is best known today as the junior officer who outfitted the new American navy of 1880–1900 with a series of remarkable inventions. But he was equally influential in transforming the strategic vision of Alfred Thayer Mahan and Stephen B. Luce into realistic operational doctrine under a practical new Navy Department organization. In addition, Fiske was one of the U.S. Navy's most prolific and lucid writers. Of Fiske's four books, *The Navy as a Fighting Machine* comes closest to being a synthesis of his wide-ranging, imaginative, and practical ideas on naval warfare. If ever a writer refuted the impression left by Mahan that enduring guidance from history is principally limited to the field of strategy, that writer was Fiske. His comprehensive treatment of all the elements of a navy as a single system—a fighting machine—is as fresh today as when he wrote it.

SERIES EDITORS

John B. Hattendorf
Naval War College
Newport, Rhode Island

Wayne P. Hughes, Jr.
Naval Postgraduate School
Monterey, California

The Navy
as a Fighting Machine

Rear Admiral Bradley A. Fiske (official U.S. Navy photograph)

REAR ADMIRAL BRADLEY A. FISKE,
U.S. NAVY

The Navy
as a
Fighting Machine

With an Introduction and Notes by
Wayne P. Hughes, Jr.

NAVAL INSTITUTE PRESS   Annapolis, Maryland

This book was originally published in 1916 by Charles Scribner's Sons, New York. Second edition published in 1918.

Introduction and notes copyright © 1988 by the United States Naval Institute, Annapolis, Maryland

Library of Congress Cataloging-in-Publication Data

Fiske, Bradley A. (Bradley Allen), 1854–1942.
    The Navy as a fighting machine / Bradley A. Fiske ; with an introduction and notes by Wayne P. Hughes, Jr.
        p.   cm.
    Reprint. 2nd ed. New York : Scribner's, 1918.
    Bibliography: p.
    Includes index.
    ISBN 0-87021-437-3
    1. Navies.   2. Naval art and science.   3. Naval strategy.
4. United States. Navy—Management.   I. Title.
V103.F4   1988
359—dc19   88-25330
                                                           CIP

Series design by Moira M. Megargee

Printed in the United States of America

CONTENTS

INTRODUCTION

B RADLEY ALLEN FISKE was the U.S. Navy's renaissance man. His contributions grew as the New Navy of 1880 grew, and the breadth of the intellectual base from which he drew his practical contributions was at least astonishing and perhaps unmatched in any navy. Fiske was an inventor who helped equip the new steel-hulled American fleet; a tactician of note in the golden age of tactical thinking; a translator of strategic vision into tough-minded plans to operate the navy in war; and a reformer of naval organization and policies on the eve of American entry into World War I.

Fiske thought of tactics like a modern operations analyst, and of naval operations as an integrated, unified system. His technical contributions to gunfire control exceeded Admiral William Sims's, and the practicality of his vision for military aviation put General Billy Mitchell's rhetoric in cool perspective.

But first and last Bradley Fiske was an operator: of ships' equipment, of ships, and of fleet formations. He fought under Admiral George Dewey at Manila Bay in 1898. He was as bold and innovative at sea as he had been in patenting inventions, taking, for example, his division of 15,000-ton armored cruisers into Key West in January 1912, the first officer who had dared to bring capital ships through that narrow channel. His life was dedicated to the combat readiness and operating efficiency of the American navy. Everything he did was measured against that end.

"I wish to draw your attention," he said to an audience at the Naval War College on 11 September 1919, "to the fact that the whole art of war consists in directing the employment of weapons." The statement was his watchword. First and last he was a naval tactician. A tactician, he believed, was devoted not only to better handling of weapons in combat, but to better peacetime preparation than the enemy through training and close association with the development of first-rate weapon systems.

After the fashion of every leader, Bradley Fiske communicated. People listened to him, whether they were technically or operationally oriented, whether progressive or conservative, and whether in the navy or outside it. He wrote six books on subjects ranging from electrical engineering to naval policy. He published sixty-two substantial essays and shorter commentaries. From 1911 to 1923 he was president of the U.S. Naval Institute, longer than any other man.

Fiske wrote as a pragmatist, a man who believed in the scientific basis of both human and mechanical activity, but who saw theory as the roots, verification through empirical evidence as the trunk, and sound practice as the fruits of the branches. Fiske wanted not only to nurture the plant but to harvest the fruit.

Bradley A. Fiske was born on 13 June 1854 along the Mohawk trail in upstate New York. He was admitted to the U.S. Naval Academy in the fall of 1870 and graduated with the Class of 1874. He married Josephine Harper of New York City in 1882.

Fiske was commissioned when the U.S. Navy was at its low ebb following the Civil War. Being inquisitive, creative, and bored with the naval routine of long peacetime cruises, at the age of twenty-two he returned to a teenage love of inventing.

In the Old Navy there was not much to work with, but an industrial revolution was under way, and Fiske was drawn to its possibilities. From a four-month course at the Naval Torpedo Station, Newport, Rhode Island, he acquired a lifelong interest in torpedoes, in due course translating interest to action with the first proposal and patent of an aerial torpedo. Owing to a series of letters to the Bureaus of Ordnance and Equipment with ideas good and bad, his name soon became known in the navy's tight little technical community. Eventually, about 1905, he would become disillusioned with the bureau system and urge reform, but for twenty years starting in 1878 he delivered his innovations by working within the system. Watching the effective synergism between his creative young mind and the cautious leadership of the technical bureaus convinces one that the bureaus of his day were not wholly hidebound. With the encouragement of the engineering community within the navy and friends prominent in the industrial community outside of it, Fiske invented and stayed abreast of the latest scientific engineering state of the art, and did so without sacrificing his reputation as a seagoing naval officer.

The following vignette from Fiske's autobiography[1] puts the early days of his career in perspective. In 1882, when Fiske was twenty-eight, the invention of electric light and the telephone piqued his interest in electricity. With the encouragement of an early mentor, Park Benjamin, he applied for a six-month leave to study it. There were no curricula in electrical engineering then; Fiske would be studying on his own. Happily, the assistant chief of the Bureau of Navigation was Bowman H. McCalla, who had been executive officer of the *Powhatan* when Fiske was a junior officer. McCalla recalled Fiske well as a free spirit with a flair for creative thinking. He

---

1. *From Midshipman to Rear Admiral* (New York: Century Co., 1919; British edition, London: T. Werner Laurie, Ltd.).

took up Fiske's request with his chief, the able and progressive Commodore John G. Walker. Walker said, "Tell Fiske that six months isn't enough, tell him to take a year." Fiske did, and was soon at his studies, during which time he had his first technical article published, sold his first patent, and began writing a textbook on electricity to bridge the gap between pure electrical theory and simple manuals to guide the construction of machinery and equipment. The book appeared in 1887, went through ten printings, and sold for twenty-two years.[2]

Thus Fiske was well positioned to contribute to the New Navy that was abuilding. His astonishing inventions and engineering achievements are what he is best remembered for today. It would take a book to record them and the full story of the influence of Fiske on the fighting quality, operational efficiency, and—no small matter—habitability of the New Navy. But a brief summary shows how Fiske married a rational, practical, utilitarian orientation with a proclivity to invent and engineer based on scientific principles. Later in life he used the perspectives of his early experience to solve problems of tactics and fleet operations.

Between 1878 and 1896 he produced a detaching device for quick release of a ship's boat launched from alongside in a seaway; an electric log to measure speed through the water; an electric depth-sounding machine; the flashing signal light for inter-ship communication; a more efficient electrical insulator; the stadimeter that we still use today for measuring range between ships; electric drive for turrets; electric gears with the power to move major caliber guns in elevation fast enough for continuous-aim fire; the first electric shell and ammunition hoists, which made big guns practical; a machine gun operated on compressed air; an electrically driven

2. *Electricity in Theory and Practice; or, The Elements of Electrical Engineering* (New York: D. Van Nostrand, 1887).

steering motor; a telescopic sight for both recoiling and non-recoiling guns; a gunnery range finder; an electric remote range transmitter to centralize range-finding high in the ship; the engine order telegraph; the rudder angle indicator; a speed and direction indicator; a steering telegraph to make control from steering aft swift and reliable; and an electrical semaphore system. He adapted telephones for shipboard use, experimented with ship-to-ship wireless radio communications, and urged—probably for the first time and certainly before Sims did—a central shipboard gunfire control station aloft that would permit continuous-aim salvo fire.

Fiske forever thought in terms of systems that integrated disparate parts. In fact, it is apparent that he started with a vision of a combat system that integrated separate parts into a unified whole, and when the parts did not exist he created them. His inventions virtually outfitted the bridge of the American warships that fought in the world wars. For efficient gunfire control he developed the telescopic sight and improved range-finders; he linked a fire-control station aloft to a below-deck central plotting room with range-keepers, which transmitted gun orders to the turrets for effective salvo fire; and he created the electrical communications to tie all stations together. Surely the cost of a year of postgraduate study was never better spent by the U.S. Navy than on Bradley A. Fiske.

Fiske believed in the scientific process, but for his purposes experimental science was king. The development of the laws of physics was for others, like his fellow Naval Academy graduate A. A. Michelson. For Fiske science dealt with understanding and applying fundamental laws to hypothesize utilitarian machinery, principally electrical and optical, all of which could be built and tested. Later he carried his bent for experimentation over into the realm of strategy and tactics. He did not take a historical approach, like Mahan and Luce. He did not structure a coherent system of thought, like Jomini,

Corbett, and, later, J. F. C. Fuller. He thought of his own works as Clausewitz thought of his: "There is no need today to labor the point that a scientific approach does not consist solely, or even mainly, in a complete system and a comprehensive doctrine. In the formal sense the present work [*On War*] contains no such system. . . . Its scientific character consists in an attempt to investigate the essence of the phenomena of war. . . . No logical conclusion has been avoided; but whenever the thread became too thin I have preferred to break it off and go back to the relevant phenomenon of experience. . . . in the practical arts the leaves and flowers of theory must be pruned and the plant kept close to its proper soil— experience."[3] Clausewitz knew war better than Fiske and wrote better about it. Fiske knew machinery better than Clausewitz and wrote well about what he understood well: the navy as a fighting machine.

For the first fifteen years of the new steel navy the bulk of its intellectual energy was expended on the creation of better ships, with Fiske contributing heavily. Meanwhile at the Naval War College, in Newport, Rhode Island, Stephen B. Luce and his protégé, Alfred Thayer Mahan, were developing a maritime philosophy which in an amazingly short time became the mantra of navies and nations, including our own. Seen to be a comer in the navy, Fiske was plucked from the pack and brought to the war college in 1896 by the president, his former Naval Academy instructor, Captain Henry C. Taylor.

Fiske's Naval War College experience was the springboard into the second phase of his career. "Taylor," wrote Fiske in his autobiography, "carried out in his own studies and practiced the principles I have tried to indicate, and he became, after Admiral Luce, our navy's principal guide in strategy.

3. Carl von Clausewitz, *On War*, edited and translated by Michael Howard and Peter Paret (Princeton, N.J.: Princeton University Press, 1976), page 61.

While all the navies owe an enormous debt to Admiral Mahan
. . . our own navy owes more to Admiral Luce and Admiral
Taylor than anybody else for determining and demonstrating
the direction in which the development of our navy should
be prosecuted, and then insisting that that direction be
followed."[4]

Rear Admiral Stephen B. Luce cast the longest shadow.
Years later Fiske dedicated his autobiography to Luce, "who
saw the light before others saw it, and led the navies toward
it." When Luce died in 1917, Fiske, as president of the Naval
Institute, reserved for himself the honor of writing "An Appreciation" of Luce in the organization's *Proceedings*. "Luce
taught the navy to think about the navy as a whole," wrote
Fiske. "He realized more clearly than any man before him . . .
that a navy is no more a collection of parts than an orchestra
is a collection of musicians. . . . Luce saw strategy as clearly
as most of us see a material object. It first appeared to him, as
he often stated, after a brief interview with General Sherman,
shortly before the fall of Savannah in our Civil War. Scales
seemed suddenly to fall from before his mental eyes," and
Luce spent the rest of his life giving the navy his vision, by
the creation of the U.S. Naval Institute and by championing
the Naval War College. "But was not the establishment of the
college," asked Fiske rhetorically, "merely an incident, and is
not the college itself merely a heap of stones, in comparison
with the thought which Luce finally planted in the mind of
the navy, and with the spirit which he put into its heart? The
agency which introduced the thought was the mind of Luce,
and the agency which infused the spirit was the spirit of Luce:
as between the two, the spirit was the finer."[5]

Luce and Taylor were the U.S. Navy's two most effective

4. Autobiography, page 67.
5. "Stephen B. Luce: An Appreciation," U.S. Naval Institute *Proceedings,* September 1917, pages 1935–1940.

exponents of a naval staff. But the bureau chiefs suspected any derogation of their powers, so in 1896, the year Fiske arrived, Taylor "employed the War College curriculum as a means of not only educating naval officers in theory, but demonstrating to them, in both hypothetical and actual situations, the functions of a general staff."[6] The problem was that the U.S. Navy was a mere collection of ships, rather than a coherent fighting force—musicians rather than an orchestra. By the time he left Newport, Fiske had become one of the reformers (among them Taylor, Sims, William Fullam, and Homer Poundstone) who wanted to see stronger central direction and better war planning.

To Fiske, Mahan had supplied the laws under which plans should be developed (see pages 49–50). What was needed was an organization that would apply the laws to effect pragmatic plans: a brain to control the muscles of the fighting machine. His solution was a staff with more authority than the purely advisory General Board that had been created in 1900. His model was the German General Staff. Part of his book consists of a rationale for central planning by career officers of the highest qualifications (a need long since met). The bulk of the book is a description of the navy as a fighting machine comprising elements that should be drawn together into a *system,* united for war. This is a timeless need that Fiske describes in a timeless way, even though he was very specific about the concrete steps to take in his own time with his own navy.

Fiske's opening salvo in the battle for reform was his Naval Institute prize-winning essay of 1905. Although it was entitled "American Naval Policy," within its eighty pages Fiske covered policy, strategy, operations, and tactics, and made

6. John B. Hattendorf, B. Mitchell Simpson, III, and John R. Wadleigh, *Sailors and Scholars: The Centennial History of the U.S. Naval War College* (Newport, RI: Naval War College Press, 1984), page 45.

unequivocal his belief that the design and construction of warships was to be guided by the officers who would fight them and the tactics they expected to use in combat. Fiske, of course, was the supreme practitioner of what he preached, and passed over rather too lightly the problem of educating officers in science and engineering to the extent required to execute this common-sense objective without detracting from their development at sea.

Close on the heels of "Naval Policy" came "The Naval Profession" in 1907, which contains his first ruminations about the navy as a fighting machine. His next major discourse on strategy and tactics was in 1911. Found amidst an outpouring of articles on fire control, tactics, and navigation, it was entitled "Naval Power," and was a fifty-three-page essay, much of which he incorporated into this book.

By now in his fifties, Fiske found sea duty, with the satisfactions of command, more appealing than in his junior officer days. He also exploited command as the best way to test his innovations, particularly with respect to fire control and maneuvering. He was commanding officer of the protected cruiser *Minneapolis,* and then, at the time of his promotion to captain in 1907, the monitor *Arkansas.* From 1908 to 1910 he commanded the armored cruiser *Tennessee.*

Immediately thereafter, as a member of the General Board in the winter of 1910–1911, Fiske proposed the use of "at least 100" airplanes for the defense of the Philippines. Fiske says he was scolded by the aid (*sic*) for operations, Richard Wainwright, for taking up its time with "wild-cat schemes," but *"I think this was the first proposal for using aeroplanes for major operations"* (Fiske's italics).[7] Fiske *wanted* to be remembered as an innovator. But with his writings, his inventions, and his urging of organizational measures to develop naval aviation, he forcefully identified himself as a

7. Autobiography, page 481.

pragmatic advocate of air power long before the technology had matured to translate vision into reality.

Fiske was promoted to rear admiral in the fall of 1911, the same year he was elected president of the U.S. Naval Institute. He took command of a four-ship armored cruiser squadron, with the USS *Washington* as his flagship. The following spring he was given the Third Battleship Division, Atlantic Fleet. A month later, when his command, temporarily eight battleships, was at Salem, Massachusetts, he spotted a seaplane on the water, waved it over to his flagship, and without much difficulty got the two young pilots to take him for a ride. In his autobiography (pp. 507–10) he takes great delight in describing the thrill of it. The year was 1912, the same year he patented plans for an air-launched torpedo. While he continued to champion naval aviation, he was also thinking about fleet combat readiness. In November 1912 he wrote a comprehensive approach to fleet tactics, so straightforward and realistic that it has been incorporated as Appendix A, to illustrate his penchant for structure, profound simplicity, and clarity of objective. His comments on fleet speed and the payoff that would accrue from operating the whole fleet exactly as it would deploy for battle seem as pertinent today as then.

In 1913 Fiske entered the third phase of his career, and found himself with a chance to promote what he and his fellow reformers believed in: the establishment of better plans for the operation of the fleet in war. As one of his last acts, Secretary of the Navy George Meyer made Fiske his aid for operations. But Meyer was a lame duck, and less than two months later was replaced by Josephus Daniels in President Woodrow Wilson's cabinet. Daniels had dogmatic attitudes about the ascendancy of civilian control, and Fiske found out in short order the difference between knowing what needs to be done and doing it in Washington. Daniels was soon dismantling the modest means then in place for military planning. Admiral Sims had seen the struggle to come and thought Fiske was not up to it. Right after Fiske took office, Sims confided in Fullam, the new aid for inspections, that he would have to carry on the fight for reform because Fiske "is constitutionally opposed to conflict of any kind." Sims was right about Fiske's temperament, but wrong about Fiske's determination, and would have to admit as much later.[8] The vigor with which Fiske pleads the case for adequate policy and planning in *The Navy as a Fighting Machine* without ever personalizing the arguments is indicative of his faith in the ultimate power of reason. Even when it came to writing his autobiography, he had to be persuaded by his publisher to include his frustrations under Daniels.

But Fiske was not above a Machiavellian stroke. In January 1915, without Daniels's knowledge, Fiske and a few assistants met in a midnight tryst with Congressman Richmond P. Hobson (who as a navy lieutenant had tried to block Santiago Harbor by blowing up the collier *Merrimac* in the narrow neck of the entrance). With the consent of only the navy's grand old man, Admiral George Dewey, from that meeting came the legislation that established the position of chief of naval operations (CNO). Although for the time being Daniels was able to reduce the power of the office as its originators conceived it, the legalization of the post and the staff by statute marked the turning point of the insurgents' battle. That sanction, along with its obvious practicality after the United States entered World War I, assured the growth of the uniformed influence that Luce, Taylor, Fiske, and the other progressives knew to be essential for professional planning.

It has been suggested that Fiske's insubordinate act cost him the honor of being the first CNO, or the privilege he valued yet more highly of commanding the fleet. Neither was

8. Paolo E. Coletta, *Admiral Bradley A. Fiske and the American Navy* (Lawrence, Kansas: the Regents Press of Kansas, 1979), page 103.

likely. Daniels and Fiske were simply too far apart. Civilian control versus professional leadership was at the philosophical heart of their quarrel. But that need not have interfered with Fiske's more pragmatic pleas to man the fleet properly, to build it up at a pace commensurate with his certain view that the U.S. would be drawn into the war in Europe, and to exercise the fleet as a unit instead of frittering away training time in what he saw as a sideshow of gunboat diplomacy in Central America. But Daniels was Wilson's loyal servant, and in 1915 Wilson's agenda was not the professional navy's. Daniels wanted an obedient assistant, and he found him in the person of the first chief of naval operations, William S. Benson. In Fiske's eyes, Daniels was "given absolute and uncontrolled power over a great machine he does not understand."[9]

Fiske was retired in June 1916, a year after leaving office as aid for operations. It was his sixty-second birthday. Despite his slight stature and suspicions since junior officer days about the robustness of his health, he lived until April 1942, dying shortly before his eighty-eighth birthday.

The output of Fiske's pen reached a climax in the five years immediately after his removal as aid. In the fall of 1915 and winter of 1916 the *North American Review* published five of his essays totaling seventy-four pages, despite efforts by Daniels to muzzle him as provocative.[10] In 1916 *The Navy as a Fighting Machine* was published. It sold well enough for a 1918 edition, which adds a longer preface but otherwise is largely unchanged. (It is this second, 1918 edition that has been chosen for the Classics of Sea Power series.) In 1919 ap-

9. Coletta, page 233.
10. "The Mastery of the World," October 1915, pages 517–526. "Naval Principles," November 1915, pages 693–701. "Naval Preparedness," December 1915, pages 847–857. "Naval Policy," January 1916, pages 63–73. "Naval Defense," February 1916, pages 216–226. "Naval Strategy," March–April 1916, pages 387–408.

peared his oft-quoted autobiography, *From Midshipman to Rear Admiral.* In 1920 followed *The Art of Fighting: Its Evolution and Progress,*[11] and in 1922, *Invention: The Master-Key to Progress.*[12]

Among his peers Fiske retained widespread respect and affection. Partly this was due to his temperament as a direct yet cooperative man, partly it was because his inventions were seen to work and to be useful, and partly it was because he had the breadth to adapt to the navy's needs as it grew. He helped first when the navy needed to build effective new warships, again when it needed to organize and operate as a fighting fleet, and again when it struggled to establish policy and plans to guide its exercises and preparations for war. He must have been a delight to work for, barring the extra demands that grew out of an irrepressible urge to innovate and experiment wherever he went.

What kind of subordinate was Fiske? As a junior officer in the wardroom he would have been like the Thoroughbred in the stable: when you saddled him up, you were in for a fast ride. This was already evident when he was a midshipman. He thought he would have stood first rather than second in his class of thirty graduates if he had enjoyed himself less, for he accumulated two hundred demerits, was stripped of rank in his first class year for cavorting within sight of the superintendent, and finished his last month at the Naval Academy under restriction. He also acquired a number of black eyes, one of which came in a fight he recalled mischievously in his autobiography. Fiske took affront at a command from an upperclassman, a midshipman notorious for being brilliant, relaxed academically, and formidable at fencing and boxing. Fiske challenged the offender, who accepted with too much

11. *The Art of Fighting: Its Evolution and Progress, with Illustrations from Campaigns of Great Commanders* (New York: Century Co., 1920).

12. *Invention: The Master-Key to Progress* (New York: E. P. Dutton and Co., 1922).

pleasure. Under arrangements of which "the details took more time than did the fight itself," he ended up on the sick list with eight days' worth of damage to his slight, 125-pound body. His more proficient opponent was A. A. Michelson.

The Navy as a Fighting Machine was written at the height of Fiske's powers and influence. It was put together in the short time between when Admiral Fiske left as Daniels's aid on 12 May 1915 and when the preface to the first edition was written on 13 September 1916. After some tidying up in Washington, he was sent by Daniels to the Naval War College, where he was given a room with a desk. He rushed into print the aforementioned series of articles for the *North American Review*. Slightly modified, five articles from the series are incorporated in his book as Chapters I, II, IV, V, and VI.

For reasons both substantive and political, his articles received a wide audience and a favorable press. Fiske's main object was to draw attention to the fleet's unreadiness, which more and more baldly he lay at the door of the secretary of the navy. He was drawn back to Washington for a series of congressional hearings on preparedness. Meanwhile the health of his wife, Jo, was failing, and she became a major burden on his time and mind. Somehow in the midst of all this he wrote *Fighting Machine*. The first edition appeared in mid-October 1916.

Both the national and the international press gave the book highly positive reviews. The American press was critical of the Democratic administration, in the main supporting readiness for war, and so was naturally sympathetic. Though Wilson himself was by then urging a naval buildup, most of the resistance lay in his own party. The *New York Times Magazine* of 5 November 1916 featured the book in a lengthy, illustrated article which picked up on Fiske's enthusiasm for war-gaming as a tool of strategic planning. Quoting no less than twenty-nine paragraphs from the book in their entirety, the article supported Fiske along the lines that "the navy is far behind the times, the Admiral declares," and "our strategy lags behind [that of the other navies of the world]."

On 15 February 1917 the London *Times Literary Supplement* devoted two long columns to the book. Since Great Britain was deep in war and the United States was not, an enthusiastic review was natural: the lead sentence is "This vigorous and suggestive volume will be read with peculiar interest by all students of naval warfare in this country, because it represents with exceptional authority the spirit and temper of a navy which has many close affinities with our own." The review picks up that "the gallant Admiral is an out and out anti-pacifist" who "argues at length that war has been so constant a feature in the history of mankind . . . so destructive a scourge to those nations which have neglected due preparations for its coming, that it might almost be thought to be an ordinance of Nature itself for the . . . chastening and final overthrow of each nation that has in the past attained greatness and lost it." This is the side of *Fighting Machine* that would naturally be emphasized in contemporary journals. But the qualities that set the book apart as a classic lie elsewhere.

Fiske wanted to show that the navy had to be designed and operated as a whole, like a well-functioning piece of machinery. His audience was anyone in favor of naval preparedness, and his aim was to give them perspective, as well as to make some cogent arguments for strengthening the role of uniformed naval leadership. The sources of his quickly assembled chapters were his past writings. The book is in a sense an anthology of Fiske, selected by Fiske. Therefore its continuity is poor, with gems of insight sparkling awkwardly apart from their chapter settings.

Fiske had no time for theory as a comprehensive and self-consistent structure. He thought in terms of things that changed and things that remained constant, and throughout his life he picked them out and wrote them down, but he wrote about things that mattered in the here and now of his own culture. There were two reasons. One was that he was a top-drawer, practicing, seagoing naval officer, who understood teamwork, believed in it, and knew his milieu as *practical*. To communicate with officers you had to speak their language, which was splashed with saltwater. The other reason was that Fiske was part engineer. Even a naval officer who regards himself as tough-minded indulges in ill-defined concepts like courage, will power, and leadership, and claims these abstract virtues as important and as his own. An engineer is allowed no such wavings of the hand. A thing he builds works well, works badly, or doesn't work. There is room for argument over the efficacy of his machine, but a machine is tangible, its output measurable, and catastrophic failure of it is obvious. Engineers see the world in concrete terms.

But Fiske was not only an engineer. He was an inventor, which was a term far more common then for what we would probably now call a scientist. Fiske himself knew the difference between engineers and scientists, and describes it neatly, on pages 178–179. Inventors are men of imagination, and it took imagination to conceive of a navy as a fighting machine, all the more so because Fiske did not have that modern paradigm, "a systems approach," to draw on. His fighting machine is a fighting system, described not at the micro (weapon system) level, but as a macro system, complete, integrated, and unified in its naval purpose.

He describes the elements of his fighting system as elements of strategy, but he makes only a few contributions to strategic thinking. Like most naval leaders of the world, Fiske wrote while under the spell of Mahan and his doctrines of sea power. Fiske shared the belief of his contemporaries in the primacy of sea power, and correctly saw the battle line as its instrument—the very muscle of the fighting machine—to gain command of the sea. But the strategic thought of this book is not undistilled Mahan. Chapter III is original, creative Fiske, and it is there that he recognizes the primacy of military decisions on the land, and where after some tortured exposition he comes to the original, striking, but fundamentally sound conclusion for his time that the primary purpose of the American naval fighting machine is to prevent a blockade. (Page 73.)

Not strategy but operations is the realm of *Fighting Machine*. Fiske deals with strategic operations (or campaigns) and combat operations (or tactics). He writes about the activities that implement strategy: operations at sea, war plans, pointed training, hardware designed to fight effectively, an effective reserve, a mobilization base, and logistical support that energizes seagoing forces in wartime. He sees the art of operating a fleet as a special skill, unappreciated outside the navy officer corps, and time-consuming and expensive.

The exposition of the naval operational art is the first characteristic that sets this book apart. Even though its intended audience is now seventy years in the past and Fiske had little concern over timelessness, and even though the book is in places a hodgepodge, still when it comes to structuring, defining, and measuring the elements that encompass the operations of a naval fighting machine, the book is remarkable for its modern insights. In fact, it is hard to think of an American book since World War II so catholic in its treatment of naval operations.

The second characteristic that sets apart this book and the mind behind it is a scientific outlook toward battle tactics. Fiske was in fact the American navy's prototype operations analyst, that is to say a man who believed the way to prepare the fleet to fight better was through quantitative thinking, descriptions of combat dynamics with models, and ceaseless exercises of the fleet, war games when the fleet was not at sea, and mathematical analyses to test the tactical and operational hypotheses that flowed from his fertile mind and which he grasped in the ideas of others. We must be careful not to overstate Fiske's genius relative to other tactical thinkers of his day, for Fiske was following on the heels of a golden age of tactical thought, and he was able to draw from the writings of men like Romeo Bernotti of Italy, Gabriel Darrieus and Ambroise Baudry of France, S. O. Makarov of Russia, and Americans like William Bainbridge-Hoff, Philip R. Alger, J. V. Chase, and William S. Sims. Most of his contemporaries thought quantitatively about tactics and gunnery effectiveness with mathematical models, even though they did not have the vocabulary to call their dynamic representations of gunfire and maneuver by that term. All but Alger were naval officers, and he was redoubtable at the Naval Academy as "Professor of Mathematics, U.S. Navy." Fiske himself might not have wanted to be set above these thinkers in the science of warfare, but he was unique as an analyst who could see operational, tactical, and technological problems all of a piece and work out solutions from a comprehensive, *Fighting Machine* perspective.

When Fiske found a need, he offered sharp insights on problems that have been quicksand for all but the deepest military philosophers. He lived in the last days of belief in rationalism, when physical science still yearned for the old deterministic universe that was being destroyed by new theories like relativity and quantum mechanics. Still to come were modern concepts that are going to influence all science, including military science—the study of nonlinear dynamic processes that have led to chaos theory, catastrophe theory, and fractals; or the modeling of stochastic processes with computer simulations. It is remarkable that his insights remain remarkably fresh, deep, trenchant, and above all communicative on some deep matters of the natural philosophy of warfare, including its art, science, and intangible mystique.

Here are a few:

- On the nature of armed force (pages 302–304) and naval power (page 52).
- On uncertainty and chance (pages 181–182).
- On the differences between forces, the combat potential of forces, and force itself applied in action against an enemy (pages 188–189 and 334–335).
- On war as art and war as science (page 147).
- On the concept of "effective skill" and its measurement (pages 337–339).
- On the logic of what in modern coin is sometimes called "moving inside the enemy's decision cycle" (page 158).
- On the uses and limits of war games and other models of warfare (pages 136–137).
- On the primacy of domination as the aim of military force (page 17). But Fiske also believed that the tactical aim of *naval combat* is straightforward attrition.
- On the ascendant roles of scouting and screening (pages 326–328).
- Why naval officers must be analysts of operations (page 190).
- Why the square law of attrition works as it does (pages 240–244).
- Why skilled warriors fight metaphorically and sometimes literally at long range (page 190), and incident thereto, why weapons will never be as effective in war as they appear to be in peace.
- Why at sea strategic defense entails a tactical offense (pages 42 and 107).

Fiske tended to write in blacks and whites. One is reminded of Harry Truman's blunt style and U. S. Grant's simple eloquence. But his pointed statements are not often overstatements, and only rarely does one feel a need to insert hedges or caveats against his bold and unequivocal positions. Bradley Fiske's rare combination of action and reflection was unmatched among naval officers of his day. He never lost the confidence of his fellow officers, even while he expressed the most comprehensive and original of ideas and invented machinery of war at the outer limits of creativity. Perhaps it was his plain-spokenness, as refreshing now as then, and as worthy of emulation. We see this in the preface to the first edition of *The Navy as a Fighting Machine*, which consists of only forty-nine words.

WAYNE P. HUGHES, JR.

The Navy
as a Fighting Machine

PREFACE TO THE SECOND EDITION

T HE FLATTERING RECEPTION given to this book, and the fact that the Conference Committee on Preparedness presented each United States Senator and Representative with a copy, give reason to feel that our people are beginning to see that the navy is important.

If the navy is important, then it is important that the people should not only support it but support it intelligently. They cannot support it intelligently unless they have clear and correct ideas about it. Like every other activity which affects the well-being of the public, such as the railroads, the press, the theatre, etc., the service given by it will be good or bad largely in proportion to the degree of knowledge of the public as to what constitutes good and bad service. If the people had no knowledge as to what constitutes good or bad railroad service the railroad service would be bad.

For this reason books like this, which set forth the simple strategical principles that govern the design, preparation, and operation of navies, have an educational value. This value, furthermore, is going to increase; because the progress of civilization and the development of new inventions are going to put an increasing number of ships out on the highway of the ocean, where no supreme law reigns, from which the chance of war is never wholly absent, and where, in time of war, the

1

commerce of each nation will have only the protection which its navy gives.

At least ninety-nine per cent of the reviews of the book, in both the United States and England, have been favorable. Only two mistakes have been pointed out. One mistake was the statement that no man had ever attained great excellence in the naval profession who entered it late in life. That I should have forgotten that Robert Blake had been a soldier, and a distinguished one, before he entered the navy, is surprising. The other mistake was the statement that the Chief of Staff of the Japanese Navy was under the Minister of Marine. Since the book appeared I have been informed by competent authority that the Chief of the General Staff of the Japanese Navy is in the same position, relatively, to the Emperor and the Minister of Marine, as is the Chief of Staff of the German Navy—that he, like the Minister of Marine, reports to the Emperor only.

The rapid changes in instruments and methods of war have been urged against the doctrine that the principles of strategy do not change; but it is merely necessary to remind the reader that the countless new mechanisms that have been developed have not altered in the slightest degree the principles of mechanics. New methods and mechanisms of all kinds are subordinate to principles; the principles are not subordinate to them, or in the least affected by them. The same principles guided Alexander when he conquered the ten richest countries in the world as guided Nelson in his contest with Villeneuve and as guide the infant aeronautic squadrons now in the strategy of the air.

Since the book was written the British Admiralty has undergone a considerable change, according to statements made in the public press, in that it has established a General Staff, in which the Chief of Staff will be free from administrative responsibilities, and able to devote most of his time to planning. This would seem to indicate that the British Admiralty is following the same idea as has governed the German and Japanese navies, and is recognizing the fact that *every undertaking of men proceeds (or should proceed) by three successive stages:*

First (and most important), planning to do, which, in military and naval life, is the task of "strategy";

Second, securing the supplies, equipments and munitions wherewith to do, which is the task of "logistics";[1]

Third, doing, which is the task of "tactics."

The course of the book, in both plan and detail, follows the lines of orthodox strategy, except in one particular, and that is that it assumes as a fact the suggestion which I made in an essay called "Naval Power," in 1907, to the effect that naval

---

1. For many years in Europe and more recently in this country, the direction of activities that fall between strategy and tactics has been called "operational art." Much of what Fiske calls strategy, especially in Part II of this book, consists of guidance in the conduct of operations (other than in combat itself) that implement strategy, which is a plan with a goal. Campaign operations are operational art in action. The term *operational art* is confusing because there are other kinds of military operations. It is awkward to allow operational art to coopt the highly utilitarian word *operations,* and the U.S. Navy has resisted doing so. Nevertheless, the Operations Plan in the American naval planning process is literally the product of operational art, and there are distinct skills associated with conducting an effective campaign that a superb strategist may not have. Churchill's strategic insight and operational meddling come to mind. Nimitz was nearly the ideal operational "artist," as exhibited by the manner in which he executed the strategic objectives directed by King and the Joint Staff. To further muddy the waters, logistics is a separate art/science, but logistics is one of the dominant considerations in "campaigning," that is, what Nimitz did effectively. Whether or not one adopts the term *operational art,* the function is distinct from strategizing, as are the skills associated with it. These skills tend to be those of officers in uniform, which is what Fiske sees and will repeatedly emphasize, though his vocabulary prohibits him from distinguishing the function.

power is essentially mechanical power, so harnessed that it can be transported across the sea and exerted on the sea.[2]

Although the idea that naval power is essentially mechanical power was ridiculed in 1907, it has never been seriously challenged, even in the numerous reviews of this book. For this reason I feel warranted in believing that it has finally been accepted, and with it the fact that a navy is an actual fighting machine, which should be designed, prepared, and operated according to the principles which govern fighting— the principles of strategy. I trust that I am correct in believing that the idea has been accepted; because it removes naval power at once from the vague position it has occupied hitherto, and puts it before us as a concrete thing: it places navies in a definite class among the activities of men, and enables every one to comprehend, in general, the principles which should govern the design, preparation, and operation of a navy.

I was led to a perception of the mechanical nature of naval power by my experiences in inventing and developing naval appliances during nearly forty years; and by realizing that nearly all the radically new naval appliances introduced into service during the past thirty years had been my own inventions, or based directly on them; that these inventions had multiplied the power of navies many times; that they had done it by multiplying the amount of destruction which any ship or navy could accomplish; that the amount of destruction which any ship or navy could accomplish was essentially mechanical; that the agencies by which this destruction was accomplished were also essentially mechanical; and that,

2. Fiske refers to "The Naval Profession," U.S. Naval Institute *Proceedings*, June 1907, pp. 475–578. The development is found on pp. 499–501. Fiske later amplified the concept in "Naval Power," published in the *Proceedings* in September 1911 (pp. 683–736). The latter essay won Honorable Mention in the Naval Institute's competition that year. Fiske draws on these two essays to describe naval power in Chapter III.

therefore, whatever increase of naval power these inventions had brought about could not have been brought about unless naval power itself were essentially mechanical.

It was not a long mental leap from this to realize that any agency whose main effort was mechanical, and whose principal instrumentalities were machines, must itself be a machine—not in the loose sense in which the word machine has often been employed, but according to a meaning which that very useful word has had for more than two thousand years, not only in the English language but in the Greek and Latin languages from which it was derived. Although the word machine has usually been applied to an arrangement of parts which are inanimate, yet both ancient and modern dictionaries contain many definitions in which the word machine is applied to arrangements of parts which are not inanimate but animate. One definition in the Standard Dictionary, for instance, is "The organization of the powers of any complex body"; and one by Webster is "Any person or organization that acts . . . through a machine-like distribution of functions." These definitions and many others show that, while the word machine is usually applied to arrangements of inanimate parts, a machine may nevertheless be composed of parts that are highly animate: in fact, Huxley says: "The human body, like all living bodies, is a *machine,* all the operations of which will sooner or later be explained on physical principles."[3]

3. Thomas H. Huxley (1825–1895), prominent English biologist and essayist. Huxley was said to have transferred an early interest in mechanical engineering to the study of living machines. His unremitting scientific rigor, advocacy of scientific education, and belief in reason made him the kind of intellectual lighthouse by which Fiske would naturally chart his course. Huxley believed "that social phenomena are as much the expression of natural laws as any others; that no social arrangements can be permanent unless they harmonize with the requirements of social statics and dynamics; and that, in the nature of things, there is an arbiter whose

Looking at a machine in this way, and picturing to ourselves all that a fighting machine should be, we realize that the highest type of fighting machine we know of is man himself. So fine a fighting machine is man, so wonderful is his co-ordination of eye and brain and lungs and will and muscle, so much interest has he always taken in fighting, and so great an influence on his history has fighting had, that we come inevitably to the thought that possibly it was within the intentions of the Almighty that men should fight!

Now a navy is essentially an organization of men, equipped with certain tools, or weapons, fitted for fighting on the sea, made into a machine so designed and prepared that it can be operated efficiently against a similar machine brought forward by an enemy. When two machines meet in war the best machine must win. Human beings may not know which one will win, but that is simply because they do not know, in advance of trial, which is the best machine. It is desirable for us, therefore, to produce the best machine we can.

How shall we do this? For answer, the reader is respectfully commended to the Preface to the First Edition and to the book itself.

Inasmuch as armies are guided by strategy as much as navies are, inasmuch as the operations of armies are essentially like those of navies, except that they are carried out on land instead of on the water, and therefore use weapons and means of transportation which are adapted to the land and not the sea, all the principles expounded in this book apply to

---

decisions execute themselves" (from his essay "Science and Culture," originally an address given at the opening of Macon College, now the University of Birmingham, 1880). These words describe Fiske's point of view, but Huxley would have thought Fiske excessive in the extent to which he likened military power to mechanical power, and smacking of materialism that Huxley rejected.

armies as well as navies; so that if such words as "ships" were replaced by such words as "camps," "naval" by "military," "cruises" by "marches," "admiral" by "general," etc., the book, without many other changes, might be published under the name "The Army as a Fighting Machine." Even under the present name, however, and without the changes indicated, the obvious bearing of its arguments on army questions may make it interesting to people interested in the army.

The book was written to show the necessity of preparing for war and conducting war according to the principles of strategy; for, while "money is the sinews of war," *strategy is the brains of war.*

BRADLEY A. FISKE.

NEW YORK, February 13, 1918.

PREFACE TO FIRST EDITION

WHAT is the navy for?

Of what parts should it be composed?

What principles should be followed in designing, preparing, and operating it in order to get the maximum return for the money expended?

To answer these questions clearly and without technical language is the object of this book.

BRADLEY A. FISKE.

U.S. NAVAL WAR COLLEGE,
NEWPORT, R.I., September 3, 1916.

CONTENTS

11

PART ONE

GENERAL CONSIDERATIONS

CHAPTER ONE

WAR AND THE NATIONS

B ECAUSE the question is widely discussed, whether peace throughout the world may be attained by the friendly co-operation of many nations, and because a nation's attitude toward this question may determine its future prosperity or ruin, it may be well to note what has been the trend of the nations hitherto, and whether any forces exist that may reasonably be expected to change that trend. We may then be able to induce from facts the law which that trend obeys, and make a reasonable deduction as to whether or not the world is moving toward peace. If we do this we shall follow the inductive method of modern science, and avoid the error (with its perilous results) of first assuming the law and then deducing conclusions from it.[1]

Men have always been divided into organizations, the first organization being the family. As time went on families were formed into tribes, for self-protection. The underlying cause for the organization was always a desire for strength; sometimes for defense, sometimes for offense, usually for both.

At times tribes joined in alliance with other tribes to attain a common end, the alliance being brought about by peace-

---

1. As Mahan was sometimes accused of doing, specifically by interpreting history to rationalize his belief in the influence of sea power as the cornerstone of national power.

15

ful agreement, and usually ceasing after the end had been attained, or missed, or when tribal jealousies forbade further common effort. Sometimes tribes joined to form one larger tribe; the union being either forced on a weaker by a stronger tribe, or caused by a desire to secure a strength greater and more lasting than mere alliance can insure.

In the same way, and apparently according to similar laws, sovereign states or nations were formed from tribes; and in later years, by the union of separate states. The states or nations have become larger and larger as time has gone on; greater numbers, not only of people but of peoples, living in the same general localities and having hereditary ties, joining to form a nation.

Though the forms of government of these states or nations are numerous, and though the conceptions of people as to the purposes and functions of the state vary greatly, we find that one characteristic of a state has always prevailed among all the states and nations of the world—the existence of an armed military force, placed under the control of its government; the purpose of this armed force being to enable the government not only to carry on its administration of internal matters, but also to exert itself externally against the armed force of another state.

This armed force has been a prominent factor in the life of every sovereign state and independent tribe, from history's beginning, and is no less a factor now. No instance can be found of a sovereign state without its appropriate armed force, to guard its sovereignty and preserve that freedom from external control, without which freedom it ceases to exist as a sovereign state.

The armed force has always been a matter of very great expense. It has always required the anxious care of the government and the people. The men comprising it have always been subjected to restraint and discipline, compelled to undergo hardships and dangers greater than those of civil life, and developed by a training highly specialized and exacting.

The armed force in every state has had not only continuous existence always, but continuous, potential readiness, if not continuous employment; and the greatest changes in the mutual relations of nations have been brought about by the victory of the armed force of one state over the armed force of another state. This does not mean that the fundamental causes of the changes have been physical, for they have been psychological, and have been so profound and so complex as to defy analysis; but it does mean that the actual and immediate instrument producing the changes has been physical force; that physical force and physical courage acting in conjunction, of which conjunction war is the ultimate expression, have always been the most potent instruments in the dealings of nations with each other.[2]

Is there any change toward peaceful methods now?

No, on the contrary; war is recognized as the most potent method still; the prominence of military matters is greater than ever before; at no time in the past has interest in war been so keen as at the present, or the expenditure of blood and money been so prodigal; at no time before has war so thoroughly engaged the intellect and energy of mankind.

In other words, the trend of the nations has been toward a clearer recognition of the efficacy of military power, and an increasing use of the instrumentality of war.

This does not mean that the trend of the nations has been regular; for, on the contrary, it has been spasmodic. If one

2. Dealing with the debate over destruction or domination as the *strategic* purpose of armed forces, Fiske takes his stand for the primacy of domination. Force—expended in battle or as latent potential—is the means to dominate. Also observe the first indication that he conceives of military force as distinct from a set of armed forces, which are not the whole basis of force in war.

17

hundred photographs of the map of Europe could be taken, each photograph representing in colors the various countries as they appeared upon the map at one hundred different times, and if those hundred photographs could be put on films and shown as a moving-picture on a screen, the result would resemble the shifting colored pieces in a kaleidoscope. Boundaries advanced and receded, then advanced again; tribes and nations moved their homes from place to place; empires, kingdoms, principalities, duchies, and republics flourished brilliantly for a while, and then went out; many peoples struggled for an autonomous existence, but hardly a dozen acquired enough territory or mustered a sufficiently numerous population to warrant their being called "great nations." Of those that were great nations, only three have endured as great nations for eight hundred years; and the three that have so endured are the three greatest in Europe now—the French, the British, and the German.

Some of the ancient empires continued for long periods. The history of practical, laborious, and patient China is fairly complete and clear for more than two thousand years before our era; and of dreamy, philosophic India for almost as long, though in far less authentic form. Egypt existed as a nation, highly military, artistic, and industrious, as her monuments show, for perhaps four thousand years; when she was forced by the barbarians of Persia into a condition of dependence, from which she has never yet emerged. The time of her greatness in the arts and sciences of peace was the time of her greatest military power; and her decline in the arts and sciences of peace accompanied her decline in those of war. Assyria, with her two capitals, Babylon and Nineveh, flourished splendidly for about six centuries, and was then subdued by the Persians under Cyrus, after the usual decline. The little kingdom of the Hebrews, hardy and warlike under Saul and David, luxurious and effeminate under Solomon, lasted but little more than a hundred years. Persia, rising rapidly by military means from the barbarian state, lived a brilliant life of conquest, cultivated but little those arts of peace that hold in check the passions of a successful military nation, yielded rapidly to the seductions of luxury, and fell abruptly before the Macedonian Alexander, lasting less than two hundred and fifty years. Macedonia, trained under Philip, rose to great military power under Alexander, conquered in twelve years the ten most wealthy and populous countries of the world—nearly the whole known world; but fell to pieces almost instantly when Alexander died. The cities of Greece enjoyed a rare pre-eminence both in the arts and sciences of peace and in military power, but only for about one hundred and fifty years: falling at last before the superior military force of Macedon, after neglecting the practice of the military arts, and devoting themselves to art, learning, and philosophy. Rome as a great nation lasted about five hundred years; and the last three centuries of her life after the death of Commodus, about 192 A.D., illustrate curiously the fact that, even if a people be immoral, cruel, and base in many ways, their existence as an independent state may be continued long, if military requirements be understood, and if the military forces be preserved from the influence of the effeminacy of the nation as a whole. In Rome, the army was able to maintain a condition of considerable manliness, relatively to the people at large, and thus preserve internal order and keep the barbarians at bay for nearly three hundred years; and at the same time exert a powerful and frequently deciding influence in the government. But the effeminacy of the people, especially of those in the higher ranks, made them the creatures of the army that protected them. In some cases, the Emperor himself was selected by the army, or by the Pretorian Guard in Rome; and sometimes the guard removed an Emperor of whom it disapproved by the simple expedient of killing him.

19

After the fall of the Western Empire in 476, when Rome was taken by Odoacer,[3] a condition of confusion, approaching anarchy, prevailed throughout Europe, until Charlemagne founded his empire, about 800 A.D., except that Constantinople was able to stand up against all outside assaults and hold the Eastern Empire together. Charlemagne's empire united under one government nearly all of what is now France, Germany, Austria, Italy, Belgium, and Holland. The means employed by Charlemagne to found his empire were wholly military, though means other than military were instituted to preserve it. He endeavored by just government, wise laws, and the encouragement of religion and of education of all kinds to form a united people. The time was not ripe, however; and Charlemagne's empire fell apart soon after Charlemagne expired.

The rapid rise and spread of the Mohammedan religion was made possible by the enthusiasm with which Mahomet imbued his followers, but the actual founding of the Arabian Empire was due wholly to military conquest, achieved by the fanatic Mussulmans who lived after him. After a little more than a hundred years, the empire was divided into two caliphates. Brilliant and luxurious courts were thereafter held by caliphs at Bagdad and Cordova, with results similar to those in Egypt, Persia, Assyria, and Rome; the people becoming effeminate, employed warriors to protect them, and the warriors became their masters. Then, effeminacy spreading even to the warriors, strength to resist internal disorders as well as external assaults gradually faded, and both caliphates fell.

From the death of Charlemagne until the fall of Con-

3. Odoacer of Rugia forced the last emperor of the Western Roman Empire, Romulus Augustulus, to abandon all pretense of sovereignty in 476 and made himself king of Italy. The event was merely the last breath of a corpse that had already been dismembered.

stantinople, in 1453, the three principal nations of Europe were those of France, Germany,[4] and England. Until that time, and dating from a time shortly before the fall of Rome, Europe was in perpetual turmoil—owing not only to conflicts between nations, but to conflicts between the Church of Rome and the civil power of the Kings and Emperors, to conflicts among the feudal lords, and to conflicts between the sovereigns and the feudal lords. The power of the Roman Church was beneficent in checking a too arrogant and military tendency, and was the main factor in preventing an utter lapse back to barbarism.

The end of the Middle Ages and the beginning of what are usually called "Modern Times" found only four great countries in the world—France, Germany, Spain, and England. Of these Spain dropped out in the latter part of the sixteenth century. The other three countries still stand, though none of them lies within exactly the same boundaries as when modern times began; and Austria, which was a part of Germany then, is now—with Hungary—a separate state and nation.

This very brief survey of history shows that every great nation has started from a small beginning and risen sometimes gradually, sometimes rapidly to greatness; and then fallen, sometimes gradually, sometimes rapidly, to mediocrity, dependence, or extinction; that the instrument which has effected the rise has always been military power, usually exerted by armies on the land, sometimes by navies on the sea; and that the instrument which has effected the actual fall has always been the military power of an adversary. In other

4. Even if one credits the Hapsburgs and the Holy Roman Empire as "Germany," placing Germany on a list of the enduring big three nations, as Fiske does repeatedly, is premature, and hints at Fiske's forthcoming praise of the German general staff, which contributed to the unification of the modern German state under Prussian leadership. The complete omission of Russia is another curiosity.

words, *the immediate instrument that has decided the rise and the fall of nations has been military power.*[5]

That this should have been so need not surprise us, since nations have always been composed of human beings, influenced by the same hopes and fears and governed by the same laws of human nature. And as the most potent influence that could be brought to bear upon a man was a threat against his life, and as it was the province of military power to threaten life, it was unavoidable that military power should be the most potent influence that could be brought to bear upon a nation.

The history of the world has been in the main a history of war and a narrative of wars. No matter how far back we go, the same horrible but stimulating story meets our eyes. In ancient days, when every weapon was rude, and manipulated by one man only, the injury a single weapon could do was small, the time required for preparation was but brief, and the time required for recuperation after war was also brief. At that time, military power was almost the sole element in the longevity of a tribe, or clan, or nation; and the warriors were the most important men among the people. But as civilization increased, the life not only of individuals but of nations became more complex, and warriors had to dispute with statesmen, diplomatists, poets, historians, and artists of various types, the title to pre-eminence. Yet even in savage tribes and even in the conduct of savage wars, the value of wisdom and cunning was perceived, and the stimulating aid of the poet and the orator was secured. The relative value of men of war and men of peace depended during each period on the condi-

5. In this Fiske challenges Mahan, probably unconsciously, for Fiske was Mahan's disciple insofar as strategy was concerned. Mahan would have stressed economic power and overseas trade, supported by naval force. Fiske is with Corbett in keeping the object of war firmly planted on the land.

tions prevailing then—in war, warriors held the stage; in peace, statesmen and artists had their day.

Naturally, during periods when war was the normal condition, the warrior was the normal pillar of the state. In how great a proportion of the time that history describes, war was the normal condition and peace the abnormal, few realize now in our country, because of the aloofness of the present generation from even the memory of war. Our last great war ended in 1865; and since then only the light and transient touch of the Spanish War has been laid upon us. Even that war ended seventeen years ago and since then only the distant rumblings of battles in foreign lands have been borne across the ocean to our ears.

These rumblings have disturbed us very little. Feeling secure behind the 3,000-mile barrier of the ocean, we have lent an almost incredulous ear to the story that they tell and the menace that they bear; though the story of the influence of successful and unsuccessful wars upon the rise and fall of nations is told so harshly and so loudly that, in order not to hear it, one must tightly stop his ears.

That war has not been the only factor, however, in the longevity of nations is obviously true; and it is also true that nations which have developed the warlike arts alone have never even approximated greatness. In all complex matters, in all processes of nature and human nature, many elements are present, and many factors combine to produce a given result. Man is a very complex individual, and the more highly he is developed the more complex he becomes. A savage is mainly an animal; but the civilized and highly educated man is an animal on whose elemental nature have been superposed very highly organized mental, moral, and spiritual natures. Yet even a savage of the most primitive or warlike character has an instinctive desire for rest and softness and beauty, and loves a primitive music; and even the most highly refined and educated gentleman raises his head a little higher, and draws his breath a little deeper, when war draws near. Thus in the breast of every man are two opposing forces; one urging him to the action and excitement of war, the other to the comparative inaction and tranquillity of peace. On the side that urges war, we see hate, ambition, courage, energy, and strength; on the side that urges peace we see love, contentment, cowardice, indolence, and weakness. We see arrayed for war the forceful faults and virtues; for peace the gentle faults and virtues. Both the forceful and the gentle qualities tend to longevity in certain ways and tend to its prevention in other ways; but history clearly shows that *the forceful qualities have tended more to the longevity of nations than the gentle.* If ever two nations, or two tribes, have found themselves contiguous, one forceful and the other not, the forceful one has usually, if not always, obtained the mastery over the other, and therefore has outlived it. If any cow and any lion have found themselves alone together, the lion has outlived the cow.

It is true that the mere fact of being a lion has not insured long life, and that the mere fact of being a cow has not precluded it; and some warlike tribes and nations have not lived so long as tribes and nations of softer fibre. This seems to have been due, however, either to the environments in which the two have lived, or to the fact that the softer nation has had available some forces that the other did not have. The native Indians of North America were more warlike than the colonists from Europe that landed on their shores; but the Indians were armed with spears and arrows, and the colonists with guns.

Now, those guns were the product of the arts of peace; no nation that had pursued a warlike life exclusively could have produced them or invented the powder that discharged them. This fact indicates what a thousand other facts of history also indicate, that civilization and the peaceful arts contribute to the longevity of nations—not only by promoting personal

24

comfort, and by removing causes of internal strife, and thus enabling large bodies of people to dwell together happily, but also by increasing their military power. Every nation which has achieved greatness has cultivated assiduously both the arts of peace and the arts of war. Every nation which has long maintained that greatness has done so by maintaining the policy by which she acquired it. *Every nation that has attained and then lost greatness, has lost it by losing the proper balance between the military and the peaceful arts; never by exalting unduly the military, but always by neglecting them, and thereby becoming vulnerable to attack.*

In other words, the history of every great nation that has declined shows three periods, the rise, the table-land of greatness, and the decline. During the rise, the military arts hold sway; on the table-land, the arts of peace and war are fairly balanced; during the decline the peaceful arts hold sway. *Facilis descensus Averni.*[6] The rise is accomplished by expending energy, for which accomplishment the possession of energy is the first necessity; the height of the table-land attained represents the amount of energy expended; the length of time that the nation maintains itself upon this table-land, before starting on the inevitable descent therefrom, represents her staying power and constitutes her longevity as a great nation.

How long shall any nation stay upon the table-land? As long as she continues to adapt her life wisely to her environment; as long as she continues to be as wise as she was while climbing up; for which climbing, she had not only to exert force, she had also to guide the force with wisdom. So we see that, in the ascent, a nation has to use both force and wisdom; on the table-land, wisdom; in the decline, neither. Among the nations of antiquity one might suppose that, because of the slowness of transportation and communication, and the feebleness of weapons compared with those of mod-

6. The descent is easy on the path to ruin.

25

ern days, much longer periods of time would be required for the rise of any nation, and also a longer period before her descent began. Yet the vast empire of Alexander lasted hardly a day after he expired, and the Grecian cities maintained their greatness but a century and a half; while Great Britain, France, and Germany have been great nations for nearly a thousand years.

Why have they endured longer than the others?

The answer is hard to find; because many causes, and some of them obscure, have contributed to the result. But, as we observe the kind of constitution and the mode of life of long-lived people, in order to ascertain what kind of constitution and mode of life conduce to longevity in people, so perhaps we may logically do the same with nations.

Observing the constitution and mode of life of the British, French, and German nations, we are struck at once with the fact that those peoples have been by constitution active, ambitious, intelligent, and brave; and that they have observed in their national life a skillfully balanced relation between the arts of peace and the arts of war; neglecting neither and allowing neither to wax great at the expense of the other. In all those countries the *first* aim has been protection from both external attack and internal disorder. Protection from external attack has been gained by military force and highly trained diplomacy; protection from internal disorder has been gained *first* by military force, and *second* by wise laws, just courts, and the encouragement of religion and of those arts and sciences that lead to comfort and happiness in living.

China may attract the attention of some as an instance of longevity; but is China a nation in the usual meaning of the word? Certainly, she is not a great nation. It is true that no other nation has actually conquered her of late; but this has been largely by reason of her remoteness from the active world, and because other nations imposed their will upon her, without meeting any resistance that required the use of war to overcome. And even China has not lived a wholly peaceful life, despite the non-military character of her people. Her whole history was one of wars, like that of other nations, until the middle of the fourteenth century of our era. Since then, she has had four wars, in all of which she has been whipped: one in the seventeenth century when the country was successfully invaded, and the native dynasty was overthrown by the Tartars of Manchuria; one in 1840, when Great Britain compelled her to cede Hong-Kong and to open five ports to foreign commerce, through which ports opium could be introduced; one in 1860, with Great Britain and France, that resulted in the capture of Pekin; and one with Japan in 1894. Since that time (as well as before) China has been the scene of revolutions and wide-spread disturbances, so that, even though a peace-loving and non-resisting nation, peace has not reigned within her borders. The last dynasty was overthrown in 1912. Since then a feeble republic has dragged on in a precarious existence, interrupted by the very short reign of Yuan Shih K'ai.[7]

This brief consideration of the trend of people up to the present time seems to show that, owing to the nature of man himself, especially to the nature of large "crowds" of men, the direction in which nations have been moving hitherto has not been toward increasing the prevalence of peace, but rather toward increasing the methods, instruments, and areas of

---

7. Prominent and influential viceroy, governor, and adviser to the emperor of China during the tumultuous period around the turn of the century. Yuan Shih K'ai was respected in the West as a leader of the reform movement that commenced around 1900. Six weeks after Sun Yat-sen became the first president of the republic proclaimed on 1 January 1912, he stepped aside in order to allow Yuan Shih K'ai to organize a provisional government. Yuan was moderately successful in restoring order in the strife-torn country until his death in 1916.

war; furthermore, that this direction of movement has been necessary, in order to achieve and to maintain prosperity in any nation.

This being the case, what forces exist that may reasonably be expected to change that trend?

Three main forces are usually mentioned: Civilization, Commerce, Christianity.

Before considering these it may be well to note Newton's first law of motion, that every body will continue in a state of rest or of uniform motion in a straight line unless acted on by some external force; for though this law was affirmed of material bodies, yet its applicability to large groups of men is striking and suggestive. Not only do human beings have the physical attributes of weight and inertia like other material bodies, but their mental organism, while of a higher order than the physical, is as powerfully affected by external forces. And though it is true that psychology has not yet secured her Newton, and that no one has yet formulated a law that expresses exactly the action of the minds and spirits of men under the influence of certain mental and moral stimuli or forces, yet we know that our minds and spirits are influenced by fear, hope, ambition, hate, and so forth, in ways that are fairly well understood and toward results that often can be predicted in advance.

Our whole theory of government and our laws of business and every-day life are founded on the belief that men are the same to-day as they were yesterday, and that they will be the same to-morrow. The whole science of psychology is based on the observed and recorded actions of the human organism under the influence of certain external stimuli or forces, and starts from the assumption that this organism has definite and permanent characteristics. If this is not so—if the behavior of men in the past has not been governed by actual laws which will also govern their behavior in the future—then our laws of government are built on error, and the teachings of psychology are foolish.[8]

This does not mean that any man will necessarily act in the same way to-morrow as he did yesterday, when subjected to the influence of the same threat, inducement, or temptation; because, without grappling the thorny question of free will, we realize that a man's action is never the result of only one stimulus and motive, but is the resultant of many; and we have no reason to expect that he will act in the same way when subjected to the same stimulus, unless we know that the internal and external conditions pertaining to him are also the same. Furthermore, even if we cannot predict what a certain individual will do, when exposed to a certain external influence, because of some differences in his mental and physical condition, on one occasion in comparison with another, yet when we consider large groups of men, we know that individual peculiarities, permanent and temporary, balance each other in great measure; that the average condition of a group of men is less changeable than that of one man, and that the degree of permanency of condition increases with the number of men in the group. From this we may reasonably conclude that, if we know the character of a man—or

8. Fiske draws many parallels between physical science and the social science of military operations, in both of which he was thoroughly informed and deeply insightful. He was a great proponent of understanding cause-and-effect relationships (which today we call models) and evidently believed they were worth seeking out as the basis of military science. Doubtless the cause-and-effect relationships of human activity tax our capacity for comprehensive understanding, if our standard is the degree of precision achieved by physical science. But Fiske seems to suggest trying to understand the dynamics of social science ("psychology has not yet secured her Newton") and believes military leadership will be wiser for having done so. His writings, here and elsewhere, are larded with elemental combat models to help describe the dynamic processes of war.

a group of men—and if we know also the line of action which he—or they—have followed in the past, we shall be able to predict his—or their—line of action in the future with considerable accuracy; and that the accuracy will increase with the number of men in the group, and the length of time during which they have followed the known line of action. Le Bon says: "Every race carries in its mental constitution the laws of its destiny."

Therefore, the line of action that the entire human race has followed during the centuries of the past is a good index—or at least the best index that we have—to its line of action during the centuries of the future.

Now, men have been on this earth for many years; and history and psychology teach us that in their intercourse with each other, their conduct has been caused by a combination of many forces, among which are certain powerful forces that tend to create strife. The strongest by far of these forces is the *ego* in man himself, a quality divinely implanted which makes a man in a measure self-protecting. This ego prompts a man not only to seek pleasure and avoid trouble for himself, but also to gain superiority, and, if possible, the mastery over his fellow men. Men being placed in life in close juxtaposition to each other, the struggles of each man to advance his own interests produce rivalries, jealousies, and conflicts.

Similarly with nations. Nations have been composed for the most part of people having an heredity more or less common to them all, so that they are bound together as great clans. From this it has resulted that nations have been jealous of each other and have combated each other. They have been doing this since history began, and are doing it as much as ever now.

In fact, mankind have been in existence for so many centuries, and their physical, moral, mental, and spiritual characteristics were so evidently implanted in them by the Almighty, that it seems difficult to see how any one, except the

Almighty himself, can change these characteristics and their resulting conduct. It is a common saying that a man cannot lift himself over the fence by his boot straps, though he can jump over the fence, if it is not too high. This saying recognizes the fact that "a material system can do no work on itself"; but needs external aid. When a man pulls upward on his boot straps, the upward force that he exerts is exactly balanced by the downward reaction exerted by his boot straps; but when he jumps, the downward thrust of his legs causes an equal reaction of the earth, which exerts a direct force upward upon the man; and it is this external force that moves him over the fence. It is this external force, the reaction of the earth or air or water, which moves every animal that walks, or bird that flies, or fish that swims. It is the will of the Almighty, acting through the various stimuli of nature, that causes the desire to walk, and all the emotions and actions of men. If He shall cause any new force to act on men, their line of conduct will surely change. But if He does not—how can it change, or be changed; how can the human race turn about, by means of its own power only, and move in a direction the reverse from that in which it has been moving throughout all the centuries of the past?

These considerations seem to indicate that nations, regarded in their relation toward each other, will go on in the direction in which they have been going unless acted upon by some external force.

Will civilization, commerce, or Christianity impart that force?

Inasmuch as civilization is merely a condition in which men live, and an expression of their history, character and aims, it is difficult to see how it could of itself act as an external force, or cause an external force to act. "Institutions and laws," says Le Bon, again, "are the outward manifestation of our character, the expression of its needs. Being its outcome, institutions and laws cannot change this character."

Even if the civilization of a given nation may have been brought about in some degree by forces external to that nation, yet it is clear that we must regard that civilization rather as the result of those forces than as a force itself. Besides, civilization has never yet made the relations of nations with each other more unselfish, civilized nations now and in the past, despite their veneer of courtesy, being fully as jealous of each other as the most savage tribes. That this should be so seems natural; because civilization has resulted mainly from the attempts of individuals and groups to enhance the pleasures and diminish the ills of life, and therefore cannot tend to unselfishness in either individuals or nations. Civilization in the past has not operated to soften the relations of nations with each other, so why should it do so now? Is not modern civilization, with its attendant complexities, rivalries, and jealousies, provocative of quarrels rather than the reverse? In what respect is modern civilization better than past civilization, except in material conveniences due to material improvements in the mechanic arts? Are we any more artistic, strong, or beautiful than the Greeks in their palmy days? Are we braver than the Spartans, more honest than the Chinese, more spiritual than the Hindoos, more religious than the Puritans? Is not the superior civilization of the present day a mechanical civilization pure and simple? And has not the invention of electrical and mechanical appliances, with the resulting insuring of communication and transportation, and the improvements in instruments of destruction, advantaged the great nations more than the weaker ones, and increased the temptation to great nations to use force rather than decreased it? Do not civilization's improvements in weapons of destruction augment the effectiveness of warlike methods, as compared with the peaceful methods of argument and persuasion?

Diplomacy is an agency of civilization that was invented to

avoid war, to enable nations to accommodate themselves to each other without going to war; but, practically, diplomacy seems to have caused almost as many wars as it has averted. And even if it be granted that the influence of diplomacy has been in the main for peace rather than for war, we know that diplomacy has been in use for centuries, that its resources are well understood, and that they have all been tried out many times; and therefore we ought to realize clearly that diplomacy cannot introduce any new force into international politics now, or exert an influence for peace that will be more potent in the future than the influence that it has exerted in the past.

These considerations seem to show that we cannot reasonably expect civilization to divert nations from the path they have followed hitherto.

Can commerce impart the external force necessary to divert nations from that path?

Since commerce bears exactly the same relation to nations now as in times past, and since it is an agency within mankind itself, it is difficult to see how it can act as an external force, or cause an external force to be applied. Of course, commercial interests are often opposed to national interests, and improvements in speed and sureness of communication and transportation increase the size and power of commercial organizations. But the same factors increase the power of governments and the solidarity of nations. At no time in the past has there been more national feeling in nations than now. Even the loosely held provinces of China are forming a Chinese nation. Despite the fundamental commercialism of the age, national spirit is growing more intense, the present war being the main intensifying cause. It is true that the interests of commerce are in many ways antagonistic to those of war. But, on the other hand, of all the causes that occasion war the economic causes are the greatest. For no thing will men fight more savagely than for money; for no thing have men fought more savagely than for money; and the greater the rivalry, the more the man's life becomes devoted to it, and the more fiercely he will fight to get or keep it. Surely of all the means by which we hope to avoid war, the most hopeless by far is commerce.

The greatest of all hopes is in Christianity,[9] because of its inculcation of love and kindliness, its obvious influence on the individual in cultivating unselfishness and other peaceful virtues, and the fact that it is an inspiration from on high, and therefore a force external to mankind. But let us look the facts solemnly in the face that the Christian religion has now been in effect for nearly two thousand years; that the nations now warring are Christian nations,[10] in the very foremost rank of Christendom; that never in history has there been so much bloodshed in such wide-spread areas and so much hate, and that we see no signs that Christianity is employing any influence that she has not been employing for nearly two thousand years.

If we look for the influence of Christianity, we can find it in the daily lives of people, in the family, in business, in politics, and in military bodies; everywhere, in fact, in Christian countries, so long as we keep inside of any organization the members of which feel bound together. This we must all admit, even the heathen know it; but where do we see any evidence of the sweetening effect of Christianity in the dealings of one organization with another with which it has no special bonds of friendship? Christianity is invoked in every warring nation now to stimulate the patriotic spirit of the nation and intensify the hate of the crowd against the enemy; and even if we

9. Fiske, the son of an Episcopal minister, was a lifelong Christian.
10. One of his infrequent references to World War I, which was under way as he wrote.

think that such invoking is a perversion of religious influence to unrighteous ends, we must admit the fact that the Christian religion itself is at this moment being made to exert a powerful influence—not toward peace but toward war! And this should not amaze us; for where does the Bible say or intimate that love among nations will ever be brought about? The Saviour said: "I bring not peace but a sword." So what reasonable hope does even Christianity give us that war between nations will cease? And even if it did give reasonable hope, let us realize that between reasonable hope and reasonable expectation there is a great gulf fixed.

Therefore, we seem forced to the conclusion that the world will move in the future in the same direction as in the past; that nations will become larger and larger and fewer and fewer, the immediate instrument of international changes being war; and that certain nations will become very powerful and nearly dominate the earth in turn, as Persia, Greece, Rome, Spain, France, and Great Britain have done—and as some other country soon may do.

Fortunately, or perhaps unfortunately, a certain law of decadence seems to have prevailed, because of which every nation, after acquiring great power, has in turn succumbed to the enervating effects which seem inseparable from it, and become the victim of some newer nation that has made strenuous preparations for long years, in secret, and finally pounced upon her as a lion on its prey.

Were it not for this tendency to decadence, we should expect that the nations of the earth would ultimately be divided into two great nations, and that these would contend for the mastery in a world-wide struggle.

But if the present rate of invention and development continues, improvements in the mechanic arts will probably cause such increase in the power of weapons of destruction, and in the swiftness and sureness of transportation and communication, that some *monster of efficiency* will have time to acquire world mastery before her period of decadence sets in.

In this event, wars will be of a magnitude besides which the present struggle will seem pygmy; and will rage over the surface of the earth, for the gaining and retaining of the mastery of the world.

CHAPTER TWO

NAVAL A, B, C

I N ORDER TO realize what principles govern the use of navies, let us first consider what navies have to do, and get history's data as to what navies in the past have done. It would obviously be impossible to recount here all the doings of navies. But neither is it necessary; for the reason that, throughout the long periods of time in which history records them, their activities have nearly always been the same.

In all cases in which navies have been used for war there was the preliminary dispute, often long-continued, between two peoples or their rulers, and at last the decision of the dispute by force. In all cases the decision went to the side that could exert the most force at the critical times and places. The fact that the causes of war have been civil, and not military, demands consideration, for the reason that some people, confusing cause and effect, incline to the belief that armies and navies are the cause of war, and that they are to be blamed for its horrors. History clearly declares the contrary, and shows that the only rôle of armies and navies has been to wage wars, and, by waging, to finish them.

It may be well here, in order to clear away a possible preconception by the reader, to try and dispel the illusion that army and navy officers are eager for war, in order that they may get promotion. This idea has been exploited by people opposed to the development of the army and navy, and has been received with so much credulity that it seriously handicaps the endeavors of officers to get an unbiassed hearing. But surely the foolishness of such an idea would promptly disappear from the brain of any one if he would remind himself that simply because a man joins the army or navy he does not cease to be a human being, with the same emotions of fear as other men, the same sensitiveness to pain, the same dread of death, and the same horror of leaving his family unsupported after his death. It is true that men in armies and navies are educated to dare death if need be; but the present writer has been through two wars, has been well acquainted with army and navy officers for forty-five years, and knows positively that, barring exceptions, they do not desire war at all.

Without going into an obviously impossible discussion of all naval wars, it may be instructive to consider briefly the four naval wars in which the United States has engaged.

The first was the War of the American Revolution. This war is instructive to those who contend that the United States is so far from Europe as to be safe from attack by a European fleet; because the intervening distance was frequently traversed then by British and French fleets of frail, slow, sailing ships, which were vital factors in the war. Without the British war-ships, the British could not have landed and supported their troops. Without the French warships the French could not have landed and supported their troops, who, under Rochambeau, were also under Washington, and gave him the assistance that he wofully needed, to achieve by arms our independence.

The War of 1812 is instructive from the fact that, though the actions of our naval ships produced little material effect, the skill, daring, and success with which they were fought convinced Europeans of the high character and consequent noble destiny of the American people. The British were so superior in sea strength, however, that they were able to send their fleet across the ocean and land a force on the shores of Chesapeake Bay. This force marched to Washington, attacked the city, and burned the Capitol and other public buildings, with little inconvenience to itself.

The War of the Rebellion is instructive because it shows how two earnest peoples, each believing themselves right, can be forced, by the very sincerity of their convictions, to wage war against each other; and because it shows how unpreparedness for war, with its accompanying ignorance of the best way in which to wage it, causes undue duration of a war and therefore needless suffering. If the North had not closed its eyes so resolutely to the fact of the coming struggle, it would have noted beforehand that the main weakness of the Confederacy lay in its dependence on revenue from cotton and its inability to provide a navy that could prevent a blockade of its coasts; and the North would have early instituted a blockade so tight that the Confederacy would have been forced to yield much sooner than it did. The North would have made naval operations the main effort, instead of the auxiliary effort; and would have substituted for much of the protracted and bloody warfare of the land the quickly decisive and comparatively merciful warfare of the sea.

In the Spanish War the friction between the United States and Spain was altogether about Cuba. No serious thought of the invasion of either country was entertained, no invasion was attempted, and the only land engagements were some minor engagements in Cuba and the Philippines. The critical operations were purely naval. In the first of these, Commodore Dewey's squadron destroyed the entire Far Eastern squadron of the Spanish in Manila Bay; in the second, Admiral Sampson's squadron destroyed the entire Atlantic squadron of the Spanish near Santiago de Cuba. The two naval victories compelled Spain to make terms of peace practically as the United States wished. Attention is invited to the fact that this war was not a war of conquest, was not a war of aggression, was not a war of invasion, was not a war carried on by either side for any base purpose; but was in its intention and its results for the benefit of mankind.

The Russo-Japanese War was due to conflicting national policies. While each side accused the other of selfish ends, it is not apparent to a disinterested observer that either was unduly selfish in its policy, or was doing more than every country ought to advance the interests and promote the welfare of its people. Russia naturally had a great deal of interest in Manchuria, and felt that she had a right to expand through the uncivilized regions of Manchuria, especially since she needed a satisfactory outlet to the sea. In other words, the interests of Russia were in the line of its expanding to the eastward. But Japan's interests were precisely the reverse of Russia's—that is, Japan's interests demanded that Russia should not do those things that Russia wanted to do. Japan felt that Russia's movement toward the East was bringing her entirely too close to Japan. Russia was too powerful a country, and too aggressive, to be trusted so close. Japan had the same feeling toward Russia that any man might have on seeing another man, heavily armed, gradually coming closer to him in the night. Japan especially wished that Russia should have no foothold in Korea, feeling, as she expressed it, that the point of Korea under Russian power would be a dagger directed at the heart of Japan. This feeling about Korea was the same feeling that every country has about land near her; it has a marked resemblance to the feeling that the United States has embodied in its Monroe Doctrine.

After several years of negotiation in which Japan and Russia endeavored to secure their respective aims by diplomacy, diplomacy was finally abandoned and the sword taken up instead. Japan, *because of the superior foresight of her statesmen,* was the first to realize that diplomacy must fail, was the first to realize that she must prepare for war, was the first to begin adequate preparation for war, was the first to complete preparation for war, was the first to strike, and in consequence was the victor. Yet Russia was a very much larger, richer, more populous country than Japan.

Russia sent large forces of soldiers to Manchuria by the trans-Siberian railroad, and Japan sent large forces there by transports across the Sea of Japan. Japan could not prevent the passage of soliders by the railroad, but Russia could prevent the passage of transports across the Japan Sea, provided her fleet could overcome the Japanese fleet and get command of the sea. Russia had a considerable fleet in the Far East; but she had so underestimated the naval ability of the Japanese, that the Russian fleet proved unequal to the task; and the Japanese gradually reduced it to almost nothing, with very little loss to themselves.

Russia then sent out another fleet. The Japanese met this fleet on the 27th of May, 1904, near the Island of Tsushima, between Korea and Japan. The battle was decided in about an hour. The Japanese sank practically all the Russian ships before the battle was entirely finished, with comparatively small loss to Japan. This battle was carried on 12,000 miles by sea route from Saint Petersburg. No invasion of Russia or Japan was contemplated, or attempted, and yet the naval battle decided the issue of the war completely, and was followed by a treaty of peace very shortly afterward.

These wars show us, as do all wars in which navies have engaged, that the function of a navy is not only to defend the coast in the sense of preventing an enemy from landing on it, but also to exert force far distant from the coast. The study of war has taught its students for many centuries that a merely passive defense will finally be broken down, and that the most effective defense is the "offensive-defensive."[1]

1. That the navy on the strategic defensive must be aggressively disposed, take risks, and conduct offensive strikes is a major verity of naval operations, and is at sharp distinction with army operations, in which the defensive, to use Clausewitz's words, is the stronger form of warfare. This

Perhaps the clearest case of a correct offensive-defensive is Nelson's defense of England, which he carried on in the Mediterranean, in the West Indies, and wherever the enemy fleet might be, finally defeating Napoleon's plan for invading England—not by waiting off the coast of England, but by attacking and crippling Napoleon's fleet off the Spanish coast near Trafalgar.

The idea held by many people that the defense of a country can be effected by simply preventing the invasion of its coasts, is a little like the notion of uneducated people that a disease can be cured by suppressing its symptoms. For even a successful defense of a coast against invasion by a hostile force cannot remove the inimical influence to a country's commerce and welfare which that hostile force exerts, any more than palliatives can cure dyspepsia. Every intelligent physician knows that the only way to cure a disease is to remove its cause; and every intelligent military or naval man knows that history teaches that the only way in which a country can defend itself successfully against an enemy is to defeat the armed force of that enemy—be it a force of soldiers on the land, or a force of war-ships on the sea. In naval parlance, "our objective is the enemy's fleet."

If the duty of a navy be merely to prevent the actual invasion of its country's coasts, a great mistake has been made by Great Britain, France, and other countries in spending so much money on their navies, and in giving so much attention to the education and training of their officers and enlisted men. To prevent actual invasion would be comparatively an easy task, one that could be performed by rows of forts along the coast, supplemented by mines and submarines. If that is the only kind of defense required, navies are hardly needed. The army

philosophy was imbedded in U.S. naval thinking, and can be seen vividly in the actions of King, Nimitz, and Halsey immediately after Pearl Harbor.

in each country could man the forts and operate the mines, and a special corps of the army could even operate the submarines, which (if their only office is to prevent actual invasion) need hardly leave the "three-mile limit"[2] that skirts the coasts. If the people of any country do not care to have dealings outside; if the nation is willing to be in the position of a man who is safe so long as he stays in the house, but is afraid to go outdoors, the problem of national defense is easy.

But if the people desire to prevent interference with what our Constitution calls "the general welfare," the problem becomes exceedingly complex and exceedingly grave—more complex and grave than any other problem that they have. If they desire that their ships shall be free to sail the seas, and their citizens to carry on business and to travel in other lands; and if they desire that their merchants shall be able to export their wares and their farmers their grain, also that the people shall be able to import the things they wish from foreign countries, then they must be able to exert actual physical force on the ocean at any point where vessels carrying their exports and imports may be threatened. Naval ships are the only means for doing this.

The possibility that an armed force sent to a given point at sea might have to fight an enemy force, brought about first the sending of more than one vessel, and later—as the mechanic arts progressed—the increasing of the size of individual vessels, and later still the development of novel types.

There are two main reasons for building a small number of large ships rather than a large number of small ships. The first reason is that large ships are much more steady, reliable, safe, and fast than small ships. The second reason is that, when designed for any given speed, the large ships have more space available for whatever is to be carried; one 15-knot ship of

2. Then the universal limit of territorial waters prescribed by international law.

20,000 tons normal displacement, for instance, has about one and a half times as much space available for cargo, guns, and what-not, as four 15-knot ships of 5,000 tons each. These two reasons apply to merchant ships as well as naval ships. A third reason applies to naval vessels only, and is that a few large ships can be handled much better together than a large number of small ships, and embody that "concentration of force" which it is the endeavor of strategy and tactics to secure. A fourth reason is the obvious one that large ships can carry larger guns than small ships.

The distinctly military (naval) purpose for which a warship is designed necessitates, first, that in addition to her ability to go rapidly and surely from place to place, she be able to exert physical force against an enemy ship or fort, and, second, that she have protection against the fire of guns and torpedoes from enemy ships and forts, against bombs dropped from aircraft, and against mines.

This means that a man-of-war, intended to exert the maximum of physical force against an enemy and to be able to withstand the maximum of punishment, must have guns and torpedoes for offense, and must have armor and cellular division of the hull for defense; the armor to keep out the enemy's shells, and the cellular division of the hull to prevent the admission of more water than can fill one water-tight compartment in case the ship is hit.

It must be admitted here that, at the present moment, torpedoes hold such large charges of explosive that the cellular division of ships does not adequately protect them. This means that a contest has been going on between torpedo-makers and naval constructors like the contest between armor-makers and gunmakers, and that just now the torpedo-makers are in the lead. For this reason a battleship needs other protection than that imparted by its cellular subdivision. This is given by its "torpedo defense battery" of minor guns of about 5-inch calibre.

By reason of the great vulnerability of all ships to attack below the water-line, the torpedo was invented and developed. In its original form, the torpedo was motionless in the water, either anchored to the ground, or floating on the surface, and was in fact what now is called a "mine." But forty-eight years ago an Englishman named Whitehead invented the automobile, auto-steering, torpedo, which still bears his name. This torpedo is used in all the navies, and is launched on its mission from battleships, battle cruisers, destroyers, submarines, and other craft of various kinds.

Most torpedoes are to be found in destroyers—long, fast, frail vessels, averaging about 700 tons displacement, that are intended to dash at enemy ships at night, or under other favorable conditions, launch their torpedoes, and hurry away. The torpedo is "a weapon of opportunity." It has had a long, slow fight for its existence; but its success during the present war has established it firmly in naval warfare.

The submarine has followed the destroyer, and some people think will supplant it; though its relatively slow speed prevents those dashes that are the destroyer's rôle. The submarine is, however, a kind of destroyer that is submersible, in which the necessities of submersibility preclude great speed. The submarine was designed to accomplish a clear and definite purpose—a secret under-water attack on an enemy's ship in the vicinity. It has succeeded so well in its limited mission that some intelligent people declare that we need submarines only—ignoring the fact that, even if submarines could successfully prevent actual invasion, they could not carry on operations at a distance from their base of supplies. It is true that submarines may be made so large that they can steam at great speed from place to place, as capital ships steam now, carry large supplies of fuel and food, house their crews hygienically, and need no "mother ship" or tender. But if submarines achieve such size, they will be more expensive to build and run than battleships—and will be, in fact, submersible battleships. In other words, the submarine cannot displace the battleship, but may be developed and evolved into a new and highly specialized type of battleship.[3]

The necessity for operating at long distances from a base carries with it the necessity for supplying more fuel than even a battleship can carry; and this means that colliers must be provided. In most countries the merchant service is so large that colliers can be taken from it, but in the United States no adequate merchant marine exists, and so it is found necessary to build navy colliers and have them in the fleet. The necessity for continuously supplying food and ammunition to the fleet necessitates supply ships and ammunition ships; but the problem of supplying food and ammunition is not so difficult as that of supplying fuel, for the reason that they are consumed more slowly.

In order to take care of the sick and wounded, and prevent them from hampering the activities of the well, hospital ships are needed. Hospital ships should, of course, be designed for that purpose before being constructed; but usually hospital ships were originally passenger ships, and were adapted to hospital uses later.

The menace of the destroyer—owing to the seaworthiness which this type has now achieved, and to the great range which the torpedo has acquired—has brought about the necessity of providing external protection to the battleships; and this is supplied by a "screen" of cruisers and destroyers, whose duty is to keep enemy destroyers and (so far as is practicable) the submarines at a safe distance.

We now see why a fleet must be composed of various types of vessels. At the present moment, the battleship is the pri-

3. Also today "some intelligent people declare that we need submarines only." Fiske makes the arguments to the contrary that still apply, including the most basic one: submarines as we know them can dispute command of the seas but cannot exercise it.

mary, or paramount type, the others secondary, because the battleship is the type that can exert the most force, stand the hardest punishment, steam the farthest in all kinds of weather, and in general, serve her country the best.

Of course, "battleship" is merely a name, and some think not a very good name, to indicate a ship that can take the part in battle that used to be taken by the "ship of the line." The reason for its primacy is fundamental: its displacement or total weight—the same reason that assured the primacy of the ship of the line. For displacement rules the waves; if "Britannia rules the waves," it is simply because Britannia has more displacement than any other Power.

The fleet needs to have a means of knowing where the enemy is, how many ships he has, what is their character, the direction in which they are steaming, and their speed. To accomplish this purpose, "scouts"[4] are needed—fast ships, that can steam far in all kinds of weather and send wireless messages across great distances. So far as their scout duties go, such vessels need no guns whatever, and no torpedoes; but because the enemy will see the scout as soon as the scout sees the enemy, and because the enemy will try to drive away the scout by gun and torpedo fire, the scouts must be armed. And this necessity is reinforced by the necessity of driving off an enemy's scouts. In foreign navies the need for getting information in defiance of an enemy's attempts to prevent it, and to drive off the armed scouts of an enemy, has been one of the prime reasons for developing "battle cruisers," that combine the speed of the destroyer with the long steaming radius of the battleship, a battery almost as strong, and a very considerable protection by armor.

4. A splendid, utilitarian term, accurately described by Fiske, "scouting" has fallen from use in the U.S. Navy, even though the function is today more important than ever. The function is described on page 326 as it was used by Fiske and his contemporaries.

The aeroplane and the air-ship are recent accessions to the list of fighting craft. Their rôle in naval warfare cannot yet be defined, because the machines themselves have not yet reached an advanced stage of development, and their probable performance cannot be forecast. There is no doubt, however, in the minds of naval men that the rôle of aircraft is to be important and distinguished.[5]

5. Fiske makes several brief references to the future of aircraft in war. He was a pioneer proponent of naval aviation, and by the time the second edition of this book was published in 1918 had written two articles for the U.S. Naval Institute *Proceedings,* "Air Power," August 1917, pp. 1701–1704, and "The Future of the Torpedo Plane," January 1918, pp. 137–143. In addition, he devoted the last three chapters of his autobiography to naval aviation and the future of the torpedo plane. Fiske was a pioneer champion of aircraft at sea, but he declines the opportunity to play the visionary in this work. An example of his remarkable foresight regarding aerial torpedoes is in Appendix B.

CHAPTER THREE

NAVAL POWER

M AHAN PROVED that sea power has exercised a determining influence on history. He proved that sea power has been necessary for commercial success in peace and military success in war. He proved that, while many wars have culminated with the victory of some army, the victory of some navy had been the previous essential. He proved that the immediate cause of success had often resulted inevitably from another cause, less apparent because more profound; that the operations of the navy had previously brought affairs up to the "mate in four moves," and that the final victory of the army was the resulting "checkmate."

Before Mahan proved his doctrine, it was felt in a general way that sea power was necessary to the prosperity and security of a nation. Mahan was not the first to have this idea, for it had been in the minds of some men, and in the policy of one nation, for more than a century. Neither was Mahan the first to put forth the idea in writing; but he was the first to make an absolute demonstration of the truth. Newton was not the first man to know, or to say, that things near the earth tend to fall to the earth; but he was the first to formulate and prove the doctrine of universal gravitation. In the same way, all through history, we find that a few master minds have been able to group what had theretofore seemed unrelated phenomena, and deduce from them certain laws. In this way they substituted reasoning for speculation, fact for fancy, wisdom for opportunism, and became the guides of the human race.[1]

The effect of the acceptance of Mahan's doctrine was felt at once. Realizing that the influence of sea power was a fact, comprehending Great Britain's secret, after Mahan had disclosed it, certain other great nations of the world, especially Germany, immediately started with confidence and vigor upon the increase of their own sea power, and pushed it to a degree before unparalleled; with a result that must have been amazing to the man who, more than any other, was responsible for it.[2]

Since the words "sea power," or their translation, is a recognized phrase the world over, and since the power of sea power is greater than ever before, and is still increasing, it may be profitable to consider sea power as an entity, and to inquire what are its leading characteristics, and in what it mainly consists.

There is no trouble in defining what the sea is, but there is a good deal of trouble in defining what power is. If we look in a dictionary, we shall find a good many definitions of power; so many as to show that there are many different kinds of

1. Even physical science has become more modest than Fiske in its claims of proof and the incontrovertibility of scientific laws. The current coin is that physical models (usually mathematical formulas) are useful descriptions of theories against which no inconsistencies have come to light. Fiske's dogmatism is a blend of, first, military forcefulness and, second, the contemporary penchant of science for deterministic and thoroughly discernible natural laws. Modern science takes a humbler stance toward epistemological questions.

As for Fiske's faith in Mahan's studies as proofs, these should be interpreted more as a reflection of contemporary beliefs of American naval officers than as modern strategic thinking. But there can be no quarrel with the importance of "a few master minds" and their contribution to military science.

2. Fiske's view on the contemporary *influence* of Mahan is not exaggerated.

power, and that when we read of "power," it is necessary to know what kind of power is meant. Clearly "sea power" means power on the sea. But what kind of power? There are two large classes into which power may be divided, passive and active. Certainly we seem justified, at the start, in declaring that the power meant by Mahan was not passive, but active. Should this be granted, we cannot be far from right if we go a step further, and declare that sea power means ability to do something on the sea.

If we ask what the something is that sea power has ability to do, we at once perceive that sea power may be divided into two parts, commercial power and naval power.

The power exerted by commercial sea power is clearly that exerted by the merchant service, and is mainly the power of acquiring money. It is true that the merchant service has the power of rendering certain services in war, especially the power of providing auxiliary vessels, and of furnishing men accustomed to the sea; but as time goes on the power contributable by the merchant service must steadily decrease, because of the relatively increasing power of the naval service, and the rapidly increasing difference between the characteristics of ships and men suitable for the merchant service and those suitable for the naval service.

But even in the past, while the importance of the merchant service was considerable in the ways just outlined, it may perhaps be questioned whether it formed an element of sea *power,* in the sense in which Mahan discussed sea power. The power of every country depends on all the sources of its wealth: on its agriculture, on its manufacturing activities, and even more directly on the money derived from exports. But these sources of wealth and all sources of wealth, including the merchant service, can hardly be said to be elements of power themselves, but rather to be elements for whose protection power is required.

In fact, apart from its usefulness in furnishing auxiliaries, it

51

seems certain that the merchant service has been an element of *weakness*. The need for navies arose from the weakness of merchant ships and the corresponding necessity for assuring them safe voyages and proper treatment even in time of peace; while in time of war they have always been an anxious care, and have needed and received the protection of fighting ships that have been taken away from the fleet to act as convoys.

If commercial sea power was not the power meant by Mahan, then he must have meant naval power.[3] And if one reads the pages of history with patient discrimination, the conviction must grow on him that what really constituted the sea power which had so great an influence on history, was *naval* power; not the power of simply ships upon the sea, but the power of a navy composed of ships able to fight, manned by men trained to fight, under the command of captains skilled to fight, and led by admirals determined to fight. Trafalgar was not won by the merchant service; nor Mobile, Manila, or Tsushima.

If sea power be essentially naval power, it may be interesting to inquire: In what does naval power consist and what are its principal characteristics?

If one looks at a fleet of war-ships on the sea, he will be impressed consciously or unconsciously with the idea of power. If he is impressed consciously, he will see that the fleet represents power in the broadest sense—power active and power passive; power to do and power to endure; power to exert force and power to resist it.

If he goes further and analyzes the reasons for this impression of power, he will see that it is not merely a mental suggestion, but a realization of the actual existence of tre-

3. Fiske departs from Mahan's belief that sea trade and the merchant marine are a source of strength. Though he evokes Mahan, he is here following his own path.

mendous mechanical power, under complete direction and control.

In mechanics we get a definition of power, which, like all definitions in mechanics, is clear, definite, and correct. In mechanics, power is the rate at which mechanical work is performed. It is ability to do something in a certain definite time.[4]

Now this definition gives us a clear idea of the way in which a navy directly represents power, because the power which a navy exerts is, primarily, mechanical; and any other power which it exerts is secondary and derived wholly from its mechanical power. The power of a gun is due wholly to the mechanical energy of its projectile, which enables it to penetrate a resisting body; and the power of a moving ship is due wholly to the mechanical energy of the burning coal within its furnaces.

It may be objected that it is not reasonable to consider a ship's energy of motion as an element of naval power, in the mechanical sense in which we have been using the word "power," for the reason that it could be exerted only by the use of her ram, an infrequent use. To this it may be answered that energy is energy, no matter to what purpose it is applied; that a given projectile going at a given speed has a certain energy, whether it strikes its target or misses it; and that a battleship going at a certain speed must necessarily have a certain definite energy, no matter whether it is devoted to ramming another ship or to carrying itself and its contents from one place to another.

Besides the mechanical power exerted by the mere motion

4. Since naval power is more complex than mechanical power, some of the kinematic relationships that follow should be taken as analogy, no matter how concise and effective. But the view that naval power "is the ability to do something [to accomplish an objective] in a certain definite time" is useful, and may be taken literally.

of the ship, and often superior to it, there is the power of her guns and torpedoes.

Perhaps the most important single invention ever made was the invention of gunpowder. Why? Because it put into the hands of man a tremendous force, compressed into a very small volume, which he could use instantaneously or refrain from using at his will. Its first use was in war; and in war has been its main employment ever since. War gives the best field for the activity of gunpowder, because in war we always wish to exert a great force at a definite point at a given instant; usually in order to *penetrate* the bodies of men, or some defensive work that protects them. Gunpowder is the principal agent used in war up to the present date. It is used by both armies and navies, but navies use it in larger masses, fired in more powerful guns.

Of course this does not mean that it would be impossible to send a lot of powder to a fort, more than a fleet could carry, and fire it; but it does mean that history shows that forts have rarely been called upon to fire much powder, that their lives have been serene, and that most of the powder fired on shore has been fired by infantry using muskets—though a good deal has been fired by field and siege artillery.

Leaving forts out of consideration and searching for something else in which to use gunpowder on a large scale, we come to siege-pieces, field-pieces, and muskets. Disregarding siege-pieces and field-pieces, for the reason that the great variety of types makes it difficult to compare them with navy guns, we come to muskets.[5]

Now the musket is an extremely formidable weapon, and has, perhaps, been the greatest single contributor to the vic-

---

5. To a modern operations analyst the reasoning that follows seems tortured, but the aim—to establish a basis for comparing the power of a navy with that of an army—was uniquely Fiske, fifty years ahead of systems analysis, and evokes the admiration of, at least, this commentator.

tory of civilization over barbarism, and order over anarchy, that has ever existed up to the present time. But the enormous advances in engineering, including ordnance, during the last fifty years, have reduced enormously the relative value of the musket. Remembering that energy, or the ability to do work, is expressed by the formula: $E = \frac{1}{2}MV^2$, remembering that the projectile of the modern 12-inch gun starts at about 2,900 f. s. velocity and weighs 867 pounds, while the bullet of a musket weighs only 150 grains and starts with a velocity of 2,700 feet per second, we see that the energy of the 12-inch projectile is about 47,000 times that of the bullet on leaving the muzzle. But after the bullet has gone, say 5,000 yards, its energy has fallen to zero, while the energy of the 12-inch projectile is nearly the same as when it started.

While it would be truthful, therefore, to say that the energy of the 12-inch gun within 5,000 yards is greater than that of 47,000 muskets, it would also be truthful to say that outside of 5,000 yards, millions of muskets would not be equal to one 12-inch gun.

Not only is the 12-inch gun a weapon incomparably great, compared with the musket, but when placed in a naval ship, it possesses a portability which, while not an attribute of the gun itself, is an attribute of the combination of gun and ship, and a distinct attribute of naval power. A 12-inch gun placed in a fort may be just as good as a like gun placed in a ship, but it has no power to exert its power usefully unless some enemy comes where the gun can hit it. And when one searches the annals of history for the records of whatever fighting forts have done, he finds that they have been able to do very little. But a 12-inch gun placed in a man-of-war can be taken where it is needed, and recent history shows that naval 12-inch guns, modern though they are, have already done effective work in war.

Not only are 12-inch guns powerful and portable, but modern mechanical science has succeeded in so placing them in our ships that they can be handled with a precision, quickness, and delicacy that have no superior in any other branch of engineering. While granting the difficulty of an exact comparison, I feel no hesitation in affirming that the greatest triumph of the engineering art in handling heavy masses is to be found in the turret of a battleship. Here again, and even inside of 5,000 yards, we find the superiority of the great gun over the musket, as evidenced by its accuracy in use. No soldier can fire his musket, even on a steady platform, himself and target stationary, and the range known perfectly, as accurately as a gun-pointer can fire a 12-inch gun; and if gun and target be moving, and the wind be blowing, and the range only approximately known, as is always the case in practice, the advantage of the big gun in accuracy becomes incomparable.

But it is not only the big projectile itself which has energy, for this projectile carries a large charge of high explosive, which exploding some miles away from where it started, exerts a power inherent in itself, that was exhibited with frightful effect at the battles of Tsushima and the Skagerrak.

This brings us to the auto-torpedo, a weapon recently perfected; in fact not perfected yet. Here is another power that science has put into the hands of naval men in addition to those she had already put there. The auto-torpedo, launched in security from below the water-line of the battleship, or from a destroyer or submarine, can be directed in a straight line over a distance and with a speed that are constantly increasing with the improvement of the weapon. At the present moment, a speed of 27 knots over 10,000 yards can be depended on, with a probability that on striking an enemy's ship below the water-line it will disable that ship, if not sink her. There seems no doubt that, in a very few years, the systematic experiments now being applied to the development of the torpedo will result in a weapon which can hardly be called inferior to the 12-inch or even 16-inch gun and will probably surpass it.

Controllability.—If one watches a fleet of ships moving on the sea, he gets an impression of tremendous power. But if he watches Niagara, or a thunder-storm, he also gets an impression of tremendous power. But the tremendous power of Niagara, or the thunder-storm, is a power that belongs to Niagara or the thunder-storm, and not to man. Man cannot control the power of Niagara or the thunder-storm; but he can control the power of a fleet.

Speaking, then, from the standpoint of the human being, one may say that the fleet has the element of controllability, while Niagara and the thunder-storm have not. One man can make the fleet go faster or slower or stop; he can increase its power of motion or decrease it at his will; he can reduce it to zero. He cannot do so with the forces of nature.

Directability.—Not only can one man control the power of the fleet, he can also direct it; that is, can turn it to the right or the left as much as he wishes. But one man cannot change the direction of motion of Niagara or the lightning-bolt.

Power, Controllability, and Directability.—We may say, then, that a fleet combines the three elements of mechanical power, controllability, and directability.

The Unit of Military Power.—This is an enormous power that has come into the hands of the naval nations; but it has come so newly that we do not appreciate it yet. One reason why we do not and cannot appreciate it correctly is that no units have been established by which to measure it.[6]

To supply this deficiency, the author begs leave to point out

6. In defining a unit of military power, Fiske is seeking to establish a theoretical foundation for its quantification, a step that modern military science continues to struggle with. He goes beyond the modern "firepower index" of effectiveness, the sum of forces such as infantry, tanks, and artillery each weighted according to its firepower relative to the other. A fire-

that, since the military power of every nation has until recently been its army, of which the unit has been the soldier, whose power has rested wholly in his musket, the musket has actually been the unit of military power. In all history, the statement of the number of men in each army has been put forward by historians as giving the most accurate idea of their fighting value; and in modern times, nearly all of these men have been armed with muskets only.

It has been said already that the main reason why the invention of gunpowder was so important was that it put into the hands of man a tremendous mechanical power compressed into a very small space, which man could use or not use at his will. This idea may be expressed by saying that gunpowder combines power and great controllability. But it was soon discovered that this gunpowder, put into a tube with a bullet in front of it, could discharge that bullet in any given direction. A musket was the result, and it combined the three requisites of a weapon—mechanical power, controllability, and directability.

While the loaded gun is perhaps the clearest example of the combination of the three factors we are speaking of, the moving ship supplies the next best example. It has very much greater mechanical power; and in proportion to its mass, almost as much controllability and directability.

The control and direction of a moving ship are very wonderful things; but the very ease with which they are exercised makes us overlook the magnitude of the achievement and the perfection of the means employed. It may seem absurd to speak of one man controlling and directing a great ship, but that is pretty nearly what happens sometimes; for sometimes the man at the wheel is the only man on board doing anything

power index is a static measure of effectiveness; he insists that dynamic properties matter—mobility, controllability, and directability.

at all; and he is absolutely directing the entire ship.[7] At such times (doubtless they are rare and short) the man at the wheel on board, say the *Vaterland,* is directing unassisted by any human being a mass of 65,000 tons, which is going through the water at a speed of 24 knots, or 27 miles, an hour, nearly as fast as the average passenger-train. In fact, it would be very easy to arrange on board the *Vaterland* that this should actually happen; that everybody should take a rest for a few minutes, coal-passers, water-tenders, oilers, engineers, and the people on deck. And while such an act might have no particular value, *per se,* and prove nothing important, yet, nevertheless, a brief reflection on the possibility may be interesting, and lead us to see clearly into the essential nature of what is here called "directability." The man at the wheel on board the *Vaterland,* so long as the fires burn and the oil continues to lubricate the engines, has a power in his hands that is almost inconceivable. The ship that he is handling weighs more than the 870,000 men that comprise the standing army of Germany.

Now can anybody imagine the entire standing army of Germany being carried along at 27 miles an hour and turned almost instantly to the right or left by one man? The standing army of Germany is supposed to be the most directable organization in the world; but could the Emperor of Germany move that army at a speed of 27 miles an hour and turn it as a whole (not its separate units) through 90 degrees in three minutes?

The *Vaterland* being a merchant ship and not fully repre-

7. Lest the significance of this be missed, consider that in a navy of World War I there were about 300 men—the commanding officers—who directed the firepower of the entire fleet, while in an army about 300,000 men—each infantryman and artillery gun captain—directed it. The consequences regarding training, doctrine, organization, and leadership were and still are profound.

senting naval power, perhaps it might be better to take, say, the *Pennsylvania*. The weight is about half that of the *Vaterland*, that is, it is nearly twice the weight of the men of the British standing army; and the usual speed is about, say, 15 knots. But in addition to all the power of the ship, as a ship, or an energy greater than that of 275,000 muskets, she has the power of all the guns, twelve 14-inch guns, and twenty-two 5-inch guns, whose projectiles, not including the torpedoes fired from four torpedo-tubes, have an energy at the muzzle equal to 750,000 muskets, seven-eighths of all the muskets in the German standing army. Now any one who has seen a battleship at battle practice knows that all the various tremendous forces are under excellent direction and control. And while it cannot be strictly said that they are absolutely under the direction and control of the captain, while it must be admitted that no one man can really direct so many rapidly moving things, yet it is certainly well within the truth to say that the ship and all it contains are very much more under the control of her captain than the German standing army is under the control of the Kaiser. The captain, acting through the helmsman, chief engineer, gunnery officer, and executive officer, can get very excellent information as to what is going on, and can have his orders carried out with very little delay; but the mere space occupied by an army of 870,000 men, and the unavoidable dispersion of its units prevent any such exact control.

In other words, the captain of the *Pennsylvania* wields a weapon more mechanically powerful than all the muskets of the German standing army: and his control of it is more absolute than is the Kaiser's control of that army.

Mechanism vs. Men.—Now what is the essential reason for the efficient direction exercised by the helmsman of the *Pennsylvania*, and the relative impotency of generals? Is it not that the helmsman acts through the medium of mechanism, while the generals act through the medium of men? A ship is not only made of rigid metal, but all her parts are fastened together with the utmost rigidity; while the parts of an army are men, who are held together by no means whatever except that which discipline gives, and the men themselves are far from rigid. In the nature of things it is impossible that an army should be directed as perfectly as a ship. The rudder of a ship is a mechanical appliance that can be depended upon to control the direction of the ship absolutely, while an army has no such a thing as a rudder, or anything to take its place. Again, the rudder is only a few hundred feet from the helmsman, and the communication between them, including the steering-engine itself, is a strong reliable mechanism that has no counterpart in the army.

The control of the main engines of a ship is almost as absolute as the control of the rudder; and the main engines are not only much more powerful than the legs of soldiers, but they act together in much greater harmony.

Inherent Power of a Battleship.—Possibly the declaration may be accepted now that a battleship of 30,000 tons, such as the navies are building now, with, say, twelve 14-inch guns is a greater example of power, under the absolute direction and control than anything else existing; and that the main reason is the concentration of a tremendous amount of mechanical energy in a very small space, all made available by certain properties of water. Nothing like a ship can be made to run on shore; but if an automobile could be constructed, carrying twelve 14-inch guns, twenty-two 5-inch guns, and four torpedo-tubes, of the size of the *Pennsylvania,* and with her armor, able to run over the land in any direction at 20 knots, propelled by engines of 31,000 horse-power, it could whip an army of a million men just as quickly as it could get hold of its component parts. Such a machine could start at one end of an army and go through to the other like a mowing-machine through a field of wheat; and knock down all the buildings in New York afterward, smash all the cars, break down all the bridges, and sink all the shipping.[8]

Inherent Power of a Fleet.—An idea of the power exertable by a fleet of modern ships may be derived from the following comparison.

When Sherman made his wonderful march to the sea from Atlanta to Savannah, he made a march whose details are historically known, which was unopposed, which was over a flat country, in good weather, and without the aid of railroad-trains. It was a march, pure and simple; and inasmuch as men are the same now as they were then, it gives excellent data of the way in which purely military or army power can move from one place to another, *while still preserving its character and exercising its functions.* Similarly, when Admiral Schroeder, in November, 1910, went from the east coast of the United States to the English Channel, his march was unopposed, its details are known, and it gave an excellent illustration of how naval power can move from one place to another, *while still preserving its character and exercising its functions.*

Now General Sherman was a man of world-wide fame, and so were some of his generals, and Sherman's fame will last for centuries. Compared with Sherman, Admiral Schroeder was obscure; and compared with Sherman's officers, Admiral Schroeder's were obscure. Sherman's soldiers, privates and all, were made glorious for the rest of their lives by having

8. In October 1915, *Popular Science Monthly* magazine published an article by Fiske, "If Battleships Ran on Land." "It was probably a coincidence," says Paolo Coletta, Fiske's biographer, "that about a year later the British produced tanks" (Coletta, *Admiral Bradley A. Fiske and the American Navy* [Lawrence, Kansas, 1979], p. 97). That article and this chapter are both children of Fiske's 1911 essay, "Naval Power" (U.S. Naval Institute *Proceedings*, January 1911, pp. 683–735).

been in Sherman's march to the sea, while Admiral Schroeder's sailors achieved no glory at all. So, the next paragraph is not intended to detract in the slightest from Sherman and his army, but simply to point out the change in conditions that mechanical progress has brought about.

The statement of comparison is simply that when General Sherman marched from Atlanta to the sea his army composed 62,000 men, and it took him twenty-five days to go about 230 land miles or 200 sea miles; and when Admiral Schroeder went from our coast to Europe he had 16 ships, and he made the trip of more than 3,000 sea miles in less than fourteen days. Disregarding twenty-eight 5-inch guns, two hundred and fifty-two 3-inch guns, and a lot of smaller guns, and disregarding all the torpedoes, Admiral Schroeder took eighty-four 12-inch guns, ninety-six 8-inch guns, eighty-eight 7-inch guns, and forty-eight 6-inch guns, *all mounted and available;* which, assuming the power of the modern musket as a unit, equalled more than 5,000,000 modern muskets.

Such an enormous transfer of absolute, definite, available power would be impossible on land, simply because no means has been devised to accomplish it. Such a transfer on land would be the transfer of ninety times as many soliders as Sherman had (even supposing they had modern muskets) over fifteen times the distance and at thirty times the speed; and as the work done in going from one place to another varies practically as the square of the speed, a transfer on land equivalent in magnitude and speed to Schroeder's would be a performance $90 \times 15 \times 30^2 = 1,215,000$ times as great as Sherman's.

This may seem absurd, and perhaps it is; but why? The comparison is not between the qualities of the men or between the results achieved. Great results often are brought about by very small forces, as when some state of equilibrium is disturbed, and vice versa. The comparison attempted is simply between the *power* of a certain army and the *power* of a certain fleet. And while it is true that, for some purposes, such as overcoming small resistance, great power may not be as efficacious as feeble power or even gentleness, yet, nevertheless, it must be clear that, for the overcoming of *great* resistance quickly great power must be applied.

The existence of a certain power is quite independent of the desirability of using it. The existence of the power is all the writer wishes to insist upon at present; the question of its employment will be considered later.

Not only is the power of a fleet immeasurably greater than that of an army, but it must always be so, from the very nature of things. The speed of an army, *while exercising the functions of an army,* and the power of a musket, while exercising its functions as a weapon of one soldier, cannot change much from what they were when Sherman went marching through Georgia. But, thanks to mechanical science, there is no limit in sight to the power to which a fleet may attain.

The power of a navy is of recent growth, but it is increasing and is going to continue to increase. Every advance of civilization will advance the navy. Every new discovery and invention will directly or indirectly serve it. The navy, more than any other thing, will give opportunity for mechanism and to mechanism. Far beyond any possible imagination of to-day, it will become the highest expression of the Genius of Mechanism, and the embodiment of its spirit.

The amount of money now being spent by the United States on its navy is so great that the expenditure can be justified only on the basis that great naval power is essential to the country.

Is it essential, and if so, why?

Primary Use for a Navy.—To answer this wisely, it may be well to remind ourselves that the principal object of all the vocations of men is directly or indirectly the acquiring of money. Money, of course, is not wealth; but it is a thing which can be so easily exchanged for wealth, that it is the thing which most people work for. Of course, at bottom, the most important work is the getting of food out of the ground; but inasmuch as people like to congregate together in cities, the thing taken out of the ground in one place must be transported to other places; and inasmuch as every person wants every kind of thing that he can get, a tremendous system of interchange, through the medium of money, has been brought about, which is called "trade." For the protection of property and life, and in order that trade may exist at all, an enormous amount of human machinery is employed which we call "government." This government is based on innumerable laws, but these laws would be of no avail unless they were carried out; and every nation in the world has found that employment of a great deal of force is necessary in order that they shall be carried out. This force is mainly exercised by the police of the cities; but many instances have occurred in the history of every country where the authority of the police has had to be supported by the army of the national government. There is no nation in the world, and there never has been one, in which the enforcement of the necessary laws for the protection of the lives, property, and trade of the people has not depended ultimately on the army; and the reason why the army could enforce the laws was simply the fact that the army had the power to inflict suffering and death.

As long as a maritime country carried on trade within its own borders exclusively, as long as it lived within itself, so long as its people did not go to countries oversea, a navy was not necessary. But when a maritime country is not contented to live within its own borders, then a navy becomes essential to guard its people and their possessions on the highways of the sea; to enforce, not municipal or national law, as an army does, but international law.

Now the desire of the people of a country to extend their trade beyond the seas seems in some ways not always a conscious desire, not a deliberate intent, but to be an effort of self-protection, or largely an effort of expansion; for getting room or employment. As the people of a country become civilized, labor-saving devices multiply; and where one man by means of a machine can do the work of a hundred, ninety-nine men may be thrown out of employment; out of a hundred men who till the soil, only one man may be selected and ninety-nine men have to seek other employment. Where shall it be gotten? Evidently it must be gotten in some employment which may be called "artificial," such as working in a shop of some kind, or doing some manufacturing work. But so long as a people live unto themselves only, each nation can practically make and use all the machinery needed within its borders, and still not employ all the idle hands; and when the population becomes dense, employment must be sought in making goods to sell beyond the sea. The return comes back, sometimes in money, sometimes in the products of the soil and the mine and the manufactures of foreign lands.

In this way every nation becomes like a great business firm. It exports (that is, sells,) certain things, and it imports (that is, buys,) certain things; and if it sells more than it buys it is making money; if it buys more than it sells it is spending money. This is usually expressed by saying that the "balance of trade" is in its favor or against it.

In a country like the United States, or any other great nation, the amount of exporting and importing, of buying and selling almost every conceivable article under the sun, is carried on in the millions and millions of dollars; and so perfect has the organization for doing this business become in every great country, that the products of the most distant countries can be bought in almost every village; and any important event in any country produces a perceptible effect wherever the mail and telegraph go.

The organization for effecting this in every country is so excellent and so wonderful, that it is like a machine.[9]

In fact, it is a machine, and with all the faults of a machine. Now one of the faults of a machine, a fault which increases in importance with the complexity of the machine, is the enormous disturbance which may be produced by a cause seemingly trivial. That such is the case with the machine which the commerce of every great nation comprises, every-day experience confirms. So long as the steamers come and go with scheduled regularity, so long will the money come in at the proper intervals and be distributed through the various channels; so long will the people live the lives to which they are habituated; so long will order reign.

But suppose the coming and going of all the steamers were suddenly stopped by a blockade. While it may be true that, in a country like the United States, no foreign trade is really necessary; while it may be true that the people of the United States would be just as happy, though not so rich, if they had no foreign trade—yet the sudden stoppage of foreign trade would not bring about a condition such as would have existed if we had never had any foreign trade, but would bring about a chaotic condition which cannot fitly be described by a feebler word than "horrible." The whole machinery of every-day life would be disabled. Hundreds of thousands of people would be thrown out of employment, and the whole momentum of the rapidly moving enormous mass of American daily life would receive a violent shock which would strain to its elastic limit every part of the entire machine.

It would take a large book to describe what would ensue from the sudden stoppage of the trade of the United States with countries over the sea. Such a book would besides be

9. With his analogy of a machine, Fiske is anticipating the methods of systems analysis, in which an entire economy is described and analyzed as a "system."

largely imaginative; because in our history such a condition has never yet arisen. Although wars have happened in the past in which there has been a blockade of our coast more or less complete, peace has been declared before the suffering produced had become very acute; and furthermore the conditions of furious trade which now exist have never existed before. Disasters would ensue, apart from the actual loss of money, owing simply to the sudden change. In a railroad-train standing still or moving at a uniform speed, the passengers are comfortable; but if that same train is suddenly brought to rest when going at a high speed, say by collision, the consequences are horrible in the extreme, and the horror is caused *simply by the suddenness of the change.* The same is true all through nature and human nature. Any sudden change in the velocity of any mass has its exact counterpart in any sudden change in the conditions of living of any man or woman, or any sudden change in the conditions under which any organization must carry on its business. The difficulty is not with individuals only, or with the organizations themselves, and does not rest solely on the personal inability of people to accommodate themselves to the losing of certain conveniences or luxuries; but it is an inertia which resists even the strenuous efforts of individuals and organizations to meet new situations promptly, and to grapple effectively with new problems.

Every organization, no matter how small, is conducted according to some system, and that system is based upon certain more or less permanent conditions, which, if suddenly changed, make the system inapplicable. The larger the organization and the more complex it is, the more will it be deranged by any change of external conditions and the longer time will it take to adapt itself to them.

The sudden stoppage of our sea trade, including our coasting trade, by even a partial blockade of our ports, would change practically all the conditions under which we live. There is hardly a single organization in the country which would not be affected by it. And, as every organization would know that every other organization would be affected, but to a degree which could not possibly be determined, because there would be no precedent, it cannot be an exaggeration to declare that the blockading of our principal ports would, entirely apart from direct loss of money and other commodities, produce a state of confusion, out of which order could not possibly be evolved except by the raising of the blockade.

In addition to the confusion brought about, there would, of course, be the direct loss of money and nonreceipt of imported things; but what would probably be the very worst thing of all would be the numbers of men thrown out of employment by the loss of foreign markets. *So long as a country can keep its people in employment, so long the people will live in comparative order.* But when there are many unemployed men in a country, not only do their families lose the means of subsistence, but the very fact of the men being unemployed leads them into mischief. Should the ports of any great commercial nation be suddenly closed, the greatest danger to the country would not be from the enemy outside, but from the unemployed people inside, unless the government gave them employment, by enlisting them in an enormous, improvised army.

It will be seen, therefore, that the blockading of the principal ports of any purely commercial country would be a disaster so great that there could not be a greater one except actual invasion. Another disaster might be the total destruction of its fleet by the enemy's fleet; but the only *direct* result of this would be that the people of the country would have fewer ships to support and fewer men to pay. The loss of the fleet and the men would not *per se* be any loss whatever to the country, but rather a gain. The loss of the fleet, however, would make it possible for the enemy's fleet to blockade our ports later, and thus bring about the horrors of which we have spoken.

While it is true that an absolute blockade of any port might be practically impossible at the present day, while it is true that submarines and torpedo-boats might compel blockading ships to keep at such distance from ports that many loopholes of escape would be open to blockade runners, yet it may be pointed out that even a partial blockade, even a blockade that made it risky for vessels to try to break it, would have a very deleterious effect upon the prosperity of the country and of every man, woman, and child within it. A blockade like this was that maintained during the greater part of the Civil War by the Northern States against the Southern States. This blockade, while not perfect, while it was such as to permit many vessels to pass both ways, was nevertheless so effective that it made it impossible for the Southern States to be prosperous, or to have any reasonable hope of ever being prosperous. And while it would be an exaggeration to state that the navy itself, unaided by the army, could have brought the South to terms; while it would be an exaggeration to state that all the land battles fought in the Civil War were unnecessary, that all the bloodshed and all the ruin of harvests and of homesteads were unnecessary, nevertheless it does seem that so long as the navy maintained the blockade which it did maintain, the people of the South would have been prevented from achieving enough prosperity to carry on an independent government; so that their revolt would have failed. The South, not being able to raise the blockade by means of their navy, might have tried to do so by sending an army into the Northern States, to whip the Northerners on their own ground; but this would clearly have been impossible.

The sentences above are not written with the intention of minimizing the services rendered by the army in the Civil War, or of detracting from the glory of the gallant officers and men who composed it, or of subtracting one jot or tittle from a grateful appreciation of their hardships and bloodshed; neither do they dare to question the wisdom of the statesmen who directed that the war should be fought mainly by the army. Their sole intention is to point out that, if a meagre naval force could produce so great an effect against a country *mainly agricultural,* a very powerful naval force, blockading effectively the principal ports of a *manufacturing country,* would have an effect so great that it can hardly be estimated.

It is plainly to be seen that the effect of a blockade against a purely commercial country by a modern navy would be incomparably greater now than it was fifty years ago, for two very important reasons. One reason is that the progress of modern engineering has made navies very much more powerful than they were fifty years ago; and the other reason is that the same cause has made countries very much more vulnerable to blockade, because it has made so many millions of people dependent upon manufacturing industries and the export of manufactured things, and forced them to live an artificial life. While the United States, for instance, does not depend for its daily bread on the regular coming of wheat from over the sea, yet millions of its people do depend, though indirectly, upon the money from the export of manufactured things; for with countries, as with people, habits are formed both of system and of mode of life, which it is dangerous suddenly to break; so that a country soon becomes as dependent upon outside commerce as a man does upon outside air, and a people suddenly deprived of a vigorous outside commerce would seem to be smothered almost like a man deprived of outside air.

A rough idea of the possible effect of a blockade of our coast may be gathered from the fact that our exports last year were valued at more than $2,000,000,000; which means that goods to this amount were sold, for which a return was received, either in money or its equivalent, most of it, ulti-

71

mately, as wages for labor. Of course no blockade could stop all of this; but it does not seem impossible that it could stop half of it, if our fleet were destroyed by the enemy. Supposing that this half were divided equally among all the people in the United States, it would mean that each man, woman, and child would lose about $10 in one year. If the loss could be so divided up, perhaps no very great calamity would ensue. But, of course, no such division could be made, with the result that a great many people, especially poor people, earning wages by the day, would lose more than they could stand. Suppose, for instance, that a number of people earning about $900 a year, by employment in export enterprises, were the people upon whom the actual loss eventually fell by their being thrown out of employment. This would mean that more than a million people—men, women, and children—would be actually deprived of the means of living. It seems clear that such a thing would be a national disaster, for any loss of money to one man always means a loss of money or its equivalent to other men besides. For instance: suppose A owes $20 to B, B owes $20 to C, C owes $20 to D, D owes $20 to E, E owes $20 to F, F owes $20 to G, G owes $20 to H, H owes $20 to I, and I to J. If A is able to pay B, and does so, then B pays C, and so on, and everybody is happy. But suppose that A for some reason, say a blockade, fails to receive some money that he expected; then A cannot pay B, B cannot pay C, and so on; with the result, that not only does J lose his $20, but nine men are put in debt $20 which they cannot pay; with the further result that A is dunned by B, B is dunned by C, and so on, producing a condition of distress which would seem to be out of all proportion to a mere lack of $20, but which would, nevertheless, be the actual result. So in this country of 100,000,000 people, the sudden loss of $1,000,000,000 a year would produce a distress seemingly out of all proportion to that sum of money, because the individual loss of every loser would be felt by everybody else.

Since to a great manufacturing nation, like ours, the greatest danger from outside (except actual invasion) would seem to be the sudden stoppage of her oversea trade by blockade, we seem warranted in concluding that, since *the only possible means of preventing a blockade is a navy,* the primary use for our navy is to prevent blockade.[10]

This does not mean that a fleet's place is on its own coast, because a blockade might be better prevented by having the fleet elsewhere; in fact it is quite certain that its place is not on the coast as a rule, but at whatever point is the best with relation to the enemy's fleet, until the enemy's fleet is destroyed. In fact, since the defensive and the offensive are so

10. The conclusion that "the primary use of our navy is to prevent blockade," expressed in those terms, was uniquely Fiske's. That he did not arrive at the conclusion casually is thrice indicated: first, his development of the supporting argument is lengthy; second, he adapts much of the argument almost verbatim from his 1911 essay, "Naval Power," so he has had five years to reconsider it; third, Coletta (p. 96) says Fiske was pleased in 1911 when the General Board did not reprimand him for asserting that the primary purpose of the navy was to prevent blockade and happy that the essay was translated for some foreign military journals.

Fiske subscribed to Mahan's emphasis on command of the sea and the decisive battle. But Fiske also saw that the goal of destroying the enemy's battle fleet was a means to an end. His conclusion as to the end is identical with Sir Julian Corbett's: navies support mankind on the land where it lives. Fiske, a sound thinker who only grappled with strategic issues late in his career, gives the naval purpose a negative twist: prevent blockade. Corbett emphasizes the positive: keep open the sea lines of communication and interdict the enemy's.

Also, Fiske was a pragmatist writing for an action-oriented audience, which was accustomed to thinking of the defense of the country. For them he was distinguishing between two mindsets: defeat the enemy fleet; or, serve the country by preventing a blockade, the first being the means to the latter end.

It is doubtful that Corbett or any other foreign theorist influenced Fiske. The very nature of his tortuous development suggests that Fiske had to work out his thesis for himself, with all the baggage of the decisive big battle to unload along the way.

inseparably connected that it is hard sometimes to tell where one begins and the other ends, the best position for our fleet might be on the enemy's coast. It may be objected that the coast of the United States is so long that it would be impossible to blockade it. Perhaps, but that is not necessary: it would suffice to blockade Boston, Newport, New York, the Delaware, the Chesapeake, and the Gulf, say with forty ships. And we must remember that blockade running would be much more difficult now than in the Civil War, because of the increased power and accuracy of modern gunnery and the advent of the search-light, wireless telegraph, and aeroplane.

It may also be objected that the blockading of even a defenseless coast would cost the blockading country a good deal of money, by reason of the loss of trade with that country. True; but war is always expensive, and the blockade would be very much more expensive to the blockaded country; and though it might hold out a long while, it would be compelled to yield in the end, not only because of the blockade itself but because of the pressure of neutral countries; and the longer it held out, the greater the indemnity it would have to pay. The expense of blockading would therefore be merely a profitable investment.

The author is aware that actual invasion of a country from the sea would be a greater disaster than blockade, and that defense against invasion has often been urged in Great Britain as a reason for a great navy; so that the primary reason for a navy might be said to be defense against invasion. But why should an enemy take the trouble to invade us? Blockade is easier and cheaper, and can accomplish almost everything that an enemy desires, especially if it be enlivened by the occasional dropping of thousand-pound shells into Wall Street and the navy-yard.

While, however, the *primary* use of naval power seems to be to prevent blockade, a navy, like any other weapon, may be put to any other uses which circumstances indicate. For instance, the Northerners in the Civil War used the navy not to prevent blockade, but to make blockade; the Japanese used the navy to cover the transportation of their armies to Manchuria and Korea; and Great Britain has always used her navy to protect her trade routes.[11]

A general statement of the various uses of a navy has been put into the phrase "command of the sea."

Of course, the probability of getting "command of the sea," or of desiring to get it is dependent on the existence of a state of war, and there are some who believe that the probability of our becoming involved in a war with a great naval nation is too slight to warrant the expense of money and labor needed to prepare the necessary naval power. So it may be well to consider what is the degree of probability.

This degree of probability cannot be determined as accurately as the probabilities of fire, death, or other things against which insurance companies insure us; for the reason that wars have been much less frequent than fires, deaths, etc., while the causes that make and prevent them are much more numerous and obscure. It seems clear, however, that, as between two countries of equal wealth, the probability of war varies with the disparity between their navies, and unless other nations are involved, is practically zero, when their

11. An argument that parallels that of modern American naval leaders against periodic attempts in the 1950s, 1960s, and 1970s to whittle down the fleet on the basis that its sole purpose is to defend the sea lines of communication between the United States and its allies. The basis of these attempts is that offensive power (represented by aircraft carriers) is a dangerous capability, risking unwarranted adventurism. The counterargument is that the construction of a defensive navy, consisting for example of convoy escorts, is a fatal philosophy, tantamount to the program of gunboats that President Jefferson built to defend our ports, thereby avoiding the risk of international involvements on the high seas. But as Fiske says, even a navy with a defensive goal must have offensive fighting power. And having constructed a balanced navy conceived for defense, why not make the relatively modest additional investment to make the navy multipurposed?

navies are equal in power; and that, other factors being equal, the *greatest probability of war is between two countries, of which one is the more wealthy and the other the more powerful.*

In reckoning the probability of war, we must realize that *the most pregnant cause of war is the combination of conflicting interests with disparity in power.* And we must also realize that it is not enough to consider the situation as it is now: that it is necessary to look at least ten years ahead, because it would take the United States that length of time to prepare a navy powerful enough to fight our possible foes with reasonable assurance of success.

Ten years, however, is not really far enough ahead to look, for the simple reason that, while we could get a great many ships ready in ten years, we could not get the entire navy ready as will be explained later. If, for instance, some change in policies or in interests should make war with Great Britain probable within ten years, we could not possibly build a navy that could prevent our being beaten, and blockaded, and forced to pay an enormous indemnity.

Is there *no* probability of this? Perhaps there is no great probability; but there certainly is a possibility. In fact, it might be a very wise act for Great Britain, seeing us gradually surpassing her, to go to war with us before it is too late, and crush us. It has often been said that Great Britain could not afford to go to war with us, because so many of her commercial interests would suffer. Of course, they would suffer for a while; but so do the commercial interests of competing railroads when they begin to cut rates. Cutting rates is war—commercial war: but it is often carried on, nevertheless, and at tremendous cost.

Just now, Great Britain does not wish to crush us; but it is certain that she can. It is certain that the richest country in the world lies defenseless against the most powerful; and that we could not alter this condition in ten years, even if we started to build an adequate navy now.

Yet even if the degree of probability of war with Great Britain, within say ten years, seems so small that we need not consider her, are there no other great Powers with whom the degree of probability of war is great enough to make it wise for us to consider them?

Before answering this question, let us realize clearly that one of the strongest reasons that leads a country to abstain from war, even to seek relief from wrongs, actual or imagined, is a doubt of success; and that that reason disappears if another country, sufficiently powerful to assure success, is ready to help her, either by joining openly with her, or by seeking war herself at the same time with the same country. As we all know, cases like this have happened in the past. Great Britain knows it; and the main secret of her wealth is that she has always been strong enough to fight any two countries.[12]

It is plain that a coalition of two countries against us is possible now. The United States is regarded with feelings of extreme irritation by the two most warlike nations in the world, one on our eastern side and the other on the western. War with either one would call for all the energies of the country, and the issue would be doubtful. But if either country should consider itself compelled to declare war, the other,

12. In fact, during much of the nineteenth century the number of British capital ships well exceeded the numbers of the next two biggest navies. Toward the end of the century, when the two-power standard was British policy, it was not so much evidence of strength as an acknowledgment that there was a limit to her dominance. See Paul M. Kennedy, *The Rise and Fall of British Naval Mastery* (New York, 1976), pp. 208–226. The American "two-ocean navy" had its roots in the Vinson-Trammell Act of 1934, and became policy with the act of that name in 1940. Its goal was similar, with Japan and the German-Italian Axis in mind.

if free at the time, might see her opportunity to declare war simultaneously. The result would be the same as if we fought Great Britain, except that our Pacific coast would be blockaded besides the Atlantic, and we should have to pay indemnity to two countries instead of to one country.

A coalition between these two countries would be an ideal arrangement, because it would enable each country to force us to grant the conditions it desires, and secure a large indemnity besides.

Would Great Britain interfere in our behalf? This can be answered by the man so wise that he knows what the international situation and the commercial situation will be ten years hence. Let him speak.

WILL THE IMPORTANCE OF NAVAL POWER INCREASE OR DECREASE?

It is clear that the importance to a country of a navy varies with two things—the value of that country's foreign trade and the probability of war.

It is also clear that, other things being equal, the probability of a country becoming involved in war varies as the value of her foreign trade; because the causes of friction and the money at stake vary in that proportion.

Therefore, *the importance to a country of her navy varies as the square of the value of her foreign trade.*[13]

In order to answer the question, therefore, we must first consider whether foreign trade—sea trade—is going to increase or decrease.

As to the United States alone, the value of our exports is about ten times what it was fifty years ago, and it promises to

13. Dubious logic.

increase. But the United States is only one country, and perhaps her increase in foreign trade has been due to conditions past or passing. So what is the outlook for the future, both for the United States and other countries? Will other countries seek foreign trade?

Yes. The recent commercial progress of Germany, Argentina, and Japan, shows the growing recognition by civilized and enterprising countries of the benefits of foreign trade, and of the facilities for attaining it which are now given by the advent of large, swift, modern steamers; steamers which are becoming larger and swifter and safer every year, more and more adapted for ocean trade. For not only have the writings of Mahan brought about an increase in the sea power of every great country; but this increase has so aroused the attention of the engineering professions that the improvement of ships, engines, and other sea material has gone ahead faster than all the other engineering arts.

The reason why the engineering arts that are connected with the sea have gone ahead more rapidly than any other arts is simply that they are given wider opportunity and a greater scope. It is inherent in the very nature of things that it is easier to transport things by water than by land; that water transportation lends itself in a higher degree to the exercise of engineering skill, to the attainment of great results.

The underlying reason for this difference seems to be that it is not possible to make any vehicle to travel on land appreciably larger than the present automobile, unless it run on rails; whereas the floating power of water is such that vehicles can be made, and are made, as large as 65,000 tons. The *Mauretania,* of 45,000 tons displacement, has been running for eight years, larger vessels are even now running and vessels larger still will undoubtedly be run; for the larger the ships, the less they cost per ton of carrying power, the faster they go, and the safer they are.

79

Sea commerce thus gives to engineers, scientists, and inventors, as well as to commercial men, that gift of the gods—opportunity. The number of ships that now traverse the ocean and the larger bodies of water communicating with it aggregate millions of tons, and their number and individual tonnage are constantly increasing. These vessels cruise among all the important seaports of the world, and form a system of intercommunication almost as complete as the system of railroads in the United States. They bring distant ports of the world very close together, and make possible that ready interchange of material products, and that facility of personal intercourse which it is one of the aims of civilization to bring about. From a commercial point of view, London is nearer to New York than San Francisco, and more intimately allied with her.

The evident result of all this is to make the people of the world one large community, in which, though many nationalities are numbered, many tongues are spoken, many degrees of civilization and wealth are found, yet, of all, the main instincts are the same: the same passions, the same appetites, the same desire for personal advantage.

Not only does this admirable system of intercommunication bring all parts of the world very closely together, but it tends to produce in all a certain similarity in those characteristics and habits of thought that pertain to the material things of life. We are all imitative, and therefore we tend to imitate each other; but the inferior is more apt to imitate the superior than vice versa. Particularly are we prone to imitate those actions and qualities by which others have attained material success. So it is to be expected, if it is not already a fact, that the methods whereby a few great nations attained success are already being imitated by other nations. Japan has imitated so well that in some ways she has already surpassed her models.

With such an example before her, should we be surprised

that China has also become inoculated with the virus of commercial and political ambitions? It cannot be many years before she will be in the running with the rest of us, with 400,000,000 of people to do the work; people of intelligence, patience, endurance, and aocility; people with everything to gain and nothing to lose; with the secret of how to succeed already taught by other nations, which she can learn from an open book.

If Japan has learned our secret and mastered it in fifty years, will China not be able to do it in less than fifty years?

Before we answer this question, let us realize clearly that China is much nearer to us in civilization than Japan was fifty years ago; that China has Japan's example to guide her, and also that any degree of civilization which was acquired by us in say one hundred years will not require half that time for another nation merely to learn. The same is true of all branches of knowledge; the knowledge of the laws of nature which it took Newton many years to acquire may now be mastered by any college student in two months.[14] And let us not forget, besides, that almost the only difficult element of civilization which other people need to acquire, in order to enter into that world-wide competition which is characteristic of the time we live in, is "engineering" broadly considered. Doubtless there are other things to learn besides; but it is not apparent that any other things have contributed largely to the so-called new civilization of Japan. Perhaps Japan has advanced enough in Christianity to account for her advance in material power, but if so she keeps very quiet about it. It may be, also, that the relations of the government to the governed people of Japan are on a higher plane than they used to be, but on a plane not yet so high as in our own country; but has any one ever seen

14. In other words, the difference between what must be discovered and what is known and taught.

81

this claimed or even stated? It may be that the people of Japan are more kindly, brave, courteous, and patriotic than they were, and that their improvement has been due to their imitating us in these matters; but this is not the belief of many who have been in Japan. One thing, however, is absolutely sure; and that is that Japan's advance has been simultaneous with her acquirement of the engineering arts, especially as applied to military and naval matters and the merchant marine.

But even supposing that China does not take part in the world-wide race for wealth, we cannot shut our eyes to the fact that Great Britain, Germany, France, Italy, Japan, Argentina, and the United States, besides others like Sweden, Norway, Belgium, Holland, Spain, and Portugal, are in the race already; and that several in South America bid fair to enter soon. Not only do we see many contestants, whose numbers and ardor are increasing, but we see, also, the cause of this increasing. The cause is not only a clearer appreciation of the benefits to be derived from commerce across the water under conditions that exist now; it is also a growing appreciation of the possibilities of commerce under conditions that will exist later with countries whose resources are almost entirely undeveloped. For four hundred years, we of the United States, have been developing the land within our borders, and the task has been enormous. At one time it promised to be the work of centuries; and with the mechanical appliances of even one hundred years ago, it would have taken a thousand years to do what we have already done. Mechanical appliances of all kinds, especially of transportation and agriculture, have made possible what would, otherwise, have been impossible; and mechanical appliances will do the same things in Tierra del Fuego and Zululand.

Mechanism, working on land and sea, is opening up the resources of the world. And now, another allied art, that of chemistry, more especially biology, is in process of removing one of the remaining obstacles to full development, by making active life possible, and even pleasant, in the tropics. It is predicted by some enthusiasts that, in the near future, it will be healthier and pleasanter to live in the tropics, and even do hard work there, than in the temperate zone. When this day comes, and it may be soon, the development of the riches of lands within the tropics will begin in earnest, and wealth undreamed of now be realized.

The opening of the undeveloped countries means a continuing increase of wealth to the nations that take advantage of the opportunity, and a corresponding backsliding to those nations that fail. It means over all the ocean an increasing number of steamers. It means the continuing increase of manufacturing in manufacturing countries, and the increasing enjoyment in them of the good things of all the world. It means in the undeveloped countries an increasing use of the conveniences and luxuries of civilization and an increasing possession of money or its equivalent. It means, throughout all the world, an increase of what we call "Wealth."

In discussing a subject so great as sea trade, while it may be considered presumptuous to look fifty years ahead, it can hardly be denied that we ought at least to try to look that far ahead.[15] To look fifty years ahead, is, after all, not taking in a greater interval of time than fifty years back; and it certainly seems reasonable to conclude that, if a certain line of progress has been going on for fifty years in a perfectly straight line, and with a vigor which is increasing very fast and shows no sign of change, the same general line of progress will probably keep up for another fifty years. If we try to realize what this means, we shall probably fail completely and become dazed

15. Fiske's insistence on the long view and the sweep of his glance is reminiscent of Herman Kahn's, and for his time more audacious. We can evaluate his speculations now in hindsight. His batting average is impressive.

by the prospect. We cannot possibly picture accurately or even clearly to ourselves any definite conditions of fifty years hence; but we certainly are warranted in concluding that by the end of fifty years, practically all of the countries of the world, including Africa, will be open to trade from one end to the other; that the volume of trade will be at least ten times as great as it is now; that the means of communication over the water and through the air will be very much better than now; and that there will be scores of appliances, methods, and processes in general use of which we have, as yet, no inkling, and cannot even imagine.

Now let us call to mind the accepted proverb that "Competition is the life of trade," and this will make us see that, accompanying this stupendous trade, extending over, and into, every corner of the world, there will be stupendous competition, involving in a vast and complicated net, every red-blooded nation of the earth.

We seem safe in concluding, therefore, that the importance of naval power will increase.

A great deal is said and written nowadays about the ability of arbitration to make wars unnecessary, and a good deal also about the possibility of an agreement among the nations, whereby armaments may be limited to forces adequate to insure that every nation shall be compelled to abide by the decision of the others in any disputed case.

In view of the number, the earnestness, and the prominence of many of the men interested in this cause; in view of the number of arbitration treaties that have been already signed; in view of the fact that arbitration among nations will simply establish a law among them like the law in any civilized country; in view of the fact that individuals in their dealings with each other sometimes surrender certain of their claims, and even rights, for the common good; in view of the fact that nations, like all business firms, like to cut down expenses, and in further view of the fact that a navy is not directly, but only indirectly, a contributor to a nation's prosperity, it seems probable that arbitration will be more and more used among the nations, and that armaments may be limited by agreement. It is clear, however, that the practical difficulties in the way of making the absolute agreement required are enormous, and that the most enthusiastic advocates of the plan do not expect that the actual limitation of armaments will become a fact for many years.[16]

After the necessary preliminaries shall have been arranged, and the conference takes place which shall settle what armament each nation may have, it is plain that it will be to the interest of each nation to keep down the armament of every other nation, and to be allowed as much as possible itself. In this way, the operation of making the agreement will be somewhat like the forming of a trust among several companies, and the advantage will lie with that nation which is the most powerful.

For this reason it would seem a part of wisdom for each country to enter the conference with as large a navy as possible.[17]

Therefore, the probability of an approaching agreement among the nations as to limitation of armaments, instead of

16. The success of arbitration, the influence of pacifists amid World War I (up to and including President Wilson, his secretary of state, William Jennings Bryan, and much of his cabinet), and hopes for peace without arms did indeed abound at the time. The League of Nations was on the immediate horizon.

17. Such was the political strategy of Woodrow Wilson when he continued the American naval buildup at the conclusion of World War I. The Democrat Wilson's legacy after his death was the Washington Naval Disarmament Treaty of 1922, negotiated by Republican leadership. Its ultimate consequences were a mixed bag. It hastened the demise of the battleship and the ascendancy of the aircraft carrier. Strategic and intermediate nuclear force reductions could very well follow a similar course today.

being a reason for abating our exertions toward establishing a powerful navy, is really a conclusive reason for redoubling them.

This brings us to the important question, "how powerful should our navy be?"

This may seem a question impossible to answer. Of course it is impossible to answer it in terms of ships and guns; but an approximate estimate may be reached by considering the case of a man playing poker who holds a royal straight flush. Such a man would be a fool if he did not back his hand to the limit and get all the benefit possible from it. So will the United States, if she fails to back her hand to the limit, recognizing the fact that in the grand game now going on for the stakes of the commercial supremacy of the world, she holds the best hand. She has the largest and most numerous seaports, the most enterprising and inventive people, and the most wealth with which to force to success all the various necessary undertakings.

This does not mean that the United States ought, as a matter either of ethics or of policy, to build a great navy in order to take unjust advantage of weaker nations; but it does mean that she ought to build a navy great enough to save her from being shorn of her wealth and glory by simple force, as France was shorn in 1871.[18]

It is often said that the reason for Great Britain's having so powerful a navy is that she is so situated geographically that, without a powerful navy to protect her trade, the people would starve.

While this statement may be true, the inference usually drawn is fallacious: the inference that if Great Britain were not so situated, she would not have so great a navy.

Why would she not? It is certain that that "tight little is-

18. In the Franco-Prussian War, a lightning-like debacle for France.

land" has attained a world-wide power, and a wealth per capita greater than those of any other country; that her power and wealth, as compared with her home area, are so much greater than those of any other country as to stagger the understanding; that she could not have done what she has done without her navy; that she has never hesitated to use her navy to assist her trade, and yet that she has never used her navy to keep her people from starving.

In fact, the insistence on the anti-starvation theory is absurd. Has any country ever fought until the people as a mass were starving? Has starving anything to do with the matter? Does not a nation give up fighting just as soon as it sees that further fighting would do more harm than good? A general or an admiral, in charge of a detached force, must fight sometimes even at tremendous loss and after all hope of local success has fled, in order to hold a position, the long holding of which is essential to the success of the whole strategic plan; but what country keeps up a war until its people are about to starve? Did Spain do so in our last war? Did Russia fear that Japan would force the people of her vast territory into starvation?

No—starvation has nothing to do with the case. If some discovery were made by which Great Britain could grow enough to support all her people, she would keep her great navy nevertheless—simply because she has found it to be a good investment.

The anti-starvation theory—the theory that one does things simply to keep from starving—does apply to some tropical savages, but not to the Anglo-Saxon. Long after starvation has been provided against, long after wealth has been secured, we still toil on. What are we toiling for? The same thing that Great Britain maintains her navy for—wealth and power.

The real reason for Great Britain's having a powerful navy

applies with exact equality to the United States. Now that Great Britain has proved how great a navy is best for her, we can see at once how great a navy is best for us. That is—since Great Britain and the United States are the wealthiest countries in the world, and since the probability of war between any two countries is least when their navies are equal in power—the maximum good would be attained by making the United States navy exactly equal to the British navy.[19]

19. "A navy second to none" was the Administration's slogan after Woodrow Wilson's switch in favor of a naval buildup in 1915. Wilson's change of heart postdated Fiske's tour as aid for operations (February 1913 to May 1915) by a scant ten weeks. On 21 July of that year President Wilson asked Secretary Daniels to assemble the best minds in the service to prepare a draft outlining an adequate defense program to present to the Congress in November. As Coletta says (p. 162), "It was Fiske's misfortune and miscalculation that he had pressed Daniels too early and too hard."

One of the critical assumptions in the concept that equality achieves deterrence is that neither side can effect a surprise attack. Equality with the possibility of surprise is destabilizing. Moreover, Fiske does not say how navies should be sized if one side is a sea power (the United States) and the other is a land power (Soviet Russia).

CHAPTER FOUR

NAVAL PREPAREDNESS

IN A PRECEDING chapter I endeavored to show why it is that the necessities of the naval defense of a country have caused the gradual development of different types of vessels, each having its distinctive work. If those different types operated in separate localities they would lose that mutual support which it is the aim of organization to secure, and each separate group could be destroyed in turn by the combined groups of an enemy. For this reason, the types or groups are combined in one large fleet, and an admiral is placed in command.

The command of a fleet is the highest effort of the naval art. Its success in time of war demands in the admiral himself a high order of mind and nerve and body; and it demands in all the personnel, from the highest to the lowest, such a measure of trained ability and character that each shall be able to discharge with skill and courage the duties of his station.

In order that the material fleet shall be efficient as a whole, each material unit must be efficient as a unit. Each ship must be materially sound; each pump, valve, cylinder, gun, carriage, torpedo, and individual appliance, no matter how small, must be in condition to perform its expected task. The complexity of a fleet baffles any mental effort, by even those most familiar with it, to grasp it fully. Each dreadnaught, battle cruiser, destroyer, submarine, collier, tender, hospital ship, scout, supply ship, and what-not, is a machine in itself, and is filled with scores—in some cases, hundreds—of highly specialized machines, operated by steam, oil, air, electricity, and water. A superdreadnaught is a machine which, including the machines inside of her, costs $15,000,000; a battle cruiser more.

The personnel is nearly as complicated as the material. Not only are there all the various ranks of commissioned officers in the line, medical corps, pay corps, marine corps, etc., but there are ten kinds of warrant officers besides; while in the enlisted personnel there are ninety-one different "ratings" in the navy, and thirteen in the marine corps, besides temporary ratings, such as gun-pointer, gun-trainer, gun-captain, etc. Each rank and rating carries its rigidly prescribed duties, as well as its distinctive uniform and pay. That such a multitudinous host of types and individuals, both material and personnel, can be actually combined in one unit fleet, and that fleet operated as a mobile directable organism by its admiral, is a high achievement of the human intellect.

How is it done?

By discipline, by training, by knowledge, by energy, by devotion, by will; by the exercise of those mental, moral, and spiritual faculties that may be grouped under the one term "mind": the same power that co-ordinates and controls a still more complex machine, the organism of the human body.

Despite its relative crudeness, a fleet possesses, more fully than any other fruit of man's endeavor, the characteristics of an organism, defined by Webster as "an individual constituted to carry on the activities of life by means of parts or organs more or less separate in function, but mutually dependent." And though it must be true that no fleet can approximate the perfection of nature's organisms, nevertheless there is an analogy which may help us to see how a complex fleet of complex vessels has been slowly evolved from the simple galley fleets of earlier days; how its various parts may be mutually dependent yet severally independent; and how all must be made to work as one vast unit, and directed as one vast unit by the controlling mind toward "the end in view."[1]

The common idea is that an army consists of a number of soldiers, and a navy of a number of ships. This idea is due to a failure to realize that soldiers and ships are merely instruments, and that they are useless instruments unless directed by a trained intelligence: that the first essential in an army and the first essential in a navy is mind, which first correctly estimates the situation, then makes wise plans to meet it, then carries out those plans; which organizes the men and designs the ships, and then directs the physical power exertable by the men and the ships toward "the end in view."

Owing to the enormous mechanical power made available in ships by the floating properties of water, machinery is more used by navies than by armies; but this does not mean that machinery can take the place of men more successfully in navies than in armies, except in the sense that navies can use more mechanical power. The abundant use of machines and instruments in navies does not mean that machinery and instruments can take the place of trained intelligence—but exactly the reverse. Under the guidance of trained intelligence, a machine or instrument can perform wonders. But it is not the machinery that does the wonders; it is the trained intelligence that devised the instrument or machine, and the trained intelligence that operates it. Let the trained intelligence err, or sleep, and note the results that follow. The *Titanic,* a mass of 40,000 tons, moving through the water at 20 knots an hour, a marvel of the science and skill of man, crashes into an iceberg, because the trained intelligence directing her errs—and is reduced at once to an inert mass of iron and brass. The

---

1. Fiske did not have systems theory to draw on, so he virtually invented it. His organism—later his "fighting machine"—is (1) a complex of entities which (2) function interactively and cooperatively to (3) accomplish an end.

mighty fleet of Russia meets the Japanese fleet in Tsushima Straits; and because the trained intelligence that directed its movements seriously erred, in an engagement decided in less than an hour, is stripped of its power and glory, and transformed into a disorganized aggregation of separate ships—some sunk, some sinking, some in flight. The Japanese fleet, on the other hand, because it is directed with an intelligence more highly trained than that which directs the Russian fleet, and because, in consequence, the officers and enlisted men perform their various duties not only in the actual battle, but in preparation for it, with a skill greater than that used in the Russian fleet, suffers but little damage in the fight—though the advantage in number and size of ships is slightly with the Russians. As a consequence of that battle, the war between Russia and Japan was decided in favor of Japan, and terms of peace were soon agreed upon. Russia lost practically all the ships that took part in the battle, and several thousand of her officers and sailors—and *she lost the whole object for which she went to war.*

The difference between the Russian and Japanese fleets that gave the victory to the Japanese was a difference in trained intelligence and in the relative degrees of preparedness which that difference caused.

During the actual battle, the intelligence was that of the officers and men in the respective fleets, in managing the two fleets, the ships themselves, and the guns, engines, and machines of all kinds that those ships contained. It is this factor—trained intelligence—that has decided most of the battles of history, and the course that nations thereafter followed. Battles have usually been fought between forces not very different in point of numbers and material, for the reason that a force which knew itself to be weaker than another would not fight unless compelled to fight; and in cases where two forces of widely differing strength have fought, the situation has usually been brought about directly by a superior intelligence. In fact, one of the most frequent and important endeavors of strategy and tactics—used triumphantly by Napoleon—has always been such a handling of one's forces as to be superior to the enemy at the point of contact—to "get the mostest men there the firstest," as General Forrest is said to have expressed it.[2]

The effect of superior-trained intelligence is greatest "at the top," but it can accomplish little unless a fine intelligence permeates the whole. A fine intelligence at the top will so direct the men below, will so select men for the various posts, and will so co-ordinate their efforts, that the organization will resemble a veritable organism: all the various organs fulfilling separately yet accurately their allotted functions; all the fire-control parties, all the gun crews, all the torpedo crews, all the engineer forces properly organized and drilled; all the hulls of the vessels, all the guns, all the torpedoes, all the multifarious engines, machines, and instruments in good material condition and correctly adjusted for use.

But it is not only in the actual battle that fine intelligence is required; it is required long before the battle and far distant from the scene—in the "admiralty" at home. The Japanese fleet set out fully manned with a highly trained, enthusiastic, and confident personnel; the Russian fleet set out manned with a poorly trained and discouraged personnel, only too well aware of their defects. The issue at Tsushima was decided before the respective fleets left their respective homes— though that issue was not then known to mortals. The battle emphasized, but did not prove, what had been proved a hundred times before: the paramount importance of preparedness; that *when two forces fight—the actual battle merely*

2. Nathan Bedford Forrest was not so backwoods as his famous misquotation would imply. Heinl is accurate: "I always make it a rule to get there first with the most men." (Robert D. Heinl, Jr., *Dictionary of Military and Naval Quotations* [Annapolis, Md., 1966].)

secures the decision as to the relative values of two completed machines, and their degrees of preparedness for use.

Preparedness of material is not, of course, so important as preparedness of personnel, because if the personnel is prepared, they will inevitably prepare the material. And the preparedness must pervade all grades: for while it is true that the preparedness of those in high command is more important than the preparedness of those in minor posts, yet there is no post so lowly that its good or its ill performance will not be a factor in the net result. An unskilful oiler may cause a hot bearing that will slow down a battleship, and put out of order the column of a squadron; a signalman's mistake may throw a fleet into confusion.

Perfect preparedness of personnel and material is essential because events follow each other so rapidly in war that no preparation can be made after it has begun. To fight is the most intense work a man can do; and a war is nothing but a fight. No matter how great or how small a war may be, no war can lose the essential qualities of a fight, or (save in the treatment of prisoners) be more brutal or less brutal when fought between two little savage tribes, than when fought between two colossal groups of Christian nations, civilized to the highest point. War is the acme of the endeavor of man. Each side determines that it will win at all costs and at all hazards; that nobody's comfort, happiness, or safety shall receive the slightest consideration; that everybody's strength and courage must be worked to the limit by night as well as by day, and that there must be no rest and no yielding to any softening influence whatever; that the whole strength and mind of the nation, and of every individual in it, must be devoted, and must be sacrificed, if need be, to the cause at stake.

In war, a navy's primary duty has usually been to protect the coast and trade routes of its country; and in order to do this, it has had to be able to oppose to an attacking fleet a defending fleet more militarily effective. If it were less effective, even if no invasion were attempted, the attacking fleet could cripple or destroy the defending fleet and then institute a blockade. In modern times an effective blockade, or at least a hostile patrol of trade routes, could be held hundreds of miles from the coast, where the menace of submarines would be negligible;[3] and this blockade would stop practically all import and export trade. This would compel the country to live exclusively on its own resources, and renounce intercourse with the outside world. Some countries could exist a long time under these conditions. But they would exist merely, and the condition of mere existence would never end until they sued for peace; because, even if new warships were constructed with which to beat off the enemy, each new and untrained ship would be sunk or captured shortly after putting out to sea as, on June 1, 1813, in Massachusetts Bay, the American frigate *Chesapeake* was captured and nearly half her crew were killed and wounded in fifteen minutes by a ship almost identical in the material qualities of size and armament—the better-trained British frigate *Shannon*.

For these reasons, every nation that has acquired and has long retained prosperity, has realized that every country liable to be attacked by any navy must either be defended by some powerful country, or else must keep a navy ready to repel the attack successfully. To do this, the defending navy must be ready when the attack comes; because if not ready then, it will never have time to get ready.[4] In regard to our own country, much stress is laid by some intelligent people—who for-

3. Fiske merely reflects current attitudes, with the submarine as the coastal defender of trade, not the attacker. His thrust is accurate that in the future the interdiction of shipping will occur farther and farther from the port terminals.

4. Although Fiske leaves personalities out of his discussion of fleet readiness, the sum and substance of his quarrel with Daniels as aid for operations, 1913–1915, was over this single issue.

get the *Chesapeake* and *Shannon*—on the 3,000 miles of water stretching between the United States and Europe. This 3,000 miles is, of course, a factor of importance, but it is not a prohibition, because it can be traversed with great surety and quickness—with much greater surety and quickness, for instance, than the 12,000 miles traversed by the Russian fleet, in 1904, in steaming from Russia to Japan.

The 3,000 miles that separate the United States from Europe can be traversed by a fleet more powerful than ours in from two to three weeks; and the fleet would probably arrive on our shores in good condition, and manned by full crews of well-trained officers and men, habituated to their duties by recent practice and thoroughly ready to fight, as the *Shannon* was. We could not meet this fleet successfully unless we met it with a fleet more militarily effective; and we could not do this unless we had in the regular service and the reserve a personnel of officers and men sufficiently numerous to man immediately all the vessels that would be needed, and to man in addition all the shore stations, which would have to be expanded to a war basis. The officers and enlisted men, of course, would have to be at least as well trained as the corresponding personnel in the attacking fleet, and have as recent and thorough practice in their respective duties; for otherwise, no matter how brave and devoted they might be, the fate of the American fleet would be the fate of the *Chesapeake*.

In order to be ready when war breaks, the first essential is a plan for preparation. Preparation is divided naturally into two parts: first, preparation of sufficient material and personnel; second, preparation of plans for the conduct of the war after it has begun. These two parts are both considered in what are technically called "War Plans."

Preparation for war has always been known to be essential. Lack of preparation has never been due to lack of knowledge, but always to neglect. The difference between the wise and the foolish virgins was not a difference in knowledge but a

96

difference in character. The difference between Alexander's little army and the tremendous army of Darius was not so much in numbers as in preparedness. Trained under Philip of Macedon for many years, organized for conquest and aggression, prepared to meet any situation that might arise, Philip's army carried Philip's son from victory to victory, and made him the master of the world. Cæsar was great in peace as well as war, but it was by Cæsar's army that Cæsar's greatness was established; and it was a thoroughness of preparation unknown before that made Cæsar's army great. Napoleon's successes were built on the splendid preparation of a mind transcendently fitted to grasp both principles and details, and on the comparatively unprepared state of his opponents.[5]

The Great Elector began in 1640 a course of laborious and scientific preparation which committed all Prussia, as well as the army, to acquiring what now we call "efficiency." As this plan developed, especially under the Elector's grandson King Frederick William, the next King found himself, as Alexander had done, the chief of an army more highly prepared for war than any other. By means of that army he made himself Frederick the Great, and raised Prussia from a minor position to the first rank of European Powers. Pursuing Frederick William's system of progressive preparation, Prussia continued her prosperous course till William I defeated Austria, then France, and founded the German Empire. This does not mean that the only result of developing national efficiency to its highest point is to secure success in war—in fact, we know that it is not. But it does mean that the same quality—efficiency—which tends to prosperity in peace tends also to victory in war.

Preparing for war was a simple thing in the olden days

5. What gives weight to Fiske's words is that his life exemplified what he preached. His peacetime contributions, technical, operational, tactical, and organizational, were unmatched.

compared with preparing now, for the reason that the implements of war are much more numerous and complicated than they used to be, especially in navies. A navy is not ready unless all preparations and plans have been made, tested, and kept up to date, to insure that all of the vessels of every kind and all the shore stations will be in material condition, fully equipped and manned by a sufficient and efficient personnel of officers and crews, in time to meet the enemy on advantageous terms, and unless the central authority has already decided what it will do, when any probable emergency shall arise. This was the condition of the German army in 1870. This was also the condition of the British navy, when war broke out in August, 1914; the British navy was ready; and therefore it was able to assume command of the sea at once, drive its enemy's commerce from the ocean, and imprison its fleets in sheltered ports.

In all countries the peace establishment of the army and navy is smaller than the war establishment, for reasons of economy, upon the assumption that there will be enough time after war is declared to get on a war basis before the enemy can strike. But since 1870, all the military nations have realized that the vital struggle of a war takes place *before* a shot is fired; that *the factors that decide which nation shall be the victor and which the vanquished are determined before the war begins;* that they are simply "functions" of preparedness. Germany was ready not only for war but for victory, because her troops were so much better trained, organized, and equipped than those of France, and her war plans so much more complete, that she was able to lay France prostrate, before the enormous resources of that country in men and material could rally in her defense.

The relative conditions in which two opposing forces will enter a war, and their relative performances afterward, will depend upon the relative excellence of the war plans made for them, and the thoroughness with which the plans are tested before war breaks. So it is not difficult to see why all the great armies have patterned after Germany, and organized special bodies of officers for the preparation and execution of war plans; and why it is that they endeavor to secure for that peculiar duty the most thorough and industrious of their officers. Owing to the nature of war itself, the principles of warfare apply in their essentials to navies as well as to armies; and so the navies have patterned after the armies and made plans whereby they can get ready to fight in fleet organization on the ocean with the greatest possible effectiveness in the shortest possible time.

During peace times every navy is maintained on a "peace basis"; only such ships and other material being kept in full commission, and only such a number of officers and enlisted men being actively employed, as the appropriations allotted by the government permit. Those ships and other material that are not actually in commission are maintained in reserve, a condition of partial readiness, of which several degrees are recognized, in which a reduced number of officers and men are kept on board, and the various structures and apparatus are kept in as high a degree of readiness as circumstances will permit. In order to man in time of war these vessels in reserve, and insure a sufficient personnel in the active fleet, a "naval reserve" is organized in each country, composed of officers and men who have had experience in the regular navy. They are compelled to undergo a specific amount of training each year, to keep themselves in readiness at all times to answer the call for active service on short notice, and to maintain such communication with the government as will make it easy to locate any man at any moment.

The act of getting ready, the passing from a state of peace to a state of readiness for fighting, is called "mobilization." Mobilization plans are an important element in war plans, but the details of any mobilization plan are of such a confidential nature that it would not be proper to discuss them in public print. There can be no impropriety, however, in making the general statement that in all navies the endeavor is made to keep the mobilization plans continually up to date, and to have them prepared in such detail that every officer and enlisted man in active service, the retired list, the naval reserve, and the naval militia, will become instantly available for a predetermined duty, and that every shore station and every necessary vessel will be ready to take part. The plans prescribe methods in very great detail whereby the ships and other vessels in reserve can be quickly put into commission with full crews of officers and men, all their various equipments, fuel, and ammunition put on board, and the vessels themselves sent out to sea to join the fleet. In addition, plans are made whereby certain auxiliaries can be fitted out at once and put into commission—such as supply ships, ammunition ships, transports, colliers, mine ships, hospital ships, etc. The mass of detailed plans, orders, and instructions is stupendous and bewildering. Years of study, trial, and rectification are required to get them into such condition that the plans can be put into immediate and effective use when war breaks out.[6] The work must be done, however, and with the utmost thoroughness, *before* war breaks out; otherwise it will never be

6. On 31 October 1914, four months after the outbreak of the First World War, Fiske offered to bet anyone on his staff, giving 2:1 odds, that the United States would be drawn into the war within two years. He had no takers. On 9 November Fiske wrote a memorandum for Secretary Daniels, which he later was to say was the most important he ever wrote and which he quotes in its entirety in his autobiography (pp. 555–560). It was rich in specific recommendations dealing with preparedness. Daniels tried to get Fiske to soften his stance, and Fiske declined. Although Fiske, as aid for operations, was in effect the spokesman for the naval officer corps, he was not unopposed by senior officers. The chief of the Bureau of Navigation (personnel) and the aid for material took Daniels's side, a costly sense of loyalty. Indicative of Fiske's natural inclination to work within the system, his exasperation is only barely discernible in this book.

done, if an active enemy is about, because he will strike at once—and then it will be too late.

In most of the great naval countries the work of mobilizing the fleet is comparatively easy, for the reason that the coastline is short and is not far from any part of the interior, enabling reserves to live in fairly close touch with the coast and with naval affairs, and so near the coast that they can get quickly to any port. But the conditions in the United States are more difficult than those in any other country, because of the enormous stretch of our coast, the great average distance from any place in our country to the coast, the difficulty of getting a naval reserve that could be of practical use (owing to the ease with which young men can make a comfortable living on land), and the perilous slowness of the nation as a whole to realize the necessity for preparedness.

As an offset to this, we have the 3,000 miles of ocean between us and Europe, and the 5,000 miles between us and Asia; and on account of this we may to a certain extent discount the danger of attack and the preparedness required to meet it. But our discount should be reasonable and reasoned out, and certainly not excessive. Fortunately the problem of how much time we should allow for mobilizing and joining the fleet is easy, as a moment's thought will show us that it must be simply the two weeks needed for a fleet to come from Europe to America; for we must realize that the report of the sailing of the hostile fleet would be the first news we should get of any hostile preparation or intent.

The general situation in which every isolated naval nation stands regarding other nations is not complicated but very plain. Each nation has, as possible opponents in its policy, certain countries. The naval forces of those countries and the time in which they can be made ready are known with sufficient accuracy for practical purposes. If any isolated naval nation wishes to carry out a policy which any of those coun-

101

tries will forcibly oppose she must either build a navy equal to that of the other country, or else be prepared to abandon any attempt to force her policies. Stating the question in another way, she can carry out only such policies as do not require for their enforcement a navy stronger than she has.

It is true that diplomacy and the jealousies of foreign powers unite to make possible the averting of war during long periods of time. Diplomacy averted war with Germany for forty-three years, but it could not continue to avert war eternally. War finally broke out with a violence unparalleled in history, and possessing a magnitude proportional to the duration of the preceding peace. "Long coming long last, short notice soon past" is a sailor's maxim about storms; and it seems not inapplicable to wars. Certain it is that the frequent wars of savage tribes are far less terrible than the infrequent wars of enlightened powers.

This indicates that, even though a nation may be able to avert war for a long time, war will come some day, in a form which the present war foreshadows; and it suggests the possibility that the longer the war is averted, the more tremendous it will be, the greater the relative unpreparedness of a slothful nation, and the sharper her punishment when war finally breaks upon her.

CHAPTER FIVE

NAVAL DEFENSE

THERE HAS NEVER been a time since Cain slew Abel when men have not been compelled to devote a considerable part of their energies to self-defense. In the early ages, before large organizations existed or the mechanic arts had made much progress, defense was mostly defense of life itself. As time went on, and people amassed goods and chattels, and organized in groups and tribes, it came to include the defense of property—not only the property of individuals, but also of the tribe and the land it occupied. Still later, defense came to include good name or reputation, when it was realized that the reputation, even of an organization, could not be destroyed without doing it an injury.

At the present day, owing to the complexity of nations and other organizations, and to the long time during which many of them have existed, the question of defense has become extremely difficult. The places in which defense has been brought to its highest excellence are the large cities of the civilized countries; for there we see that defense of the life, property, and reputation of every individual has been carefully provided for. This has been made possible by the intimate intermingling of the people, the absence of racial rivalries, and the fact that the interests of all are identical in the matter of defense of life, property, and reputation; since, no matter how bad any individual may be, he wishes that others shall be good, in order that he himself may be safe.

The defense of reputation has two aspects: the practical and the sentimental. The practical aspect regards the defense of that element of reputation which affects ability to "make a living"; while the sentimental aspect is concerned with the purely personal reputation of the individual, or with the reputation of an organization or a nation. The sentimental aspect is much more important, especially in enlightened nations, than is realized by some who have not thought much about it; for there is, fortunately, in every decent man a craving for the esteem and even the affection of his fellow men; and a knowledge that, no matter how wealthy or powerful he may be, he cannot be happy if he knows that he is despised.

The fact that individuals organize to acquire the strength of united effort brings about, among organizations, a spirit of competition like that among individuals. It is more intense, however, because no man alone can get up the enthusiasms that ten men acting together can get up, and ten men cannot get up as much as a thousand. The longer any organization is maintained, the sharper this spirit of rivalry grows to be, owing to the feeling of clanship that propinquity and material interests evoke. Its acme is found in those organizations called nations, that have lived together, nourished from the same soil, for generations; where the same loves and jealousies and hates that they now feel were felt by their fathers and their grandfathers and great-grandfathers for centuries back. Among a people possessing the potentialities of national solidarity and greatness this feeling waxes into a self-sacrificing devotion to the nation and to the land that bore them.

That there should be such a thing is sometimes deplored; because patriotism, like all human qualities, has its bad side and its unfortunate effects. If it were not for patriotism there would probably be no war, and the greatest suffering that the world endures would thus be obviated. But if it were not for patriotism there would be no competition among nations; and in any one nation there would be no national spirit, no endeavor on the part of every man to do his part toward making her strong, efficient, and of good repute or toward making the people individually prosperous and happy. In the same way, on a smaller scale, many people deplore the necessity of competition among organizations, saying that it is ruthless and selfish; that it stamps out the individual; that it makes every man a mere cog in a money-getting machine; that it brings about strife, hatred, jealousies, and sometimes murders; that, if it were not for competition, all men would live together in peace.

This may be so; but if it were not for competition there would probably be little of that strenuous endeavor without which no effective progress in advancing the welfare of men has ever yet been made. Of course, it may be that what we call "progress" has really not advanced the welfare of men; that the savage in Samoa is as happy as the millionaire in New York; that knowledge itself is not an unmixed benefit; and if we accept this view, we may logically declare that competition, progress, and patriotism are all disadvantages. But who will go so far? It seems to be a fact that we cannot get something for nothing: that every plus has its minus, every joy its pain; that if men succeed in passing beyond the savage state, and in overcoming the forces of nature, so that they can live in houses with every modern luxury and convenience, they must pay for it by a condition of competition that causes personal jealousies among individuals, commercial wars among organizations, physical wars among nations.

Yet the instinctive desire of every one is for peace and comfort, for the maximum of good with the minimum of exertion; and therefore the normal person dislikes to see interjected into human life the abominable confusion of war. From this it comes about that every nation, even if it consciously brings about a war, always endeavors to make it appear that the other party is the aggressor. For this reason in every country the army and navy are said to be for the "defense" of the country. No nation, no matter how aggressive its policy may secretly be, openly declares that it intends to provoke aggression. This does not mean that any nation ever deliberately raises an army and navy for aggression, and then consciously deceives the world in regard to its intention; for men are so constituted as to feel more or less unconsciously that their interests and desires are proper and those of their opponent wrong; and every nation is so firmly persuaded of the righteousness of its own policies as to feel that any country which exhibits antagonism toward these policies is trying to provoke a fight.

Now these policies, especially after a nation has adhered to them for long, seem vital in her eyes, and they usually are so. To Great Britain, whose major policy is that she must be mistress of the seas, it is vital that she should be. Her people are surrounded by the ocean, and unless they are willing simply to eke out an agricultural existence, it is essential that she should be able to manufacture articles, send them out in ships to all parts of the world, and receive in return money and the products of other lands. In order that she may be able to do this, she must feel sure that no power on earth can restrain the peaceful sailing to and fro of her exporting and importing ships. This assurance can be had only through physical force; it can be exerted only by a navy. Germany has been gradually coming into the same position, and the same clear comprehension, owing to the increase of her population, the growth of their desire for wealth, and their realization of the control by Great Britain and the United States of large areas of the surface of the earth. Germany's determination to break down, at least in part, that overpowering command of the sea which Great Britain wields has been the result. The ensuing rapid growth and excellence of Germany's navy and merchant marine brought Germany and England into sharp competition. Military and naval men have seen for years that these competing nations would have to go to war some day in "self-defense."

In the minds of some people the idea of what constitutes "defense" is rather hazy, and "defense" is deemed almost synonymous with "resistance." Perhaps the clearest idea of what constitutes "defense" is given in a sentence in Webster's Dictionary, that reads: "The inmates of a fortress are *defended* by its guns, *protected* by its walls, and *guarded* against surprise by sentries."

The distinction is important, and the partially aggressive character of defense it indicates is exemplified in all walks of human and brute life. Any animal, no matter how peaceably inclined, will turn on his aggressor—unless, indeed, he runs away. No one ever saw any brute oppose a merely passive resistance to attack. Every man recognizes in himself an instinct to hit back if he is hit. If it be an instinct, it must have been implanted in us for a reason; and the reason is not hard to find in the universal law of self-protection, which cannot be satisfied with the ineffectual method of mere parrying or resisting.

Naval defense, like military defense, therefore, is not passive defense only, but contains an element of "offense" as well. When the defense contains in large measure the element of offense, it is said in military parlance to be "offensive-defensive"; and the most effective defensive is this offensive-defensive. When a defending force throws off its defensive attitude entirely and advances boldly to attack, it is said to have "assumed the offensive"; but even this assumption, especially if it be temporary—as when a beleaguered garrison makes a sortie—does not rob the situation of its defensive character.[1]

---

1. Fiske reflects his culture, which believes, correctly, that even on the defensive a fleet must use its mobility and strike blows where the enemy is

For these reasons the dividing line between offense and defense is very vague; and it is made more vague through a realization by all military people that the offense has certain decided advantages over the defense (unless the defense has the advantage of position); so that when strained relations between two nations come, each is so fearful that the other will take the offensive first, when the two nations are near each other, that it is apt to take the offensive first—in real *self-defense!* A striking illustration is the action of certain European Powers in the latter part of July, 1914.

In addition to the sincere convictions of either party, there is also apt to be considerable yielding to the temptation to persuade the world that the other party is the aggressor, merely to get the sympathy that usually goes to the innocent victim—the support of what Bismarck called "the imponderables." Few wars have been frankly "offensive," like the conquests of Alexander, Cæsar, and Pizarro, at least in modern times; each side has usually claimed (and often sincerely believed) that its action was demanded in self-defense and that its cause was just.

To some in the United States naval defense means merely defense against invasion. This notion is of recent growth, and certainly was not held by the framers of our Constitution. Section 8 of Article I defines the powers of Congress; and

---

vulnerable, while evading decisive battle. Army men, leaning on Clausewitz, assert a preference to assume a defensive posture on the battlefield until the enemy is weakened enough to counterattack. The U.S. Navy fought World War II according to the tenets Fiske enunciates. Immediately after Pearl Harbor, Nimitz initiated hit-and-run carrier strikes in the Central Pacific. Early in 1942 King sponsored the April bombing of Tokyo. Two months after the Battle of Midway, naval forces retook Guadalcanal, and the subsequent year-long Solomons Campaign is now called our offensive-defensive phase, a period of temporizing activity to blunt the Japanese offensive and also gain time to build up a combat force advantage sufficient for the navy's swift offensive sweep across the central Pacific in 1944.

although eight of the eighteen paragraphs deal exclusively with measures of defense on sea and land, only one of those paragraphs (the fifteenth) deals with invasion. The first paragraph reads:

> The Congress shall have power to lay and collect taxes, duties, imposts, and excises, *to pay the debts and provide for the common defense and general welfare of the United States;* but all duties, imposts, and excises shall be uniform throughout the United States.

The juxtaposition of the words "common defense" and "general welfare" in this admirably written paragraph could hardly have been accidental, or have been due to any other cause than a juxtaposition of those ideas in the minds of the Constitution's framers. And what more natural connection can there be between any two ideas than between those of common defense and general welfare, since the general welfare of no country has ever continued long unless it was defended. Now the general welfare of every maritime power has always been intimately concerned with its sea-borne commerce. It is only by means of sea-borne commerce, for instance, that Americans can live in the way Americans wish to live. "General welfare" means more than mere existence. A mere existence is the life a savage lives. Furthermore, the general welfare of a country requires the safety of its exported and imported goods while on the sea, and includes the right of its citizens to travel with safety in every land, to buy and sell in foreign ports, to feel a proper measure of self-respect and national respect wherever they may go, and to command from the people of the lands they visit a proper recognition of their claims to justice.

Naval defense may, therefore, be said to consist of three parts:

1st—Defense of the coast against bombardment and invasion.

2d—Defense of the trade routes traversed by ships carrying the exports and imports of the country.

3d—Defense of the national policy, including defense of the nation's reputation, honor, and prestige.[2]

Of these, defense of the coast against bombardment and invasion is the easiest, and defense of the national policy the most difficult; because in preventing bombardment and invasion the defender has the strategical advantage of being nearer home than the adversary; while in the defense of a country's policy, a naval force may have to "assume the offensive," and go even to the far distant coasts of the enemy—as the Russian fleet went to Tsushima, where it met its death.

In that part of naval defense which is concerned with trade routes, the strategical advantage must go, in general, to that side which is the nearer to the locality where the decisive battle may occur.

In laying down a policy of naval defense, however, it is not necessary to consider these three parts separately, because no nation can ever tell whether in the distant future its naval defense will have to be used directly for any one of the three, or for all. In general terms, it may be stated that in nearly all naval wars the fleet has been used more for the defense of the nation's policy than for the actual defense of the coasts or the trade routes. This does not mean that there has never been a bombardment or invasion, or that the defense of trade routes may not have been the cause of the war itself; but it does mean that in actual wars bombardment or invasion has been rare, the capture of merchant vessels has played a minor part, and the deciding events have been battles between two fleets, that were often far from the land of either.[3]

2. Still applicable today. The U.S. forward strategy is totally consistent. However, since the advent of SSBNs, the conclusion (in the next sentence of the text) is obsolete that defense against bombardment is easiest.

3. This was a common belief among American naval officers, but is wrong. Most naval operations had been against the shores.

110

Owing to the fact that within modern times most of the important countries of the world have been those of continental Europe, with frontiers contiguous, and in fact identical, the defense of a country has been largely committed to the army, and most of the wars have been on land. The country standing in exception to this has been Great Britain, whose isolated and insular situation demanded a defense that was strictly naval. The tremendous advance in recent times of the engineering arts, by which ships became larger and faster, and able to carry more powerful and accurate guns than ever before, has enhanced the value of naval power and enabled Great Britain to reach all over the surface of the earth, and become more powerful than any continental nation. Thus she has made out of the very weakness of her position a paramount tower of strength.

Naval defense was taken up systematically in Great Britain in the eighth century by King Offa,[4] to whom is credited the maxim, "He who would be secure on land must be supreme at sea"; but it must have dropped to a low ebb by 1066, for William of Normandy landed in England unopposed.[5] Since that time Great Britain's naval defense, committed to her navy, has increased steadily in effectiveness and power, keeping pace with the increase in the national interests it defended, and utilizing all the growing resources of wealth and science which the world afforded. Until the present crisis, Great Britain's naval defense did its most important work during Napoleon's time, when Great Britain's standing, like the standing of every other European nation, was subjected to a strain that it could hardly bear. So keenly, however, did the

4. King of Mercia, A.D. 757 to 796. To him is also ascribed the great earth wall along the Welsh border known as "Offa's dike."

5. William got ashore unopposed because the Saxon King Harold had been fighting a Norse invasion near York. He rushed south but was too late to prevent the Norman conqueror's forces from establishing a fateful beachhead. It was the last successful invasion of Britain.

nation and the nation's great leader, Pitt,[6] realize the situation that the most strenuous measures were adopted to keep the navy up, press-gangs even visiting the houses of subjects of the King, taking men out and putting them by force on board his Majesty's ships. But the British navy, even more than the British army, brought Great Britain safe out of the Napoleonic danger, and made the British the paramount nation of the world.

Since then Great Britain has waxed more and more powerful, her avowed policy being that her navy should be equal to any other two; realizing that her aloofness in point of national characteristics and policy from all other nations made it possible that a coalition of at least two great nations might be pitted against her at a time when she could not get an ally. Accompanying the growth of the British navy has been the establishment of British foreign trade, British colonies, and British bases from which the navy could work, and the general making of a network of British commerce and British power over the surface of the earth. No other nation has ever dominated so large a part of the surface of the globe as has Great Britain during the last two centuries; and she has done it by means of her naval power. This naval power has been, in the language of Great Britain, for the "imperial defense"; not for coast defense alone, but for the defense of all the imperial interests, commercial and political, and even the imperial prestige. And this defense of prestige, it may here be remarked, is not a vainglorious defense, not an exhibition of a swaggering, swashbuckling spirit, but a recognition of the fact that the minds of men are so constituted that the prestige of an individual, an organization, or a nation has a practical value and is an actual force. No government that appreciates its respon-

6. William Pitt was prime minister during the French Revolution and Napoleonic Wars through 1806. He was arguably England's greatest wartime minister.

112

sibilities will willingly risk the prestige of the nation which it governs, because it knows that any weakening of it will be followed by a weakening of influence and a consequent increase of difficulty in attaining some "end in view."

The greatness of the British navy, compared with that of the British army and the other elements of Great Britain's government, has taken on magnified dimensions during the last half century. So long as war-ships used sails as their principal motive power, so long were they forced to employ methods of construction and equipment that forbade the efficient employment of high-power guns, the attainment of great speed, and the use of instruments of precision; so long, in other words, was their military effectiveness prevented from increasing greatly. But when the British navy decided to abandon sail power altogether and propel their ships by steam, a new phase was entered upon, in which every resource of the engineering arts and the physical sciences was called into requisition; and now, on board a dreadnaught, battle cruiser, destroyer, or submarine, can be found the highest examples of mechanical and electrical art and science. Every material resource which the brain and wealth of man can compass is enlisted in her naval defense; and in order to take advantage of the rapidity and certainty of movement they afford for operating fleets and ships, there has been a great advance in methods of operation, or, in military parlance, "staff work." To assist this work, the radio, the cable, and even the humble typewriter have contributed their essential share, with the result that to Great Britain's naval defense there has been devoted an extraordinary degree of efficiency, continuous effort, a more varied activity, and a larger expenditure of money than to any other object of man's activity.

The United States navy, to which is committed the naval defense of the United States, has followed the same lines as the British; and its task, while in some ways easier, is in other ways more difficult. Perhaps the chief reason why the naval defense of Great Britain is so difficult is the extreme closeness of her borders to the borders of her possible foes—for the English Channel is only twenty-three miles across from Dover to Calais. And yet the very narrowness of the Channel there lends a certain element of assistance to the defender of either coast against an enemy like Germany, because it enables the defender, by simply protecting that narrow area, to prevent an enemy from passing to the sea or from it, except by going around the British Isles. But while it is interesting thus to compare the tasks of two navies by comparing the lengths of coast line, populations, wealth, and areas of their countries, or their distances from possible antagonists, such comparisons are really misleading; for the reason that all nations are on a par in regard to the paramount element of national defense, which is defense of national policy. It was as important to Belgium as it was to Germany to maintain the national policy, and the army of Belgium was approximately as strong as that of Germany in proportion to her wealth, area, and population; but nevertheless the Belgian army was routed, and Belgium was conquered by the German army.[7]

Much has been written to prove that the sole reason for the possession of the paramount navy by Great Britain is that the soil of Great Britain cannot support her people. In an essay, entitled "Naval Power," which I contributed to the *United States Naval Institute* in 1911,[8] the fallacy of this was shown; and it was pointed out that even if Great Britain grew more than enough to feed her people, life could be made unendurable to the 60,000,000 living there (or to the people in any civilized and isolated country) by an effective blockading fleet. *The question of how great a navy any country needs depends, not on the size, but on the policies of that country,*

7. In August 1914.
8. U.S. Naval Institute *Proceedings*, June 1911, pp. 683–736. Chapter V is the kernel of that essay.

and on the navies of the countries that may oppose those policies. The navy that a country needs is a navy that can defend its policies, both offensively and defensively. If, for instance, the United States does not wish to enforce any policy that Great Britain would oppose, or to oppose any policy that Great Britain would enforce, then we may leave her navy out of consideration. But if we decide that we must maintain a certain policy which a certain country may oppose, then we must have a navy at least equal to hers; because we do not know whether we should have to meet that navy near our coast, or near hers, or far away from both. For the reason, furthermore, that a war with a European Power might occur at a period of strained relations with some Asiatic Power, we must realize the temptation to that Asiatic Power to seize the opportunity and attack us on the Pacific side, knowing that we should need all our navy on the Atlantic side. This seems to mean that in order to have an effective naval defense (since we are precluded by our policy from having European allies and no South American country could give us any effective naval help) we must have on each ocean a fleet as strong as that of any nation on that ocean against whose wishes we may have to enforce a policy—or against whose policy we may have to oppose resistance.

The essential requirement of any defense is that it shall be adequate; because an inadequate defense will be broken down, while the attack will retain a large proportion of its original strength. In the *United States Naval Institute,* in 1905,[9] the present writer showed, by means of a series of tables, how, when two forces fight, the force which is originally the more powerful will become gradually more powerful, relatively to the weaker, as the fight goes on. That, for

9. "American Naval Policy," U.S. Naval Institute *Proceedings,* January 1905, pp. 1–80, the U.S. Naval Institute's prize essay for that year. Fiske was then a commander.

instance, if two forces start with the relative powers of 10 and 8, the weaker force will be reduced so much more rapidly than the stronger that when it has been reduced to zero the stronger force will have a value of 5.69. The values mentioned indicated the actual fighting strength—strength made up of all the factors—material, physical, and psychic—that constituted it. Of course, none of these factors can ever be accurately compared; but nevertheless the tables seemed to prove that in a contest between two forces whose total strengths are as 10 and 8 one force will be reduced to zero, while the other will be reduced not quite one-half.[10]

One of the lessons drawn was "the folly of ineffectual resistance." Doubtless a clearer lesson would have been "the folly of ineffectual preparedness"; because, when the decision as to resistance or non-resistance is forced upon a nation, the matter is so urgent, the military, political, and international conditions so complex, and the excitement probably so intense that a wise decision is very difficult to reach; whereas the question of what constitutes effectual preparedness is simple, and needs merely to be approached with calm nerves and an open mind.

Inasmuch as the psychic element in defense is the strongest single element, it is apparent that if the decision is reached to prepare an effectual defense the nation must be absolutely united, and must appreciate at its full value the debilitating influence of opposition to the measure; for, no matter how much money a nation may expend, no matter how many lives it may sacrifice, its defense cannot have an efficiency proportional to the effort if a considerable number of its citizens are permitted to oppose it.

10. Fiske is describing the "square law" phenomenon. He returns to it with a fuller explanation in Chapter X, pp. 240–245, and again in Chapter XII, pp. 314–320.

In our own country there has been so much talking and writing recently about defense, that there is danger of the question coming to be considered academic; though no question is more practical, no question is more urgent. *Defense must defend.*

CHAPTER SIX

NAVAL POLICY

E VERY COUNTRY that has a satisfactory navy has acquired
it as the result of a far-seeing naval policy, not of opportunism or of chance. The country has first studied the question thoroughly, then decided what it ought to do, then decided how to do it.

Naval policy has to deal with three elements: material, personnel, and operations, which, though separate, are mutually
dependent. A clear comprehension of their actual relations
and relative weights can be obtained only by thorough study;
but without that comprehension no wise naval policy can
be formulated, and therefore no satisfactory navy can be
established.

The most obvious thing about a navy is its material: the
ponderous battleships, the picturesque destroyers, the submarines, the intricate engines of multifarious types, the radio,
the signal-flags, the torpedo that costs $8,000, the gun that
can sink a ship 10 miles away.

The United States navy ever since its beginning in 1775 has
excelled in its material; the ships have always been good, and
in many cases they have surpassed those of similar kind in
other navies. This has been due to the strong common sense
of the American people, their engineering skill, and their inventive genius.[1] The first war-ship to move under steam was

1. Fiske the scientist-engineer is well qualified to assess the American

the American ship *Demologos*, sometimes called the *Fulton the First*, constructed in 1813; the first electric torpedoes were American; the first submarine to do effective work in war was American; the first turret ship, the *Monitor*, was American; the first warship to use a screw propeller was the *Princeton*, an American; the naval telescope-sight was American. American ships now are not only well constructed, but all their equipments are of the best; and to-day the American battleship is the finest and most powerful vessel of her class in the world.

Our personnel, too, has always been good. The American seaman has always excelled, and so has the American gunner. No ships have ever been better handled than the American ships; no naval battles in history have been conducted with more skill and daring than those of American ships; no exploits in history surpass those of Cushing, Hobson, and Decatur.

In operations, however, in the handling of the navy as a whole, we have never excelled; though no better individual fleet leaders shine in the pages of all history than Farragut and Dewey.[2] The strategical operating of our material and personnel has not been in accordance with carefully laid plans, but has been left largely to the inspiration of the commander on the spot, both in peace and in war. Material has suffered from lack of a naval policy, but only quantitatively, because material is a subject that the people understand. Personnel has suffered more, because the people fail to realize the amount

navy's technological merit, and does so without exaggeration.

2. Regarding American naval heroes, Fiske might better have ended the sentence at the semicolon. Farragut and Dewey were competent and the best fleet leaders we had to offer, but until World War II the United States had no commanders to rival the world's best. This is the shrewd and conciliatory communicator speaking, not the objective critic, for he cannot here say we had none, and Dewey was one of Fiske's lifelong sponsors.

of training needed to make a personnel competent to perform their tasks successfully, in competition with the highly trained men of other navies. But operations have suffered incomparably more than material and personnel; because naturally the people do not comprehend the supreme importance of being ready, when war breaks out, to operate the material and personnel skilfully against an active enemy, in accordance with well-prepared strategic plans; nor do they realize how difficult and long would be the task of preparing and testing out those plans. Therefore, they fail to provide the necessary administrative machinery.[3]

In fact, the kind and amount of machinery needed to conduct operations skilfully and quickly cannot be decided wisely until the country adopts some naval policy; and in naval policy the United States must be admitted to have lagged behind almost every other civilized country. Spurred as we were to exertion by the coming of the Revolutionary War, we constructed hastily, though with skill, the splendid ships that did service in that war. But after the war, interest in the navy waned; and if it had not been for the enormous tribute demanded by the pirates of the Barbary coast from our government, and a realization of the fact that not only was it cheaper to build ships and fight the pirates than to pay the tribute, but paying the tribute was a disgraceful act, our navy would have run down even more than it did. Yet even with this warning, 1812 found our navy in a desperate condition. Rallying to the emergency, though too late to accomplish much practical result, we built a number of excellent ships, against the votes of many highly influential men in Congress. These ships did gallant service, and redeemed the reputation of Americans from

3. Since this was written, the Congress has so enlarged the scope of the Office of the Chief of Naval Operations as to make it a General Staff. (Author's note, added to the second edition, to which Fiske doubtless would have liked to add three cheers, even though modesty prohibited him from saying that he was the most important single individual to bring about this pivotal organizational achievement.)

the oft-repeated charge of being cowards and merely commercial men, though they were too few to prevent the blockade which British squadrons maintained on our Atlantic coast. After the war, the navy was again allowed to deteriorate; and although our ships were excellent, and the officers and men were excellent, and although the war with Mexico supplied some stimulation, the War of the Rebellion caught us in a very bad predicament. The country rose to this emergency too slowly, as before; but the enemy were even less prepared than we, so that during the four years of the Civil War we were able to construct, man, and buy several hundred ships of various kinds; with the result that, at the end of the war, our navy, if not quite so powerful as Great Britain's, was at least very close to it, and with a recent experience in actual war which the British navy did not possess.

After that war, the same story was repeated. The people convinced themselves that they would never again be forced to go to war; that they had seen the folly of it, and the misery of it, and would devote themselves thereafter to the delightful pursuits of peace. Gradually the fighting ships of the ironclad class were allowed to go to pieces; gradually even the larger ships of the wooden sailing class fell into disrepair; gradually the idea of war faded from the minds even of naval officers; gradually squadrons and fleets, as such, were broken up, and our ships were to be found scattered singly over all the seas, and swinging idly at their anchors in pleasant ports.

Fortunately, Admiral Luce and a very few other officers had learned the salient lessons of war during the Rebellion, and sturdily stood up against the decadent tendency of the times. Against much opposition, Luce succeeded in founding the Naval War College at Newport, where the study of war as an art in itself was to be prosecuted, and in enlisting Captain Mahan in the work. In a few years Mahan gave to the world that epochal book, "The Influence of Sea Power upon History" (embodying his lectures before the War College), which stirred the nations of Europe to such a realization of the significance of naval history, and such a comprehension of the efficacy of naval power, that they entered upon a determined competition for acquiring naval power, which continues to this day.

Meanwhile, a little before 1880, the people became aroused to the fact that though the country was growing richer, their navy was becoming weaker, while the navies of certain European countries were becoming stronger. So they began in 1880 the construction of what was then called "the new navy." The construction of the new ships was undertaken upon the lines of the ships then building abroad, which were in startling contrast with the useless old-fashioned American ships which then were flying our flag.

The construction of the material of the navy has progressed since then, but spasmodically. At every session of Congress tremendous efforts have been made by people desiring an adequate navy, and tremendous resistance has been made by people who believed that we required no navy, or at least only a little navy. The country at large has taken a bystander's interest in the contest, not knowing much about the pros and cons, but feeling in an indolent fashion that we needed some navy, though not much. The result has been, not a reasonable policy, but a succession of unreasonable compromises between the aims of the extremists on both sides.

Great Britain, on the other hand, has always regarded the navy question as one of the most difficult and important before the country, and has adopted, and for centuries has maintained, a definite naval policy. This does not mean that she has followed a rigid naval policy; for a naval policy, to be efficient, must be able to accommodate itself quickly to rapid changes in international situations, and to meet sudden dangers from even unexpected quarters—as the comparatively recent experience of Great Britain shows. At the beginning of this century the British navy was at the height of its splendor and self-confidence. Britannia ruled the waves, and Britannia's ships and squadrons enforced Britannia's policies in every sea. The next most powerful navy was that of France; but it was not nearly so large, and seemed to be no more efficient, in proportion to its size. Owing to Britain's wise and continuing policy, and the excellence of the British sailor and his ships, the British navy proudly and almost tranquilly held virtual command of all the seas.

But shortly after this century began, British officers discerned a new and disturbing element gradually developing on the horizon. The first thing which roused their attention to it was the unexpected attack of the Japanese torpedo-boats on the Russian squadron in Port Arthur. No war had been declared, and the Russian squadron was riding peacefully at anchor. The suddenness of the attack, and the distinct though incomplete success which it achieved, startled the British into a realization of the fact that there had been introduced into warfare on the sea methods and tactics requiring *a higher order of preparation* than had ever before been known; that the scientific methods which the Germans employed so effectively on land in 1870 had been adapted by the Japanese to naval warfare, and would necessitate the introduction into naval policies of *speedier methods* than had hitherto been needed.

Another event which had happened shortly before showed that naval policies would have to be modified, if they were to utilize recent advances in scientific methods. This event was the unprecedented success at target practice of H. M. S. *Terrible,* commanded by Captain Sir Percy Scott, which proved that by a long and strenuous training and the adoption of instruments of precision, it was possible to attain a skill in naval gunnery never attained before. Up to this moment the British navy had almost despised gunnery. Inheriting the traditions brought down from Howe, Rodney, and Nelson, permeated with the ideals of the "blue-water school," proud of being British seamen, proud of the pure white of their ships, enamoured of the stimulating breeziness of the quarterdeck and bridge, imbued with almost a contempt for such mathematical sciences as were not directly used in practical navigation, British naval officers exalted seamanship as the acme of their art, and took little interest in gunnery. All the battles of the past had been won by dash and seamanship and dogged persistence. Ships had always fought close alongside each other. No science had ever won any naval battle of the past, so why should they bother with science now—and why should they bother with target practice, except just enough to insure that the battery was in order, and that the men were not afraid of their guns? Besides, target practice dirtied the ship—a sacrilege to the British naval officer.

But the events of the war between Japan and Russia, especially the naval battles of Port Arthur, August 10, 1904, and the Sea of Japan, May 27, 1905, riveted their attention on the fact that something more than seamanship and navigation and clean ships would be needed, if the British navy was to maintain its proud supremacy on the sea; for in these battles, overwhelming victories were won purely by superior skill in gunnery, strategy, and tactics.

To these causes of awakening was added one still greater, but of like import—the rapid rise of the German navy from a position of comparative unimportance to one which threatened the British navy itself. The fact became gradually evident to British officers that the German navy was proceeding along the same lines as had proceeded the German army. Realizing the efficiency of the German Government, noting the public declarations of the German Emperor, observing the excellence of the German ships, the skill of the German naval officers, and the extraordinary energy which the German people were devoting to the improvement of the German navy—the British navy took alarm.

So did the other navies.

Beginning about 1904, Great Britain set to work with energy to reform her naval policy. Roused to action by the sense of coming danger, she augmented the size and number of vessels of all types; increased the personnel of all classes, regular and reserve; scrapped all obsolete craft; built (secretly) the epochal *Dreadnought,* and modernized in all particulars the British navy. In every great movement one man always stands pre-eminent. The man in this case was Admiral Sir John Fisher, first sea lord of the admiralty, afterward Lord Fisher.[4] Fisher brought about vital changes in the organization, methods, and even the spirit of the navy. He depleted the overgrown foreign squadrons, concentrated the British force in powerful fleets near home, established the War College, inculcated the study of strategy and tactics, appointed Sir Percy Scott as inspector of target practice, put the whole weight of his influence on the side of gunnery and efficiency, placed officers in high command who had the military idea as distinguished from the idea of the "blue-water school," and imbued the entire service with the avowed idea that they must get ready to fight to the death, not the French navy, with its easygoing methods, but the German navy, allied perhaps with some other. At the admiralty he introduced methods analogous to those of the General Staff, to maintain the navy ready for instant service at all times, to prepare and keep up to date mobilization plans in the utmost detail, and to arrange plans for the conduct of war in such wise that after a war should break out, all the various probable situations would have been studied out in advance.

The work required at the admiralty, and still more in the fleet—night and day and in all weathers—taxed mental and

4. John Arbuthnot Fisher, first Baron Fisher; first sea lord, 1903–1909, during the modernization of the British navy; forceful, articulate, imaginative, and ruthless. As a seagoing officer he was one of the earliest to appreciate the need for more accurate long-range gunnery, hence his sponsorship of Percy Scott. In Whitehall he produced HMS *Dreadnought,* Britain's first all-big-gun battleship, and many of her successors.

physical endurance to the limit; but the result was complete success; for when war broke out on the 1st of August, 1914, the British navy was absolutely ready. Many complaints have appeared in print about the unreadiness of Great Britain; but no one who knows anything of the facts supposes that these criticisms include Great Britain's navy.

The United States navy in the early part of this century occupied, relatively to others, a very ill-defined position; but the increased interest taken in it by our people after the Spanish War, combined with the destruction of the flower of the Russian fleet in the Russo-Japanese War, and the crushing blow inflicted on the French navy by the maladministration of Camille Pelletan, resulted in placing our navy, about three years ago, in a position second only to Great Britain's—a position which it recently has lost. Owing to a common origin and language, our navy has always followed the British navy, though at a somewhat respectful distance; and while it is true that in point of mechanical inventions we are ahead, in seamanship, navigation, and engineering on a par, and in gunnery and tactics not far behind, yet we must admit that in policy and in policy's first cousin, strategy, we are very far in the rear.

There are many reasons why this should be, the first being that the British navy has nearly always lived under more stimulating conditions than we, because the probability of war has seemed greater, and because the United States has underestimated what reasonable probability there has been, and failed to realize how tremendously difficult would be the task of getting ready for it. Owing to the present war, our people have gradually come to see that they must get more ships and other material; but they realize this as only a measure of urgency, and not as a matter of policy. If the emergency passes us by in safety, the people may see in this fact only a confirmation of their notion that war can be postponed *ad infinitum,* and may therefore fail to take due precautions for the future. If so, when we at last become involved in a sudden war, we shall be as unprepared as now; and, relatively to some aggressive nation which, foreseeing this, may purposely prepare itself, we shall be more unprepared.

A curious phase of the navy question in our country is the fact that very few people, even the most extreme partisans for or against a large navy, have ever studied it as a problem and endeavored to arrive at a correct solution. Few have realized that it is a problem, in the strictest sense of the word; and that unless one approaches it as such his conclusions cannot be correct except by accident.

In Germany, on the other hand, and equally in Japan, the question has been taken up as a concrete problem, just as definite as a problem in engineering. They have used for solving it the method called "The Estimate of the Situation," originated by the German General Staff, which is now adopted in all the armies and navies of civilized countries for the solution of military problems. Previous to the adoption of this method the general procedure had been such as is now common in civil life, when a number of people forming a group desire to make a decision as to what they will do in any given contingency. The usual procedure is for some one to suggest that a certain thing be done, then for somebody else to suggest that something else be done, and so on; and then finally for the group to make a decision which is virtually a compromise. This procedure is faulty, and the decisions resulting are apt to be unwise; because it is quite possible that some very important factors may be overlooked, and equally possible that some other factors be given undue weight. Furthermore, a measure advocated by a man who has the persuasive and emotional abilities of the orator is more apt to be favorably considered than a measure advocated by a man not possessing those abilities.

In the "Estimate of the Situation" method, on the other hand, the orator has no opportunity, because the procedure is

127

simply an accurate process of reasoning. It is divided into four parts. The first part consists of a careful study of the "mission," ending in a clear determination of what the "mission" really is—that is, *what is the thing which it is desired to do?* The second part consists of a careful study, and eventually a clear comprehension, of the difficulties in the way; the third part consists of a careful study, and eventually a clear comprehension, of what facilities are available with which to overcome the difficulties; the fourth part consists of a careful study of the mission, difficulties and facilities, in their mutual relations, and a "decision" as to what should therefore be done.

Military and naval people are so thoroughly convinced of the value of this method that they always employ it when making important decisions, writing down the various factors and the successive steps in regular order and in complete detail.

In this country, while naval and military people use this method in their comparatively minor problems, the country at large does not use it in deciding the major problem—that is, in deciding how much navy they want, and of what composition. They do not take even the first step toward formulating a naval policy, because they do not study the "mission" of the navy—that is, *they do not study the international and national situations and their bearing on the need for a navy.* Yet until they do this they will not be in a sufficiently informed condition of mind to determine what the "mission" is—that is, what they wish the navy to be able to do—because, before they can formulate the mission they must resolve what foreign navy or navies that mission must include. If they decide that the mission of the navy is to guard our coast and trade routes against the hostile efforts of Liberia the resulting naval policy will be simple and inexpensive; while if they conclude that the mission of our navy is to guard our coast and trade routes against the hostile acts of *any* navy the resulting naval policy will be so difficult and costly as to tax the brain and wealth of the country to a degree that will depend on *the length of time that will elapse before the date at which the navy must be ready to fulfil that mission.*[5]

This factor reminds us of another factor: *the minimum time in which the navy can get ready to fulfil a given mission* (for instance, to protect us against any navy): and we cannot decide the mission correctly without taking this factor into account. For example, it would be foolish to decide that the mission of our navy is to protect us *now* against any navy, including the greatest, when it would take us at least twenty years to develop and train a navy to accomplish that task; and it would be equally foolish to decide that the mission is to protect us against any navy *except* the greatest, because such a decision could rest on no other ground than present improbability of conflict with the greatest navy, or improbability for the very few years ahead (say two or three) which we poor mortals can forecast.

This reasoning seems to indicate that the first step in formulating a naval policy for the United States is to realize that any conclusion as to which navies should be included in the mission of our navy must not exclude any navy about whose peaceful conduct toward us we can entertain a reasonable doubt, *during the period of time which we would require to get ready to meet her.* For instance, inasmuch as it would take us at least twenty years to get ready to protect ourselves against the hostile efforts of the British navy, we cannot exclude even that navy from a consideration of the mission of

5. In the foregoing we see the difference between a strategic theorist who aims to describe the proper basis of sound policy and strategy, and Fiske, the practical man who wanted to transform strategic insight (Mahan's) into decisions and achievements. He resorts to the estimate of the situation as the decision-making vehicle. The estimate as the basis for decision was second nature to all naval officers who had attended the U.S. Naval War College from early in this century through World War II.

our own, unless we entertain no doubt of the peaceful attitude of that navy toward us for at least that twenty years.

Clearly, the problem is not only very important but very difficult—perhaps the most difficult single problem before the country; and for this reason, naval officers have long marvelled that the leading minds of the country do not undertake it. Perhaps one reason is that they do not know how difficult it is: that they do not realize the extraordinary complexity of modern ships and engines, and the trained skill required to handle them; that they do not realize what Great Britain now realizes, that we must prepare for one of the most stupendous struggles ever carried on; that we must have a personnel both of officers and enlisted men trained to the highest point, because they will have to meet officers and enlisted men trained to the highest point; that the training must be such that the skill produced can be exercised by night and day, in cold and heat, in storm and calm, under circumstances of the utmost possible difficulty and danger; that, while it takes four years to build a ship and get her into the fleet as an effective unit, it takes much longer to train an enlisted petty officer as he should be trained, and a lifetime to train officers of the upper grades. Perhaps also our leading minds do not realize the intellectual requirements of the higher realms of the naval art, or comprehend what the examples of Alexander, Cæsar, Napoleon, Nelson, and Farragut prove: that, *in the real crises of a nation's life her most valuable asset is the trained skill in strategy that directs the movements of her forces.*

Further than this, they may not realize that the greater the danger which they must avert, the earlier they must begin to prepare for it, because the more work in preparation will have to be performed; and yet realization of this truth is absolutely vital, as is also realization of the fact that we have no military power as our ally, and therefore must be ready to meet alone a hostile attack (though perhaps in the far-distant future) from *any* foreign power. To see that this is true it is merely necessary to note the facts of history and observe how nations that have long been on terms of friendship have suddenly found themselves at war with each other; and how countries which have always been hostile have found themselves fighting side by side. In the present war, Great Britain is allied with the two countries toward which, more than toward any other, she has been hostile; and she is fighting the country to which, more than any other, she is bound by ties of consanguinity and common interests. The history of war is so filled with alternations of peace and war between every pair of contiguous countries as to suggest the thought that the mere fact of two countries having interests that are common is a reason why their respective shares in those interests may conflict; that countries which have no common interests have nothing to fight about; that it is only for things in which two nations are interested, and which both desire, that those two nations fight.

If our estimate of the situation should lead us to the decision that we must prepare our navy in such a way that, say twenty years hence, it will be able to protect the country against any enemy, we shall then instinctively adopt a policy. The fact of having ahead of us a definite, difficult thing to do, will at once take us out of the region of guesswork, and force us into logical methods. We shall realize the problem in its entirety; we shall see the relation of one part to another, and of all the parts to the whole; we shall realize that the deepest study of the wisest men must be devoted to it, as it is in all maritime countries except our own. The very difficulties of the problem, the very scope and greatness of it, the fact that national failure or national success will hinge on the way we solve it, will call into action the profoundest minds in all the nation. We shall realize that, more than any other problem before the country, this problem is urgent; because in no other problem have we so much lost time to make up for, and in no other work of the government are we so far behind the great nations that we may have to contend against.

Great Britain was startled into a correct estimate of the situation ten years ago, and at once directed perhaps the best of her ability to meet it. Certain it is that no other department of the British Government is in such good condition as the navy; in no other department has the problem been so thoroughly understood, and so conscientiously worked out, or the success been so triumphant.

The underlying reason for this is not so much the individual courage and ability of the officers and men, or even their skill in handling their ships and squadrons, as the fact that Great Britain has followed a definite naval policy; so that the British nation has had a perfectly clear realization of what it wishes the navy to do, and the navy has had a perfectly clear realization of how to do it.

The United States has not yet made a correct estimate of the naval situation; she has not yet reached the point that Great Britain reached ten years ago. Great Britain apprehended the danger, and took action before it was too late. Shall the United States take action now or wait until it is too late?[6]

6. By the time the second edition was published in 1918, the answer to Fiske's rhetorical question was a major naval buildup. The capital ships of the "navy second to none" were authorized and funded. Nevertheless, the navy was still shaking off the strictures of Mahan's emphasis on the battle fleet and was only starting to build escorts for the crucial battle against German U-boats in the Atlantic. Admiral William S. Sims, in London in 1917, was the first to see the need and press for many more destroyers.

PART TWO

NAVAL STRATEGY

CHAPTER SEVEN

GENERAL PRINCIPLES

S TRATEGY IS DIFFICULT of definition; but though many definitions have been made, and though they do not agree together very well, yet all agree that strategy is concerned with the preparation of military forces for war and for operating them in war—while tactics is the immediate instrument for handling them in battle.[1] Strategy thinks out a situation beforehand, and decides what preparations as to material, personnel, and operations should be made.

Many books have been written on strategy, meaning strategy as applied to armies, but very few books have been written on naval strategy. The obvious reasons are that armies in the past have been much larger and more important than navies; that naval men have only recently had the appliances on board ship for writing on an extensive scale; and that the nature of their occupation has been such that continuous application of the kind needed for thinking out prin-

---

1. See footnote 1, page 3. Observe that Fiske sees strategy as composed of two parts, preparations and operations. It is not uncommon to define strategy as preparation (determining objectives and laying plans), and distinguish the operations of forces as operational art. The distinction was not in Fiske's vocabulary when he wrote. Nevertheless, an excellent description of operational art as it applies to a navy will be found in the succeeding pages. Also see p. 347.

ciples and expounding them in books, has only recently been possible.[2]

Most of the few existing books on naval strategy deal with it historically, by describing and explaining the naval campaigns of the past and such land campaigns as illustrate principles that apply to sea and land alike. Perhaps the best books are those of Darrieus[3] and Mahan.

Until about fifty years ago, it was only by experience in actual war, supplemented by laborious study of the campaigns of the great commanders, and the reading of books on strategy which pointed out and expounded the principles involved in them, that one could arrive at any clear idea of strategy.

But wars have fortunately been so infrequent, the information about them has often been so conflicting, and so many results have been due to chance, that, in default of experience, the mere reading of books did not lead to very satisfactory results, except in the case of geniuses; and therefore war problems and war games were devised, in which the various factors of material and personnel were represented, and made as true to life as possible.

The *tactical* games resulting, which naval strategists now play, employ models of the various craft used in war, such as battleships, submarines, etc., and are governed by rules that regulate the movements of those craft on a sort of big chessboard, several feet square, that represents an area of water several miles square. The *strategic* games and problems are based on principles similar to those on which the tactical games are based, in the sense that actual operations are car-

2. This observer believes the reason lies principally in the demands on naval officers to operate machinery efficiently, and to the fact that the number of trigger pullers in the ships and aircraft of a navy are two or three orders of magnitude fewer than in an army.

3. *War on the Sea: Strategy and Tactics* by Captain Gabriel Darrieus, French Navy, translated by Philip R. Alger (Annapolis, Md., 1908).

ried on in miniature; but naturally, the strategical operations cover several hundred miles, and sometimes thousands. The aim of both the tactical and the strategic games is to determine as closely as possible the laws that decide victory or defeat; and therefore, for any country, the material, personnel and operations it should employ. Naturally the results obtained are not quite so convincing as those of actual war or battle; but they are more convincing than can be attained in any other way, as yet devised, especially as many of the operations of the game-board that turn out well in games are tried out afterward by the fleet in peace maneuvers. War games and problems may be compared to the drawings that an architect makes of a house which some one wants to build; the plans and drawings are not so realistic as a real house, but they are better than anything else; and, like the war games, they can be altered and realtered until the best result seems to have been attained, considering the amount of money allowed, and other practical conditions.[4]

The idea of devising war games and war problems seems to have originated with Von Moltke; certainly it was first put in practice by his direction. Shortly after he became chief of the General Staff of the Prussian army in 1857, he set to work to carry out the ideas which he had had in mind for several years, while occupying minor posts, but which he had not had the power to enforce. It seems to have become clear to his

4. Fiske has not the word "model" to assist him, so he uses an example of a model: an architect's plan of a real house. He is abreast of the best technical thinking today, which is that war gaming and fleet exercises must reinforce each other in tactical development. Note that Fiske first says the aim of war games is developmental, i.e., to produce better tactics, as opposed to their other major employment, for training officers and testing operational plans. But then he will go on to describe gaming for these latter functions, so the presumption must be that he makes no distinction between the two. Gaming for a research and development purpose is technically harder than gaming for training.

mind that, if a chess-player acquired skill, not only by playing actual games and by studying actual games played by masters, but also by working out hypothetical chess problems, it ought to be possible to devise a system whereby army officers could supplement their necessarily meagre experience of actual war, and their necessarily limited opportunities for studying with full knowledge the actual campaigns of great strategists, by working out hypothetical, tactical, and strategic problems. Von Moltke succeeded in devising such a system and in putting it into successful operation. Hypothetical problems were prepared, in which enemy forces were confronted with each other under given circumstances of weather, terrain, and distances, each force with its objective known only to itself: for instance, you are in command of such and such a force at such and such a place; you have received orders to accomplish such and such a purpose; you receive information that the enemy, comprising such and such troops, was at a certain time at a certain place, and marching in a certain direction. What do you do?

Classes of army officers were formed, and compelled to work out the problems exactly as boys at school were compelled to work out problems in arithmetic. The skill of individual officers in solving the problems was noted and recorded; and the problems themselves, as time went on and experience was gained, were made more and more to conform to probable situations in future wars with Austria, France, and other countries, actual maps being used, and the exact nature and magnitude of every factor in each problem being precisely stated.

By such work, the pupils (officers) acquired the same kind of skill in solving strategic and tactical problems that a boy acquires in solving problems in arithmetic—a skill in handling the instruments employed. Now the skill acquired in solving any kind of problem, like the skill developed in any art, such as baseball, fencing, or piano-playing, does not give a man skill merely in doing a thing identically like a thing he has done before: such a skill would be useless, for the reason that identical conditions almost never recur, and identical problems are never presented. Similar conditions often recur, however, and similar problems are often presented; and familiarity with any class of conditions or problems imparts skill in meeting any condition or any problem that comes within that class. If, for instance, a man memorizes the sums made by adding together any two of the digits, he is equipped to master any problem of addition; and if he will practise at adding numbers together, he will gradually acquire a certain ability of mind whereby he can add together a long row of figures placed in a sequence he never saw before, and having a sum he never attained before. Or a pianist, having acquired the mastery of the technic of the keyboard and the ability to read music, can sit down before a piano he never sat at before and play off instantly a piece of music he never saw before.

Doubtless Moltke had ideas of this kind in mind when his plans for educating strategists and tacticians by problems on paper and by games were ridiculed by the unimaginative, and resisted by the indolent; and certainly no man was ever proved right more gloriously than Moltke. In the war with Austria in 1866, the Prussian army defeated the Austrian at Sadowa or Königgrätz in nineteen days after the declaration of war. In the war with France in 1870, the Prussian army routed the French and received the surrender of Napoleon III in seven weeks and two days, not because of superior courage or experience in war, but by more scientific strategy. As Henderson[5]

5. Colonel G. F. R. Henderson, 1854–1903, was one of Great Britain's most esteemed instructors at the Royal Military College, Sandhurst. For a summary of Henderson's thought and influence, see Jay Luvaas, *The Education of an Army* (London, 1964), Chapter 7. The succeeding quotations by Fiske are probably from *The Science of War,* published posthumously in

says: "Even the French generals of divisions and brigades had had more actual experience (in war) than those who led the German army corps. Compared with the German rank and file, a great part of their non-commissioned officers and men were veterans, and veterans who had seen much service. Their chief officers were practically familiar with the methods of moving, supplying, and maneuvering large masses of troops; their marshals were valiant and successful soldiers. And yet the history of modern warfare records no defeats so swift and complete as those of Königgrätz and Sedan. The great host of Austria was shattered in seven weeks; the French Imperial army was destroyed in seven weeks and three days; and to all intents and purposes the resistance they had offered was not much more effective than that of a respectable militia. But both the Austrian and the French armies were organized and trained under the old system. Courage, experience, and professional pride they possessed in abundance. Man for man, in all virile qualities, neither officers nor men were inferior to their foes. But one thing their generals lacked, and that was education for war. Strategy was almost a sealed book to them." Also, "Moltke committed no mistake. Long before war had been declared every possible precaution had been made. And these included much more than arrangements for rapid mobilization, the assembly of superior numbers completely organized, and the establishment of magazines. The enemy's numbers, armaments, readiness, and efficiency had been submitted to a most searching examination. Every possible movement that might be made, however unlikely, had been foreseen; every possible danger that might arise, however remote, discussed and guarded against"; also, "That the

---

1906. Henderson was also an intense student of the American Civil War, his great classic being *Stonewall Jackson and the American Civil War* (London, 1913, two volumes), the purpose of which was to train soldiers to solve operational and tactical problems.

Prussian system should be imitated, and her army deprived of its monopoly of high efficiency, was naturally inevitable. Every European state has to-day its college, its intelligence department, its schools of instruction, and its course of field maneuvers and field firing."

Strategy may be divided into two parts, war strategy and preparation strategy; and of these two, preparation strategy is by far the more important.[6]

War strategy deals with the laying out of plans of campaign after war has begun, and the handling of forces until they come into contact with the enemy, when tactics takes those forces in its charge. It deals with actual situations, arranges for the provisioning, fuelling, and moving of actual forces, contests the field against an actual enemy, the size and power of which are fairly well known—and the intentions of which are sometimes known and sometimes not. The work of the strategist in war is arduous, pressing, definite, and exciting; and results are apt to follow decisions quickly. He plays the greatest and oldest game the world has ever known, with the most elaborate instruments, and for the largest stakes. In most wars, the antagonists have been so nearly equal in point of personnel and material that the result has seemed to be decided by the relative degrees of skill of the strategists on both sides. This has been the verdict of history; and victorious commanders in all times and in all lands have achieved rarer glories, and been crowned with higher honors, than any other men.

Preparation strategy deals with the laying out of plans for supposititious wars and the handling of supposititious forces

6. Doubtless the importance of strategic planning and training before war was underestimated in the U.S. Navy of 1900 to 1916. But an emphasis on the two swift wars of German unification (1866 and 1870) results in undervaluing what Fiske calls war strategy and its role in a longer war.

against supposititious enemies; and arranges for the construction, equipment, mobilization, provisioning, fuelling,
and moving of supposititious fleets and armies. War strategy
is vivid, stimulating and resultful; preparation strategy is dull,
plodding, and—for the strategist himself—apparently result-
less. Yet war strategy is merely the child of preparation strategy. The weapons that war strategy uses, preparation strategy
put into its hands. The fundamental plans, the strength and
composition of the forces, the training of officers and men,
the collection of the necessary material of all kinds, the arrangements for supplies and munitions of all sorts—the very
principles on which war strategy conducts its operations—
are the fruit of the tedious work of preparation strategy. Alexander reaps the benefit of the preliminary labors of his father,
Philip; William is made German Emperor by the toil of
Moltke.

The work of laying out a supposititious campaign, involving supposititious operations against a supposititious enemy,
requires of the strategist a thorough estimate of the situation,
including a careful estimate of the forces of the enemy, in
material and personnel, and of the strategy that will probably govern his operations—whether he will act on the
defensive, or assume the offensive; if he is to act on the
defensive, how and where will he base his forces, how far will
he operate away from his own shores? And if he is to act
on the offensive, what direction will his operations take; will
he secure an advance base; and if so, where? And as the
character of the enemy's operations will depend on the personnel of the enemy General Staff and of the high commanders afloat, who comprise the personnel, and what are their
characteristics?

To decide these questions correctly requires considerable
acquaintance with the enemy country, its navy and its policy,
a full knowledge of the strategy, personnel, and material of

that navy, and a sound conception of strategy itself. But to decide the questions correctly is essential, because the decision will form the basis of the future plans.

Naturally, as the plan is entirely supposititious and is to take effect at some indefinite time in the future, all the factors that will be in existence at that time cannot be foretold exactly, and therefore must be estimated. This will necessitate several alternate hypotheses; and a war plan including mobilization and operations must be made out, based on each hypothesis. For instance, on the hypothesis that the enemy will take the offensive, one set of plans will have to be prepared on the basis that we shall also take the offensive, and another on the basis that circumstances may be such at that time as to make it wise for us to resort to the defensive; while on the hypothesis that the enemy is to remain on the defensive, a set of plans very different from the other two as to both mobilization and operations must be devised.

Each set of the plans just suggested may also have to be divided into two or more parts. On the basis that the enemy will remain on the defensive, for instance, the circumstances when the hour for action comes, such as the fact of his being quite unprepared, may indicate the advisability of an attack on him as sudden as it can be made; while, on the other hand, circumstances such as the fact of his being thoroughly prepared may render it necessary for us to send a larger force than we could get ready quickly, especially if the enemy coast be far away, and may therefore indicate the advisability of deliberate movements, and even a protracted delay before starting.

But no matter what plan is to be followed, a detailed plan for every probable contingency must be prepared; and it must be elaborated in such detail that it can be put into operation instantly when the fateful instant comes; because the enemy will put his plans into operation at the same time we do, and the one whose plans are executed first will take a long step toward victory.

Not only must the plans provide some means whereby the plans themselves shall get into full operation instantly when war breaks; other plans must also provide that all the acts which those plans contemplate must be performed. Not only must the plans provide that all the prearranged orders for putting the *Kearsarge* into full commission shall be instantly sent by mail, telegraph, and telephone to the proper officials, but other plans must also provide means whereby the officers and men shall actually march on board the *Kearsarge*, her ensign and commission pennant be displayed, all the fuel, ammunition, provisions, and equipment be on board and the *Kearsarge* sail at once, and join the commander-in-chief at sea.

Doubtless the most complicated and comprehensive plans are those for sending a large expedition on an offensive mission to a far-distant coast, especially if that coast be guarded by an efficient navy, if it have outlying islands that would afford good bases for her destroyers and submarines, and if there are not good harbors which our fleet could seize as advance bases, from which to prosecute its future operations. The complexity of the task of planning such an expedition, taking due account, but not exaggerated account, of all the factors, favorable and adverse, is appalling; but the task must be undertaken and accomplished. The most tedious part is the logistics—the arrangements for supplying the fleet on the way and in the distant theatre of operations with the necessary provisions, equipment, and ammunition and, above all, the fuel. The average superdreadnaught consumes about 460 tons of coal per day at full speed, and about 108 tons at 10 knots; and coal or other fuel for all the dreadnaughts, battle cruisers, cruisers of various classes, scouts, destroyers, submarines, ships, aircraft of different kinds, hospital ships, ammunition ships, transports, and the fuel ships themselves, must be provided by means that *must not fail.*[7]

While the work of planning an offensive movement to a distant coast is the most tedious and complex, the work of planning a defensive measure against a sudden attack on the coast needs the most concentration of effort; for whatever the plans require to be done must be done at once. This necessitates that the orders to be issued must be as few as possible; that they be as concise and clear as possible; that the things to be done be as few and as simple as possible, and that all possible foresight be exercised to prevent any confusion or misunderstanding, or any necessity on the part of any one for requesting more instructions.[8]

When the fateful instant comes, the final command to mobilize puts into execution whichever of the plans already made is to be followed; and for this reason it is clear that the various plans must be kept separate from each other, and each set of plans must include all the various orders that must be signed for carrying it into effect, including the particular word or phrase that directs the execution of that particular set of plans.

It is the story that the final order to the British navy in the early part of August, 1914, was the word "Go." All the units went immediately, understandingly, unitedly; and the greatest machine the world has ever known was almost instantly in

7. This paragraph superbly demonstrates that the skills of operational art and operational logistics are virtually indistinguishable. For his time Fiske's breadth of understanding was remarkable. It was his comprehensive knowledge, rather than any incisive strategic thought, that gave value to his writings. He was an operator with a scientific outlook toward the problems of warfare.

8. Wise counsel for modern planners, who have the communications and computer storage capacity to create massive plans, orders and signals, threatening to saturate the comprehension of the men who must act on them.

operation at full speed. No such stupendous feat, physically considered, had ever been done before.[9] The mobilization of the Prussian army in 1870 and of the German army about August 1, 1914, were as great performances mentally and strategically, but not physically, by reason of the relative feebleness of the forces set in motion. This relative feebleness was due, of course, to the insignificance of muskets compared to navy guns, of railway-trains compared to battleships, etc.— an insignificance far from being neutralized by the greater number of the units, for one 14-inch shell has an energy equal to that of about 60,000 muskets, and no army contains anything approximating the powerfulness of a battleship.

Not only, however, must the strategist make plans in peace for preparations that culminate in mobilization, and simply insure that the navy shall be ready in material and personnel when war breaks; he must also make plans for operating the navy strategically afterward, along each of the various lines of direction that the war may take. In other words, the work of preparation strategy in making war plans may be divided into two parts—mobilization and operation.

The plans of mobilization deal naturally with all the activities concerned, material and personnel, and endeavor to arrange a passing from a state of peace to a state of war in the quickest possible time, and with the least chance of errors and omissions. A considerable degree of imagination is required, an almost infinite patience, and a perfect willingness to work indefinitely without any reasonable expectation of getting tangible results. A more hopeless task can hardly be given any man or body of men than that of working out plans, general and detailed, day after day, for contingencies that will probably never happen, and to guard against dangers that will

9. Fiske may be taken literally, in view of the fact that he has anticipated the possibility of instant naval mobilization with his discussion of the inherent power, directability, and controllability of a fleet on pages 57 and 58.

probably never come; preparing tables, diagrams, and schedules which are almost certainly doomed to rest forever in the sepulchre of the confidential files.

Yet this work is basic. Perhaps it is for that reason that it is obscure and dull; basic work is apt to be so. The spectacular success of an individual in any walk of life is often but the crowning of the unrecognized, and often utterly unknown work—of other men.[10]

Strategy is not a science only; it is an art as well; and although the art cannot be practised in its perfection until after the science is well comprehended, yet the art of strategy was born before the science was.[11] This is true of all those departments of man's activity that are divided into sciences and arts, such as music, surgery, government, navigation, gunnery, painting, sculpture, and the rest; because the fundamental facts—say of music—cannot even attract attention until some music has been produced by the art of some musician, crude though that art may be; and the art cannot advance very far until scientific methods have been applied, and the principles that govern the production of good music have been found. The unskilled navigators of the distant past pushed their frail craft only short distances from the land, guided by art and not by science; for no science of navigation then existed. But the knowledge gradually gained, passing first from adept to pupil by word of mouth, and afterward recorded on the written and then the printed page, resulted first in the realization of the fact that various apparently unrelated phenomena were based on the same underlying principles; and resulted later in the perception, and still later in the definite expression, of

10. Or, to paraphrase Fiske's contemporary and fellow inventor, Thomas A. Edison, naval operations are one percent inspiration and ninety-nine percent perspiration.

11. The relationship between military art and science has never been better expressed.

those underlying principles. Using these principles, the navigator expanded the limits of his art. Soon we see Columbus, superbly bold, crossing the unknown ocean; and Magellan piercing the southern tip of the American continent by the straits that now bear his name.

But of all the arts and sciences, the art and science that are the oldest and the most important; that have caused the greatest expenditure of labor, blood, and money; that have been the immediate instruments of more changes and greater changes in the history of the world than any other, are the art and the science of strategy.

Until the time of Moltke the art of strategy, like most arts, was more in evidence than the science. In fact, science of any kind is a comparatively recent product, owing largely to the more exact operations of the mind brought about by the birth of the science of measurement, and the ensuing birth and development of the mechanic arts. Before Moltke's time campaigns were won by wise preparation and skilful execution, as they are now; but the strategical skill was acquired by a general or admiral almost wholly by his own exertions in war, and by studying the campaigns of the great commanders, and reflecting upon them with an intensity that so embedded their lessons in his subjective mind that they became a part of him, and actions in conformity with those lessons became afterward almost automatic. Alexander and Napoleon are perhaps the best illustrations of this passionate grasping of military principles; for though both had been educated from childhood in military matters, the science of strategy was almost non-existent in concrete form, and both men were far too young to have been able to devote much time or labor to it. But each was a genius of the highest type, and reached decisions at once immediate and wise, not by inspiration, but by mental efforts of a pertinacity and concentratedness impossible to ordinary men.

It was because Von Moltke realized this, realized the folly of depending on ability to get geniuses on demand, and realized further the value of ascertaining the principles of strategy, and then expressing them so clearly that ordinary men could grasp and use them, that he conceived and carried into execution his plan; whereby not only actual battles could be analyzed, and the causes of victory and defeat in each battle laid bare to students, but also hypothetical wars and battles could be fought by means of problems given.

The first result of a course of study of such wars and battles, and practice with such problems, was a skill in decision a little like that developed in any competitive game, say tennis, whist, chess, poker, boxing, and the like—whereby any action of your adversary brings an instantaneous and almost automatic reply from you, that you could not have made so skilfully and quickly before you had practised at the game; and yet the exact move of your adversary, under the same conditions, you had never seen before. Of course, this skill was a development, not of the science, but of the art, as mere skill always is; but as skill developed, the best methods for obtaining skill were noted; and the principles governing the attainment of success gradually unveiled themselves, and were formulated into a science.

Naturally, strategy is not an exact science like mathematics, physics, or engineering—at least not now. Whether it ever will be cannot be foretold. The reason that strategy (like medicine and most other sciences concerning human beings) is not an exact science is simply because it involves too many unknown quantities—quantities of which our knowledge is too vague to permit of our applying exact methods to them, in the way in which we apply exact methods to the comparatively well-known quantities and elements in the so-called "exact sciences." But a science may be a science even if it is not an exact science; we may know certain important principles sufficiently well to use them scientifically, even if we do not know them with sufficient exactness to permit us to use them as confidently as we should like. We may know, for instance, that it is folly to divide a military force in the presence of an active enemy into such small forces, and at such distances apart, as to let the enemy defeat each small force, one after the other, even if we do not know exactly how far it would be safe to separate two forces of a given size, in the presence of an enemy of a given power. It is well to know a fact in general terms, even if we do not know it in precise terms: it is well to know in general terms that we must not take prussic acid, even if we do not know exactly how much is needed to kill.

So the studies and problems instituted by Von Moltke, and copied in all the armies and navies of the world, have brought about a science of strategy which is real even though not exact, and which dwells in the mind of each trained strategist, as the high tribunal to which all his questions are referred and by whose decisions he is guided; just as the principles of medicine are the guide alike of the humblest and the most illustrious practitioner, wherever the beneficent art of medicine is practised.

It is clear that, in order to be skilful in strategy (in fact, in any intellectual art), not only must a man have its scientific principles firmly imprinted on his mind, but he must make its practice so thoroughly familiar to his mental muscles that he can use strategy as a *trained* soldier uses his musket—automatically. Inasmuch as any man requires years of study and practice—say, of chess—in order to play chess well enough to compete successfully with professional chess-players, it seems to follow that any man must require years of study and practice of the more complicated game of strategy, in order to play strategy well enough to compete successfully with professional strategists. The game of chess looks easy to a beginner; in fact, the kind of game that he thinks chess to be is easy. But after he has learned the moves, he finds the intricacies of the game developing more rapidly than he can master them, and discovers that chess is a game which some men spend their lifetime studying. The full realization of this fact, however, does not come to him until after defeats by better players have forced into his consciousness the almost infinite number of combinations possible, the difficulty of deciding on the correct move at any juncture, and the consequences that follow after wrong moves.

So with strategy. The ease and certainty with which orders can be transmitted and received, the precision with which large forces can be quickly despatched from place to place, and the tremendous power exertable by those forces, tend to blind the mind to the fact that transferring any force to any place is merely making a "move," and that the other player can make moves, too. If a man were never to be pitted in strategy against another player, either in games or in actual war, the "infinite variety" of strategy would never be disclosed to his intelligence; and after learning how to make the moves, he might feel willing to tackle any one. Illustrations of this tendency by people of great self-confidence are numerous in history, and have not been missing even in the present war, though none have been reported in this country as occurring on the Teuton side. There has always been a tendency on the part of a ruling class to seize opportunities for military glory, and the ambition has often been disproportioned to the accompanying ability and knowledge—sometimes on the part of a King, prince, or man of high nobility, sometimes on the part of a minister, sometimes on the part of an army or navy man, who has been indebted to political or social influence for his place. But within the past fifty years, especially since the establishment of the General Staff in Prussia and the studies of Von Moltke, the overshadowing importance of strategy has been understood, the necessity of comprehending its principles and practising its technique has been appreciated, and attempts to practise strategy by persons inexpert in strategy have been deprecated.

The game of strategy, while resembling in many ways the game of chess, differs from it, of course, in the obvious element of personal danger. It also differs from it in an equally important but less obvious way—its relation to the instruments employed; for in chess those instruments (pieces) are of a number and character fixed by the rules of the game; whereas in strategy the number and character of the instruments (ships, etc.) employed are determined by strategy itself, assisted by engineering. Germany realizes this, and therefore has established and followed a system whereby the character of the various material and personnel units of the navy, and even the number of them (under the restrictions of the money allotted), are decided by a body of men who are highly trained in strategy and engineering.

There is an intimate connection between policy and strategy, and therefore between naval policy and naval strategy; and while it is difficult to draw the line exactly which separates policy and strategy, it may be said in general that policy is the concern of the government, and strategy is the concern of the navy and army, to be employed by them to carry out the policy.

As naval policy and naval strategy are so intimately connected in their essence, it is apparent that the naval policy of a country and its naval strategy should be intimately connected in fact; for the policy cannot be properly carried out if the strategy that tries to execute it is not good, or if the policy requires more naval force or skill than the navy can bring to bear; and the strategy cannot be good if it is called upon to execute a policy impossible to execute, or if the exact end in view of the policy is not distinctly known. Some of the greatest mistakes that have been made by governments have been made because of a lack of co-ordination between the government and its navy, so that the policy and the strategy could not work together. We see an illustration of this throughout the history of France, whose civil and naval authorities have not worked harmoniously together, whose naval strategy has apparently been opportunistic and short-sighted, and whose navy in consequence has not been so successful as the large sums of money spent upon it might lead one to expect.

Across the English Channel we see a totally different state of things. In Great Britain the development of the navy has been going on for more than twelve hundred years, ever since King Offa declared that "he who would be secure at home must be supreme at sea." For about eight hundred years thereafter the development was carried on energetically, but in an opportunistic fashion, following the requirements of the hour. In 1632, however, the Board of Admiralty was established; and with occasional interruptions, especially prior to 1708, the board has continued in existence ever since. A coherent policy of development has thereby been assured, and a wisdom of strategy established which more than any other single factor has made Great Britain the mistress of the seas, and almost the mistress of the world.

The wisdom of her strategy has been due largely to the fact of the close touch maintained between the civil government, including Parliament, and the navy; for by its very constitution the Board of Admiralty includes some of the highest officers of Parliament, the cabinet, and the navy. Its presiding officer is a member of the cabinet, and also member of Parliament; four of the officers are naval officers, high in rank, character, and attainments; and the junior civil lord is a civilian versed in naval matters. All the orders for great movements of the fleets and ships are directed by this board and signed by its secretary, the board, by a fiction of the law, being considered an individual replacing the lord high admiral—which it did, in 1632. The board is supposed to meet every day with all the members present, the vote of each member carrying as

153

much weight as that of any other member. Naturally, the first lord of the admiralty being a cabinet officer and a member of Parliament, has a far greater influence on broad questions than any other member; and the first sea lord being the person of the most experience in naval matters, has the most weight on strictly naval questions. Theoretically, however, neither of these gentlemen can carry a measure opposed to the others; and any member, even a junior, has equal opportunity with the others to bring up and discuss any question and to attempt to procure its passage by the full board; but in 1869 the first lord at that time, Mr. Childers, brought about a change whereby the first lord was made personally responsible to the government. This vastly increased the power of the first lord, relatively to the others.

Two other navies, the German and the Japanese, which with the British, are the most efficient navies in the world, have systems somewhat different from the British. In Germany and Japan the Emperor is the head of the navy, and there is no civilian between him and it. In Germany there is no minister of marine, unless the Emperor himself may be said to be the minister, which he practically is; and the navy is divided into three parts, each under an admiral. The three parts are the General Staff, which deals with war plans and fundamental questions; the naval cabinet, which deals with matters of personnel; and the administrative section, which has to do with questions of material, including money, and the getting of money from Parliament. In Japan the minister of marine is by law a naval officer, and under him is a chief of staff, also a naval officer. The minister of marine has the direction of the navy as a whole, but the ideas of the chief of staff are supposed to be carried out in matters that are strictly naval. The Japanese naval officer has a higher regard for the office of chief of staff than for that of minister of marine, because it is given for professional excellence only.

It might seem at first sight that in Germany and Japan there would be danger of a lack of co-ordination between the civil and the naval authorities, and a tendency for the navy to become unduly self-assertive. Of course, one reason why there is no such danger is that the governments of those countries are controlled by men who, though civilians, have great knowledge of international affairs, and of military and naval subjects; another reason is that the navy is so vital a matter, accurate knowledge about it is so general, and interest in it so wide-spread and intense, that there is no great gulf fixed between naval people and civilians. Still another reason is the fact that in each country the Emperor is trained in military and naval duties as well as in civil duties, and therefore can effect in his own person the co-ordination of the civil and the naval authority: that is, of policy and strategy.[12]

Such automatic and complete co-ordination is desirable not only in preventing the unnatural barrier between the civil and the military authority which exists in some countries such as ours, but in lightening the labors and enlightening the deliberations of the strategists. If, for instance, a bold policy is to be enforced, and a large sum of money allotted for material and personnel, the strategists will be led to recommendations different from those to which they would be led if a cautious policy were to be pursued, and a small sum of money to be allotted.

Germany did not turn her eyes seriously toward the navy until the Emperor William II read Mahan's book, "The Influence of Sea Power upon History." Previous to that epochal event, Germany had relied on her army to protect her inter-

12. One of Fiske's blind spots is his treatment of naval operations as separable from army operations. His admiration for the Japanese system of command would have been tempered if he had been able to observe the disharmony between army and navy policy before and during World War II, in part because there was no way to mediate their differences except by the emperor himself.

ests and enforce her rights, being led thereto by the facts of her history and the shortness of her coast-line. But the strategically trained mind of William grasped at once the situation laid bare by Mahan; and his military training led him to quick decision and prompt action. The necessary machinery was soon set in motion, with the amazing result that in twenty years the German navy became the second in power and perhaps the first in efficiency in the world.

Was this feat accomplished by prodigal expenditures in building vessels and other material of all kinds, and enlisting and commissioning a large number of officers and men? No, the expense was less than that of building our navy, even if a liberal allowance be made for the relative cheapness of things in Germany; and the mere enlisting and commissioning of officers and men was the simplest part of the undertaking.[13]

How was it accomplished? In the simplest way imaginable: by following Moltke's plan of solving hypothetical war problems, and adapting the military war game (*Kriegspiel*) to naval forces; playing numberless war games, and deciding from those games the naval strategy best adapted to Germany's needs—not only in matters of general principle, not only as to tactics, training, education, co-operation with the army, and the size of fleet required to carry out the policy of the nation—but also as to the composition of the fleet, relative proportions of vessels of the various types, and the characteristics of each type. Nothing was left to chance; nothing was decided by guessing; no one man's dictum was accepted. The whole problem was attacked in its entirety, and a general solution found; and after this, the various divisions and subdivisions of the problem were attacked and solved, in obedience to the same principles, in accordance with the results obtained at *Kriegspiel*.

13. The rapid development of a highly effective German navy was indeed a remarkable achievement, worthy of study and respect.

If a very large and complicated engine of new pattern is to be built by any engineering company, no casting of the smallest kind is made until general plans have been outlined, detailed plans prepared from these, and then "working plans" made for the workmen. From the working plans, the workmen construct the various parts; sometimes in number several hundred. Finally, the whole intricate machine is put together, and the motive power applied. Then all the parts, great and small, begin their allotted tasks, each part perfectly adapted to its work, not too large and not too small; all working together in apparent confusion, but in obedience to law—fulfilling exactly the will of the designing engineer. So, the vast and new machine of the German navy was designed in the drafting-room of the *Kriegspiel;* and though it has been gradually strengthened and enlarged since then, each strengthening piece and each addition has been designed in accordance with the original plan, and has therefore harmonized with the original machine. Thus the navy has expanded smoothly, symmetrically, purposefully. No other result was to be expected: the strategy having been correct, the result was correct also.[14]

Perhaps one contributing factor to the success of the German navy has been her staff of officers highly trained in strategy by *Kriegspiel,* that insures not only sound advice in gen-

14. German naval strategy before both world wars has been severely criticized for following Mahan's emphasis on a battle fleet too literally. In a subsequent book of this series one of Germany's own astute naval strategists will evaluate it. The discussion of foreign organizations in the next several paragraphs is most useful to a modern reader as an indication of careful study of organization and policy by a leader who was in the middle of controversy over what the American system should look like. It is hard to find a leader in uniform today who has taken a comparative approach or sought organizational wisdom by looking overseas. Our debates, principally over the Joint Chiefs of Staff and its influence, have drawn almost exclusively on our own history and experience.

eral, but also insures that at any time, night or day, a body of competent officers shall be ready at the admiralty to decide what action should be taken, whenever any new situation is reported. This factor is most important; because in naval and military operations, even in time of peace, but especially in war, events follow each other so rapidly, and momentous crises develop so suddenly, that the demand for action that shall be both wise and instantaneous is imperative. The chessplayer can linger long over his decisions, because his opponent cannot make his next move meanwhile; but in warfare no such rule or condition can exist. In war, time is as vital a factor as any other: and the strategist, who, like Napoleon, can think faster and decide more quickly and accurately than his antagonist is, *ceteris paribus,*[15] sure to win; and even if *ceteris* are not quite *paribus,* his superior quickness and correctness will overcome great handicaps in material and personnel, as the lives of all the great strategists in history, especially Alexander and Napoleon, prove convincingly. To bring a preponderating force to bear at a given point ahead of the enemy—to move the maximum of force with the maximum of celerity—has always been the aim of strategy: and probably it always will be, for the science of strategy rests on principles, and principles never change.

Thus, while we see in Great Britain's navy an example of the effect of a strategy continuous and wise, conducted for three hundred years, we see in the Japanese and German navies equally good examples of a strategy equally wise, but of brief duration, which started with the example of the British navy, and took advantage of it.

The German and Japanese navies did not follow the British navy slavishly, however; for the national military character of their people required the introduction and control of more

15. Other things being equal.

military and precise methods than those of the primarily sailor navy of Great Britain. We see, therefore, a curious similarity between the German and Japanese navies, and very clear evidence in each of the engrafting of purely military ideals on maritime ideas. And we see not only this, we see the reaction on the British navy itself of the ideals of the German and the Japanese, and a decided change during the last ten years from the principles of "the blue-water school"; as evidenced mainly by the institution of a Naval War College, including a war staff, the employment at the admiralty of General Staff methods, though without the name; and the introduction into naval methods, especially naval gunnery, of mathematical procedures.

Previous to the Russo-Japanese War, ten years ago, the strategy of the British navy may be characterized as physical rather than mental, depending on a superior number of ships and men; those ships and men being of a very high grade individually, and bound together by a discipline at once strict and sympathetic. All the personnel from the highest admiral to the humblest sailor prided themselves on being "British seamen," comrades of the sea, on whom their country placed her ultimate reliance. Maneuvers on a large scale were held, target practice was carried on with regularity—and navy ships carried the banner of Saint George over every sea, and displayed it in every port. Tactics and seamanship filled the busy days with drills of many kinds; but strategy, though not quite forgotten, did not command so large a portion of the officers' time and study as it did in Germany and Japan. The rapid success of the Germans and Japanese, however, in building up their navies, as instanced by the evident efficiency of the German fleet almost under the nose of England, and the triumph of the Japanese fleet in Tsushima Strait startled the British navy out of her conservatism, and caused her to proceed at full speed toward the modernization of her strategy. With the quick decision followed by quick action that characterizes the seaman everywhere, the British instituted a series of reforms, and prosecuted their efforts with such wisdom and such vigor, that, in the brief space of ten years, the British navy has been almost revolutionized. As in all such movements, the principal delay was in bringing about the necessary mental changes; the mental changes having been accomplished, the material changes followed automatically.

The change whereby the German and Japanese navies became preceptors to their preceptor is like changes that occur in every-day life, and is one of many illustrations of how a young and vigorous individual or organization, endowed with proper energy and mentality, can appropriate whatever is valuable for its purposes from its elders, and reject whatever those elders have had fastened on them by circumstances or tradition, and develop a superior existence. It is a little like the advantage which a comparatively new city like Washington has over an old city like Boston, in being started after it was planned, instead of being started haphazard, without being planned at all.

The United States navy was started not like the city of Washington, but like the city of Boston. It was modelled on the British navy; but since the United States has never taken an interest in its navy at all comparable with that taken by Great Britain in its navy, and since our navy has been built up by successive impulses from Congress and not in accordance with a basic plan, the lack of harmoniousness among its various parts reminds one of Boston rather than of Washington. Owing to the engineering and inventive genius of our people and the information we got from Europe, inferiority has not occurred in the units of the material: in fact, in some ways our material is perhaps the best of all. Neither has inferiority been evidenced in the personnel, as individuals; for the excellent physique and the mental alertness of the American have shown themselves in the navy as well as in other walks of life.

In strategy, however, it must be admitted that we have little reason to be proud.[16] We do very well in the elementary parts of the naval profession. In navigation, seamanship, gunnery, and that part of international law that concerns the navy we are as good as any. But of the higher branches, especially of strategy, we have little clear conception. How can we have? Strategy is one of the most complex arts the world contains; the masters in that art have borne such names as Alexander, Cæsar, Nelson, and Napoleon. Naval strategy is naval chess, in which battleships and other craft take the place of queens and other pieces. But it is a more complicated game than chess, for the reason that not only are there more kinds of "pieces," but the element of time exerts a powerful influence in strategy while it does not even exist in chess. The time element has the effect not only of complicating every situation, but also of compelling intense concentration of mind, in order to make decisions quickly; and often it forces decisions without adequate time for consideration, under circumstances of the utmost excitement, discomfort, and personal peril.

One dislikes intensely to criticise his own country, even to himself. But when a naval officer is studying—as he should continually do—what must be done, in order to protect his country from attack by some foreign foe, it would be criminal folly for him to estimate the situation otherwise than honestly; and to do this, it is necessary to try to see where his country is weak and where strong, relatively to the possible foes in question. If we do this, and compare the strategical methods employed by—say Germany and us—we are forced to admit that the German methods are better adapted to producing economically a navy fitted to contend successfully in war against an enemy. In Germany the development of the

16. In this commentator's judgment, the actions of Fiske and a few other of the navy's best uniformed thinkers voided his own criticism virtually as he wrote it. U.S. naval strategic planning was highly effective prior to World War II.

navy has been strictly along the lines of a method carefully devised beforehand; in our country no method whatever is apparent, at least no logical method. Congress, and Congress alone, decides what vessels and other craft shall be built, how many officers and men shall wear the uniform.[17] It is true that they consult the report of the secretary of the navy, and ask the opinions of some naval officers; and it is true that the secretary of the navy gets the opinions of certain naval officers including the General Board, before making his report. But both the secretary and Congress estimate the situation from their own points of view, and place their own value on the advice of naval officers. And the advice of these naval officers is not so valuable, possibly, as it might be; for the reason that it is really irresponsible, since the advisers themselves know that it will not be taken very seriously. The difference between the advice of men held responsible for the results of following their advice, and the advice of men not so held responsible, is well recognized, and is discussed fully in the reports of the Moody and the Swift Boards on the organization of the Navy Department.[18] Furthermore, our officers do not have the machinery of the *Kriegspiel* to help them. It is true that at the Naval War College, a war-game apparatus is installed and

17. *Déjà vu* here. By its obsolete system of annual appropriations, the Congress of the United States effectively perpetuates the problem.

18. Fiske was only one of several forceful officers, among them Sims, Henry C. Taylor, William Swift, and William F. Fullam, who, starting around 1900, espoused a strong military staff. The Moody Board, appointed by President Theodore Roosevelt and headed by Secretary of the Navy William H. Moody, and the Swift Board, appointed by Secretary George Meyer and headed by Admiral Swift, convened in 1909 and arrived at recommendations in line with the reformers. Consistent with the board's recommendations, Meyer maintained four military aids (for operations, material, inspections, and personnel) while he was secretary from 1909 to 1913. Since these were never sanctioned by Congress, Daniels, who was his successor, felt free to weaken their influence, including that of Fiske.

that war games are played, and war problems solved; but the officers there are very properly engaged in the regular work of a war college, in educating officers in the principles of warfare, and have little time for other work. It is also true that the war games and problems there do lead occasionally to recommendations by the War College to the General Board as to various matters; but the connection between the conclusions of the War College and the decisions of Congress via the General Board and the secretary of the navy is so fragile and discontinuous, that it may truthfully be said that the influence of the war games at our War College has but a faint resemblance to the determining force of the *Kriegspiel* in Berlin.

It is often said that Germany is an empire and the United States a republic, and that *therefore* the military methods of Germany cannot be employed here. The inference is not necessarily correct, however, as is shown by the excellence of the army of France; for, France, although a republic, insists that military strategy only shall control and direct the army. The American Congress can do the same with the American navy. Whether Congress shall so decide or not, the decision will undoubtedly be wise; and we of the navy will do our utmost to make the navy all it should be. In this connection, it should be noted that:

1. Germany has been following a certain strategic system regarding the navy; we a system different from that of any other navy, which has been used now for about one hundred and forty years. Both systems have been in operation for a time sufficiently long to warrant our comparing them, by comparing the results they have achieved.

2. The German navy has been in existence a much shorter time than the American navy, belongs to a much less populous and wealthy country, and yet is not only about 30 per cent larger in material, and more than 100 per cent larger in trained personnel, but if we judge by maneuvers carried on in

both peace and war, is much better in organization, morale, and capacity for doing naval work upon the ocean. We do not, of course, know what Germany has been doing since the war began on August 1, 1914; but all accounts show that Germany, like all the other belligerent Powers, has been adding units of material and personnel to her navy much more rapidly than they have been destroyed; as well as perfecting her strategy, under the influence of the war's stimulus. Leaving out of consideration, however, what she may have been doing since the war began, and neglecting any unauthenticated accounts of her status before it started, we know positively that in 1913 the maneuvers of the German fleet were executed by a force of 21 battleships, 3 battle cruisers, 5 small cruisers, 6 flotillas of destroyers (that is 66 seagoing torpedo vessels), 11 submarines, an airship, a number of aeroplanes and special service ships, and 22 mine-sweepers—all in one fleet, all under one admiral, and maneuvered as a unit. *This was nearly three years ago, and we have never come anywhere near such a performance.* In January, 1916, the United States Atlantic fleet, capable as to both material and personnel of going to sea and maneuvering together, consisted of 15 battleships and 23 destroyers, 2 mine-depot ships, and 1 mine-training ship, and 4 tugs fitted as mine-sweepers—with no submarines, no aircraft of any kind, no scouts (unless the *Chester* be so considered, which was cruising alone off the coast of Liberia, and the *Birmingham*, which was flag-ship to the destroyer flotilla). This was the only fleet that we had ready to fight in January, 1916; because, although more battleships could have been put into commission, this could have been done only by putting out of commission certain smaller vessels, such as cruisers and gunboats; and the battleships would have had to be put into commission very hurriedly, filled up with men fresh from other ships, and no more ready to fight in the fleet against an enemy (whose ships were fully manned with well-trained officers and men, accustomed to

164

the details of their respective ships, and acquainted with each other) than the *Chesapeake* was ready to fight the *Shannon*.[19]

3. In case our system is not so good as that of—say Germany—or of any other country having a system equally excellent, we shall *never* be able to contend successfully against that navy, under equal strategic conditions, unless we have an excess over her in numbers of personnel and material sufficient to counteract our inferiority in efficiency.

The efficiency of a navy or an army is exactly what the strategic system makes it. Eleven thousand Greeks under Miltiades, highly efficient and thoroughly trained, defeated 100,000 Persians at Marathon. A Greek fleet under Themistocles defeated and almost destroyed a much larger Persian fleet at Salamis. With an army of less than 35,000 men, but highly trained by Philip of Macedon, his father, Alexander, in only twelve years conquered ten of the most wealthy and populous countries of the world. Cæsar, Alaric, Attila, Charlemagne, and all the great military men from the greatest antiquity down to the present moment have trained and organized bodies of soldiers and sailors, under systems suited to the times, and then waged successful war on peoples less militarily efficient. Cortez conquered Mexico, and Pizarro conquered Peru; the British, French, and Spanish subdued the Indians of

19. It was in this battle off Boston during the War of 1812 that the dying captain of the *Chesapeake*, James Lawrence, uttered the words that Oliver Hazard Perry immortalized at the Battle of Lake Erie: "Don't give up the ship!" With more courage than good sense, Lawrence had taken the ill-prepared *Chesapeake* against one of the best-trained ships in His Majesty's navy. Lawrence had just taken command, and had done so with extreme reluctance, fully knowing the *Chesapeake*'s poor state of readiness. Fleet readiness was naturally Fiske's passion as aid for operations. Elements of the fleet were heavily occupied with supporting Wilson's gunboat diplomacy off Mexico, Santo Domingo, and Haiti, which Fiske saw as detracting from *fleet* readiness. He seems oblivious to the German U-boat operations, which by the time of the second edition were the principal threat, consumed as he was with concentrating and training the battle line.

North America, and during the latter half of the nineteenth century nearly all the land in the world that was "unoccupied" by Europeans or their descendants was taken in possession by European Powers. Great Britain is now mistress of about one-quarter of the land and the population of the globe. Russia, France, Germany, and the United States govern most of the remainder.

These results were brought about almost solely by the exercise of military force:—and of this force, physical courage was not a determining element, because it was just as evident in the conquered as in the conquerors. The determining element was strategy that (under the behest of policy) prepared the military and naval forces in material and personnel before they were used, and directed their operations, while they were being used.

Of all the single factors that have actually and directly made the history of the world, the most important factor has been strategy.

CHAPTER EIGHT

DESIGNING THE MACHINE

T HE MOST IMPORTANT element connected with a navy is the strategy which directs it, in accordance with which all its plans are laid—plans for preparation before war and plans for operations during war. Strategy is to a navy what mind is to a man. It determines its character, its composition, its aims; and so far as external conditions will permit, the results which it accomplishes.

It is possible for certain features connected with a navy to be good, even if the strategy directing it be faulty; or for those features to be faulty, even if the strategy directing it be good. Experience has shown, however, that, in any organization the influence of the men at the top, and the effect of the policy they adopt, is so great that the whole organization will in the main be good or bad according to the kind of men that control it, and the methods they employ. The better the discipline of the organization, the more completely the quality of the management will influence the whole, and the more essential it becomes that good methods be employed. Good discipline means concentration of the effort of the organization; and the more concentrated any effort is, the more necessary that it be directed aright. The simplest illustration of this is seen in naval gunnery; for there the effect of good fire-control is to limit the dispersion of the various shots fired, relatively to each other; to make a number of shots fired simultaneously to bunch closely together, that is to concentrate; getting away from the shotgun effect, and approximating the effect of a single shot. Obviously, if the fire-control and the skill of the gunners are so great that the shots fall very close together, the chance of hitting the target is less than if the shots did not fall close together, if the range at which the guns are fired is incorrect. A mathematical formula showing the most effective dispersion for a given error in range was published in the *Naval Institute* by Lieutenant-Commander B. A. Long, U.S.N., in December, 1912.[1]

So, we see that if the strategy directing a navy is incorrect, we can accomplish little by improving the discipline, and may do harm; when unwise orders have been given in the past, those orders have sometimes been disobeyed with beneficial effect. Neither would it avail much to improve the details of the material or personnel, or to spend much money; for there is no benefit to be derived from building fine ships, if they are to be captured by the enemy. If the Russian fleet sent to Tsushima had been weaker than it was, the loss to Russia would have been less.

Inasmuch as strategy, however, includes all the means taken to make a navy effective, it is obvious that a good strategical direction will be more likely to result in good discipline and good material than would a poor strategy. But this is not necessarily so, for the reason that a strategy may be in the main

1. Pages 1601–1604. In the U.S. fleet's 1911 gunnery exercises many salvoes had been observed to miss completely because the patterns were tight relative to the range errors. The tight fall of shot created an all-hit-or-no-hit effect. Several officers observed that if dispersion in range were built into the salvoes, at least some hits would have occurred. Long worked out a formula for the proper amount of dispersion to crank in, given an average error in ranging. Fiske inserted a brief comment (p. 1605) agreeing with Long's formula, but he also pointed out that the real culprit was poor rangefinding. On this page Fiske likens tight discipline and training to a tight salvo pattern, and correct strategy to good rangefinding so that the well-directed salvo will hit the target.

faulty, and yet be good in certain ways—especially in attention to details, for which a high degree of mentality is not required. In the same way, an individual who is shortsighted and imperfectly educated may be a most excellent and useful member of society, provided he is not permitted to use power in matters beyond his vision. An illustration of how an incorrect point of view does not necessarily injure, but may even benefit in details is shown by certain militia regiments, which are able to surpass some regiments of the regular army in many details of the drill, and in general precision of movement.

In fact, a very wise strategical direction has as one of its most important functions the division of study and labor among various lines of action, and in deciding which lines are important and which not: and for this reason may—and often does—limit labor, and therefore perfection of result, along lines which a less wise strategy would not limit. Illustrations of the casting aside of rigid and difficult forms of drill during the past fifty years in armies, and the substitution of more easy methods are numerous. This does not indicate, however, that a wise strategy may not encourage rigid forms of drill, for the army which is directed with the greatest strategical skill is the German, and no army has more precise methods, not only of procedure, but of drill. The Prussian army of Frederick William which Frederick the Great inherited was not more rigidly drilled in some particulars than the German army of to-day, fought by Frederick the Great's great-great-great-grandnephew, William II.

So we see that a wise and far-sighted strategy does not necessarily either frown on or encourage attention to details; it merely regulates it, deciding in each case and for each purpose what degree of attention to detail is best.

The most obvious work of naval strategy, and therefore the work that impresses people most, is in directing naval forces against an enemy in war. But it is clear that before this can be done effectively strategy must first have made plans of preparation in time of peace; and it is equally clear that, previous to this, strategy must first determine the units of the force and their relation to each other: it must, in other words, design the machine.

Evidently, therefore, *the work of strategy is threefold: first, to design the machine; second, to prepare it for war; and, third, to direct its operations during war.*

A navy being a machine composed of human and material parts, it is clear that the work of designing it correctly should take account of all the parts at the outset; and not only this— the whole design should be completed before any parts are made and put together if the best results are to be obtained. This is the practice in making material machines in manufacturing establishments—and no other practice there could be successfully pursued. It is the outcome of the experience of tens of thousands of men for many years—and the result of the expenditure of tons of money.

This remark as to manufacturing establishments does not include the development of new ideas, for which experimentation or original research is needed; because it is sometimes necessary, when venturing into untrodden fields, to test out by mere trial and error certain parts or features before determining enough of their details to warrant incorporating them in the drawing of the whole machine. Similarly, some experiments must be made in the methods, organization, and material of the naval machine; but in this case, as in the case of manufacturing establishments, the experimental work, no matter how promising or alluring, must be recognized as of unproved and doubtful value; and no scheme, plan, or doctrine must be incorporated in the naval machine, or allowed to pose as otherwise than experimental, until successful trials shall have put it beyond the experimental stage.

The naval machine consists obviously of two parts, the personnel and the material; these two parts being independent, and yet mutually dependent, like the parts of any other organism. Obviously, the parts are mutually dependent not only in the quantitative sense that the more numerous the material parts the more numerous must be the personnel to operate them, but also in the qualitative sense that the various kinds of material determine the various kinds of personnel that must be provided to operate them with success. Gunners are needed to handle guns, and engineers to handle engines.

In this respect, personnel follows material. In the galley days only two kinds of personnel were needed—sailors to handle the galleys (most of these being men merely to pull on oars)—and soldiers to fight, when the galleys got alongside of the enemy. Ship organization remained in a condition of great simplicity until our Civil War; for the main effort was to handle the ships by means of their sails, the handling of the simple battery being a very easy matter. Every ship was much like every other ship, except in size; and in every ship the organization was simple and based mostly on the necessities of handling the ship by rails.

The first important change from this condition followed the departure of the Confederate ironclad *Virginia* (*Merrimac*) carrying 10 guns and 300 men from the Norfolk Navy Yard on the 8th of March, 1862, and her sinking hardly two hours afterward the Union sloop of war *Cumberland*, carrying 24 guns and 376 men; and then destroying by fire the Union frigate *Congress*, carrying 50 guns and 434 men. The second step was taken on the following day, when the Union *Monitor*, 2 guns and 49 men, defeated the *Merrimac*. These two actions on two successive days are the most memorable naval actions in history from the standpoint of naval construction and naval ordnance, and perhaps of naval strategy; because they instituted a new era—the era of mechanism in naval war.

The next step was the successful attack by the Confederate "fish-torpedo boat" *David*, on the Union ironclad *Housatonic* in Charleston harbor on February 17, 1864; and the next was the sinking of the Confederate ironclad *Albemarle* by a spar torpedo carried on a little steam-launch commanded by Lieutenant W. B. Cushing, U.S.N., on October 27, 1864.

These four epochal events in our Civil War demonstrated the possibilities of mechanism in naval warfare, and led the way to the use of the highly specialized and scientific instruments that have played so important a part in the present war. During the half-century that has intervened since the *Monitor* and *Merrimac* ushered in the modern era, since the five brave crews of the *David* lost their lives, and since Cushing made his amazing victory, a contest between the sailor and the scientist has been going on, as to which shall be deemed the ultimate master of the sea.[2] As in many contests, the decision has gone unqualifiedly to neither; for he who sails the sea and braves its tempests, must be in heart and character a sailor—and yet he who fights the scientific war-craft of the present day cannot be merely a sailor, like him of the olden kind, but must be what the New York *Times,* a few years ago, laughingly declared to be a combination quite unthinkable, "a scientific person and a sailor."[3]

Each year since the fateful 8th of March, 1862, has seen some addition to the fighting machinery of navies. Some appliances have been developed gradually from their first beginnings, and are to-day substantially what they were at first—but of course improved; among these are the turret, the automobile torpedo, the telescope-sight, the submarine, and

2. That is to say, the "scientist" competed by introducing new technical capabilities that allowed the *Virginia* (*Merrimac*) of ten guns to sink two ships carrying sixty-four guns between them; and the *Monitor* of two guns to fight off the *Virginia* of ten. These and subsequent scientific achievements broke the mold of all prior standards for comparison of combat power. Fiske had devoted his life to exploiting scientific potential and transforming it into weapon systems that dominated the "sailor" who had only courage and tradition to depend upon.

3. This obscure quotation could have had Fiske as its target.

the gyrocompass. Many other appliances found favor for a while and then, having demonstrated the value of what they attempted and did perform, were gradually supplemented by improved devices, doing the same thing, but in better ways; in this class are many forms of interior-communication apparatus, especially electrical. Still other appliances are adaptations to ship and naval life of devices used in civil life—such as the telephone, electric light, and radio.

Each of these appliances has required for its successful use the educating of men to use it, and frequently the creation and organization of entirely new branches of the service; an illustration is the radio corps in each of our large ships. At the present time the attitude of officers and of the department itself is so much more favorable to new appliances that a clear probability of a new device being valuable is a sufficient stimulus to bring about the education of men to use it; but a very few years ago many devices were lost to us because they were considered "not adapted to naval use." Now we endeavor to adapt them.[4]

The present complexity of our material is therefore reflected in the complexity of the organization of our personnel; and as it is the demands of material that regulate the kind of personnel, and as a machine must be designed and built before men can learn to use it, it follows that our personnel must lag behind our material—that our material as material must be better than our personnel as personnel.

It may be answered that all our material is first invented, then designed, and then constructed by men; that men create our material appliances (though not the matter of which they are composed), that the created cannot be better than the creator, and that therefore it is impossible for our material to be better than our personnel. But to this objection it may be

4. Thanks in no small part to Fiske's rapport with the leaders of the Old Navy while the New Navy was created, from 1880 to 1910.

pointed out that only a very small proportion of our personnel are employed in creating; that most of them are engaged merely in using the material with whatever degree of skill they possess, and that, if a man uses an instrument with perfect skill, he then succeeds merely in getting out of that instrument all that there is in it. A soldier's musket, for instance, is a very perfect tool—very accurate, very powerful, very rapid; and no marksman in the world is so skilful that he can shoot the musket with all the accuracy and speed of which the gun itself is capable.

This indicates that the personnel of a navy is harder to handle than the material, and that therefore the most effort is required to be expended on the personnel. The strength of any system depends on the strength of its weakest part; in any organism, human or material, effort is best expended on the weak points rather than on the strong.

Recognition of this principle is easy, but carrying out the principle in practice is most difficult. One reason is the difficulty of seeing always where the weak spot is; but a greater difficulty is due to the fact that the principle as above stated must be modified by the consideration that things which are important need attention more than things that are unimportant. A weak point in any organism deserves attention more than a strong point of the same order of importance, or than a strong point in the same class; but not, necessarily more than a strong point of a higher order of importance, or a strong point in another class. It may be more beneficial, for instance, to drill an ineffective turret crew than to try to reduce friction in a training gear already nearly frictionless; or it may be more beneficial to overcome the faults of a mediocre gun-pointer than to develop still more highly the skill already great of another gun-pointer; but, on the other hand, it may be less beneficial to drill boat crews at boat-sailing, even if they need it, than to drill them at landing as armed forces on the beach, though they may do that pretty well; or it may be better not to have boat drill at all and to get under way for fleet drill, even though the ships are very expert at it.[5]

It is true that in any endeavor where many things are to be done, as in a navy, it is important that nothing be neglected; and yet, under the superintendence of any one, there are some things the doing of which requires priority over other things. The allotting of the scientifically correct amount of time, energy, and attention to each of the various things claiming one's attention is one of the most difficult, and yet one of the most important problems before any man. It requires an accurate sense of proportion.

Naturally the problem increases in complexity and importance the higher the position, and the greater the number of elements involved—being more difficult and important for instance in the office of the commander-in-chief of a fleet, whose time and attention have to be divided among multitudinous matters, than in that of captain of a single ship. For this reason, *the higher one is in position, the more imperative it is that he understand all elements involved, and estimate properly their various weights.* The success or non-success of a man in high authority depends largely on how his sense of proportion leads him to allot his time.

But a matter fully as important as the allotment of time and attention to the consideration of various matters by the various members of the personnel is the allotment of money for the various items, especially of the material; for, after all, every navy department or admiralty must arrange its demands for ships, guns, men, etc., with reference to the total amount of money which the nation will allot. For this purpose, only one good means of solution has thus far been devised—the game-board.

5. Then as now the fleet had certain drills used to measure efficiency by, as Fiske says, "things that are unimportant" to combat effectiveness, but which nevertheless carried great weight because they contributed to smartness for appearance's sake.

The game-board, naturally, tries out only the units that maneuver on the ocean; it does not try out the mechanism inside those units, because they can be tried out best by engineering methods. The province of the game-board is merely to try out on a very small scale, under proper conventions or agreements, things that could not be tried out otherwise, except at great expense, and very slowly; to afford a medium, half-way between actual trials with big ships and mere unaided reasoning, for arriving at correct conclusions. When the game-board is not used, people conferring on naval problems can do so only by forming pictures in their own minds, endeavoring to describe those pictures to the others (in which endeavor they rarely perfectly succeed) while at the same time, trying to see the pictures that are in the minds of the others—and then comparing all the pictures. The difficulty of doing this is shown by a little paragraph in "The Autocrat of the Breakfast Table," in which Dr. Holmes[6] points out that when John and Thomas are talking, there are really six persons present—the real John, the person John thinks himself to be, the person Thomas thinks him to be, the real Thomas, the person Thomas thinks himself to be, and the person John thinks him to be. The conditions surrounding John and Thomas are those of the simplest kind, and the conversation between them of the most uncomplicated character. But when—not two people but—say a dozen or more, are considering highly complicated questions, such as the House Naval Committee discuss when officers are called to testify before them, no two of the twenty congressmen can form the

6. Oliver Wendell Holmes, father of the chief justice of the same name, was a physician turned author. He helped James Russell Lowell found the *Atlantic Monthly* in 1857 and sustain it through the depression of that year with twelve good-humored essays. These were published together as *The Autocrat of the Breakfast Table* in 1858. Holmes is also credited with saving the original USS *Constitution* from the woodpile by his stirring poem "Old Ironsides," written as a young man barely out of college.

176

same mental picture when an officer uses the word—say "fleet." The reason is simply that very few of the congressmen hearing that word have ever seen a fleet; none of them know exactly what it is, and every one forms a picture which is partly the result of all his previous education and experience; which are different from the previous education and experience of every other congressman on the committee. Furthermore, no one of the officers uses words exactly as the other officers do; and the English language is too vague (or rather the usual interpretation put on words is too vague) to assure us that even ordinary words are mutually understood. For instance, the question is asked: "Do you consider it probable that such or such a thing would happen?" Now what does the questioner mean by "probable," and what does the officer think he means? Mathematically, the meaning of "probable" is that there is more than 50 per cent of chance that the thing would happen; but who in ordinary conversation uses that word in that way? That this is not an academic point is shown by the fact that if the answer is "no" the usual inference from the answer is that there is no need for guarding against the contingency. Yet such an inference, if the word "probable" were used correctly by both the questioner and the answerer, would be utterly unjustified, because the necessity for taking precautions against a danger depends not so much on its probability or improbability, as on the degree of its probability; and to an equal degree on the greatness of the danger that impends. If the occurrence of a small mishap has a probability say of even 75 per cent, there may be little necessity of guarding against it; while if the danger of total destruction has a probability as low as even 1 per cent, we should guard against it sedulously.[7]

7. Like a modern operations analyst Fiske argues for quantification not from any illusion as to the accuracy of the numbers but for clarity of communication.

177

The more complicated the question, the more elements involved, the more difficult it is to settle it wisely by mere discussion. The effort of the imagination of each person must be directed not so much to getting a correct mental picture of what the words employed describe, as to getting a correct picture of what the person using the words desires them to describe. Any person who has had experience in discussions of this character knows what an effort this is, even if he is talking with persons whom he has known for years, and with whose mental and lingual characteristics he is well acquainted: and he also knows how much more difficult it is when he is talking with persons whom he knows but slightly.

It may here be pointed out how greatly the imaginations of men differ, and how little account is taken of this difference in every-day life. In poetry and fiction imagination is recognized; and it is also recognized to some extent in painting, inventing, and, in general, in "the arts." But in ordinary life, the difference among men in imagination is almost never noticed. Yet a French proverb is "point d'imagination, point de grand general";[8] and Napoleon indicated a danger from untrained imagination in his celebrated warning to his generals not to make "pictures" to themselves of difficulties and disasters.

The difference in imagination among men is shown clearly by the difference—and often the differences—between inventors and engineers, and the scarcity of men who are both inventors and engineers. Ericsson repudiated the suggestion that he was an inventor, and stoutly and always declared he was an engineer. This was at a time, not very long ago, when it was hardly respectable to be an inventor; when, even though men admitted that some inventors had done valuable work, the work was supposed to be largely a chance shot of a more or less crazy man. Yet Ericsson was an inventor—though he

8. No imagination, no great general.

178

was an engineer. So were Sir William Thompson (afterward Lord Kelvin), Helmholtz, Westinghouse, and a very few others; so are Edison and Sperry. Many inventors, however, live in their imaginations mainly—some almost wholly. Like Pegasus, they do not like to be fastened to a plough or anything else material. Facts, figures, and blue-prints fill their souls with loathing, and bright generalities delight them. The engineer, on the other hand, is a man of brass and iron and logarithms; in imagination he is blind, in flexibility he resembles reinforced concrete. He is the antipodes of the inventor; he despises the inventor, and the inventor hates him. Fortunately, however, there is a little bit of the inventor in most engineers, and a trace of the engineer in most inventors; while in some inventors there is a good deal of the engineer. And once in a while we meet a man who carries both natures in his brain. That man does marvels.

Despite the great gulf normally fixed, however, between the engineer and the inventor, most of the definite progress of the world for the past one hundred years has been done by the co-ordination of the two; a co-ordination accomplished by "the man of business."

Now the inventor and engineer type do not exist only in the world of engineering and mechanics, though it is in that world that they are the most clearly recognized; for they exist in all walks of life. In literature, inventors write novels; in business life, they project railroads; in strategy, they map out new lines of effort. In literature, the engineer writes cyclopædias; in business, he makes the projected railroads a success; in strategy, he works out logistics and does the quantitative work.

In that part of strategy of which we are now thinking—the designing of the naval machine—the inventor and the engineer clearly have two separate lines of work: one line the conceiving, and the other line the constructing, of strategic and tactical methods, and of material instruments to carry out

179

those methods. Clearly, these two lines of work while independent are mutually dependent; and, if properly carried out are mutually assistant. The coworking of the inventor and the engineer is a little like that coworking of theory and practice, which has been the principal factor in bringing about the present amazing condition of human society commonly called "Modern Civilization."

The shortcomings of human speech are most evident in discussing complicated matters; and for this reason speech is supplemented in the engineering arts by drawings of different kinds. No man ever lived who could describe a complicated machine accurately to a listener, unless that machine differed but little from a machine with which the listener was acquainted. But hand a drawing of even a very complicated machine to a man who knows its language—and the whole nature of the object is laid bare to him; not only its general plan and purpose, but its details, with all their dimensions and even the approximate weights. So, when the forces representing a complicated naval situation are placed upon the gameboard, all the elements of the problem appear clearly and correctly to each person; the imagination has little work to do, and the chance for misunderstanding is almost negligible. Of course, this does not mean that the game-board can decide questions with absolute finality. It cannot do this; but that is only because conditions are represented with only approximate realism, because the rules of the game may not be quite correct, and because sufficient correct data cannot be procured. The difficulties of securing absolute realism are of course insuperable, and the difficulties of getting absolutely correct data are very great. The more, however, this work is prosecuted, the more clearly its difficulties will be indicated, and therefore the more effectively the remedies can be provided. The more the game-board is used both on ship and shore, the more ease will be found in getting correct data for it, and the more correctly conclusions can then be deduced.

These remarks, while intended for tactical games, seem to apply to strategical games as well; for both the tactical and the strategical games are simply endeavors to represent actual or probable situations and occurrences in miniature, by arbitrary symbols, in accordance with well-understood conventions.

War games and war problems have not yet been accepted by some; for some regard them as games pure and simple and as academic, theoretical, and unpractical. It may be admitted that they are academic and theoretical; but so is the science of gunnery, and so is the science of navigation. In some ways, however, the lessons of the game-board are better guides to future work than "practical" and actual happenings of single battles: for in single battles everything is possible, and some things happen that were highly improbable and were really the result of accident. After nearly every recent war there has been a strong move made toward the adoption of some weapon, or some method, that has attained success in that war. For instance, after our Civil War, many monitors were built, and the spar torpedo was installed in all our ships; after the battle of Lissa, the ram was exploited as the great weapon of the future; the Japanese War established the heavily armed and armored battleships on a secure foundation; and the early days of the present war caused a great rush toward the submarine. Yet, in most cases, the success was a single success or a very few successes, and was a little like the throw of a die, in the sense that the result was caused in great measure by accident; that is, by causes beyond the control of man, or by conditions that would probably not recur.

The game calls our attention to the influence of chance in war, and to the desirability of our recognizing that influence and endeavoring to eliminate it, when reasoning out the desirability or undesirability of a certain weapon or a certain method. Of course, every thoughtful person realizes that few effects in life are due to one cause only, and that most effects are due to a combination of many causes; so that, if any weapon or method succeeds or fails, it is illogical to infer from that one fact that the weapon or method is good or bad. A common illustration is the well-known fact that a marksman may hit the target when his aim is too high or too low, provided that he has erroneously set his sight enough too low or too high to compensate; whereas if he had made only one error instead of two, he would have missed. "Two wrongs cannot make a right," but two errors can compensate each other, and often do. The theory of the Probability of Errors recognizes this. In fact, if it were not true that some errors are plus and some minus, all errors in gunnery (in fact in everything) would be additive to each other, and we should live in a world of error.

The partial advantage of the game-board over the occurrences of actual war, for the purpose of studying strategy, lies largely in its ability to permit a member of trials very quickly; the trials starting either with identical situations, or with certain changes in conditions. Of course, the game-board has the tremendous disadvantage that it presents only a picture, and does not show a real performance; but the more it is used, and the more fleets and game-boards work together, the more accurate the picture will become, and the more correctly we shall learn to read it.

One limitation of the game-board is that it can represent weather conditions only imperfectly—and this is a serious limitation that may or may not be remedied as time goes on. The theory of the game-board is in fact in advance of the mechanism, and is waiting for some bright inventive genius for the remedy. Until this happens, the imagination must do the best it can, and the effect of a certain kind of weather under the other conditions prevailing will have to be agreed upon by the contestants.

The term "war game" is perhaps unfortunate, for the reason that it does not convey a true idea of what a "war game" is. The term conveys the idea of a competitive exercise, carried on for sport; whereas the idea underlying the exercise is of the most serious kind, and has no element of sport about it, except the element that competition gives. A war game may be simply a game of sport—and sometimes it is so played; but the intention is to determine some doubtful point of strategy or tactics, and the competitive element is simply to impart realism, and to stimulate interest. When two officers, or two bodies of officers, find themselves on different sides of a certain question, they sometimes "put it on the game-board," to see which side is right.

This statement applies most obviously to tactical games; but it applies to strategic games as well; for both are inventions designed to represent in miniature the movements of two opposing forces. The main difference between strategic and tactical games is the difference in size. Naturally, the actual means employed are different, but only so different as the relative areas of movement necessitate. In the strategic games, the opposing forces are far apart, and do not see each other; in the tactical games, they operate within each other's range of vision.[9]

War games when played for the purpose of determining the value of types of craft and vessels of all kinds, may take on almost an infinite variety of forms; for the combinations of craft of different kinds and sizes, and in different numbers, considered in connection with the various possible combinations of weather, climate, and possible enemy forces, are so numerous as to defy computation.

9. But not for long. Even at Jutland tactical maneuvers were confounded by the way the fleets were spread out, and by the poor visibility, which was perhaps 10 percent of the distance across a circle that encompassed the ships on both sides. Moreover, though tactical discussions admitted the dire possibilities of night attacks, especially by torpedo boats, tactical games played night actions badly or not at all. Until computer-assisted games came along, the play of naval aircraft on the game floor of the Naval War College was a great complication.

In practice, however, and in a definite problem, the number of factors can be kept down by assuming average conditions of weather, using the fairly well-known enemy force that would appear in practice, and playing games in which the only important variable is the kind of vessel in question. For instance, in the endeavor to ascertain the value of the battle cruiser, games can be played in which battle cruisers are only on one side, or in which they are more numerous, or faster or more powerful on one side than on the other.

Naturally, the games cannot be as valuable practically as they otherwise would be, unless they consider the amount of money available. For instance, if games are played to ascertain the most effective number and kinds of craft for which to ask appropriations from Congress at next session, the solution, unless a money limit were fixed, would be impossible. In other words, the amount of money to be expended must be one of the known or assumed factors in the problem.

As this amount can never be known, it must be assumed; and, in order that the whole value of the games may not be lost, in case the amount assumed were incorrect, it is necessary to assume a number of possible sums, the upper limit being above the probable amount to be received, and the lower limit below it, and then work out the answer to the problem, under each assumption.

Of course, this procedure would be laborious, but most procedures are that bring about the best results. Suppose that such a procedure were followed for, say, a year, and that a number of plans, all worked out, were presented to Congress when it met: plan No. 1, for instance, consisting of such and such craft showing (according to the results of the games) the best programme, if $100,000,000 were to be appropriated for the increase of the navy; plan No. 2, if $90,000,000 were to be appropriated; plan No. 3, if $80,000,000 were to be appropriated, and so on. Each plan being concisely and clearly stated, and accompanied by drawings, sketches, and descriptions, Congress could easily and quickly decide which plan it would adopt.

This scheme would have the obvious advantage over the present scheme that the professional questions would be decided by professional men, while the financial question would be decided by Congress, which alone has the power to decide it. At present, the laymen on the House Naval Committee spend laborious days interrogating singly, and on different days, various naval officers, who naturally do not always agree. Finally, the House Naval Committee decides on a programme and recommends it to the House. The House discusses it most seriously (the professional points more seriously than the financial point), and decides on something. Then the Senate Committee, using the House decision as a basis, recommends something to the Senate, and the Senate then decides on something more or less like what the Senate Committee recommends. Then the whole question is decided by a Conference Committee of three senators and three members of the House. It is to be noted that this committee decides not only how much money the country shall spend on the navy, but also what kinds of vessels navy officers shall use to fight in the country's defense; how many officers there shall be, and how they shall be divided among the various grades![10]

Attention is requested here to the *ease* with which a decision can be made, *provided one does not take into account all of the factors of a problem, or if he is not thoroughly acquainted with them;* and attention is also requested to the *impossibility* of making a *wise* decision (except by chance) unless one understands *all* the factors, takes *all* into consideration, and then combines them *all*, assigning to each its proper weight. From one point of view, every problem in life

10. Most observers of the defense budget process would agree that it has regressed since the time of Fiske's wise appeal for a macro approach, which would have caused the Congress to determine the level of funds and naval officers to determine what strategy the funds would support.

is like a problem in mathematics; for if all the factors are added, subtracted, multiplied, and divided correctly (that is, if they are combined correctly), and if correct values are assigned to them, the correct answer is inevitable. In most of the problems of life, however, certainly in the problems of strategy, we do not know all of the factors, and cannot assign them their exactly proper weights; and therefore we rarely get the absolutely correct answer. The best that any man can do is to estimate the factors as accurately as he can, judge as correctly as he can their interaction on each other, and then make his own conclusion or decision.

When a man can do this well in the ordinary affairs of life, he is said to be "a man of good judgment"; when he can do it well in a certain line of work—say investments in real estate—he is said to have good judgment in real estate. The use of the word "judgment" here is excellent, because it expresses the act of a judge, who listens patiently to all the evidence in a case and then gives his decision. And the act of the judge, and the act of any man in coming carefully to any decision, consist mainly in estimating the relative values of all the factors, and their relations to each other ("sizing them up" is the expressive slang), and then perceiving with more or less correctness what the answer is. Some men do not have good judgment; some men highly educated, brilliant, and well-meaning, seem never to get quite the correct answer to any problem in life. They are said to be unsuccessful and no one knows why. Perhaps they lack that instinctive sense of proportion that some men have—a sense as real as an "ear for music"; or perhaps they lack a willingness or a capability to think about a situation with sufficient intentness to force a clear picture of the situation with all its various features upon the mental retina.

The ability to make a mental picture, be it of a machine, of any group of material objects, such as the various units of a fleet organized as such, or of any other situation, varies with different men; but like every other kind of ability, it can be strengthened by practice, and assisted by appropriate means. In the engineering arts, the practice is gotten by observing and remembering actual machines; and the assistance is given by drawings of different kinds. In strategy, the practice is given by observing and remembering the movements of actual fleets; and the assistance by means of drawings of different kinds, and by war problems, and the game-board. The game-board represents a number of successive pictures, and is not very different in principle from moving-pictures. In fact, the suggestion has been made repeatedly for several years and is now in process of development that the various situations in tactical games might advantageously be photographed on films and afterward projected in rapid succession on a screen.

One of the curious limitations of the naval game board, both in tactical and strategic games, is that it takes no account of personnel; that it assumes that all the various units are manned by crews that are adequate both in numbers and in training. Of course, it would be impracticable to test say the relative values of kinds of vessels, unless all the factors of the problem were the same, except the two factors that were competing. Therefore the limitation mentioned is not mentioned as a criticism, but simply to point out that the game-board, in common with most of the other means of discussion in naval matters, has gradually led people to think of naval matters in terms of material units only. That such an unfortunate state of affairs has come to pass can be verified by reading almost any paper, even professional, that speaks about navies; for one will be confronted at once with the statement that such and such a navy consists of such and such ships, etc. Since when has a navy consisted of brass and iron? Since when has the mind and character of man taken a place subordinate to matter? At what time did the change occur whereby the instrument employed dominated the human being who employed it? That this is not an academic point, or an unimportant thing to bear in mind is evidenced by countless facts in history. In order not to tire the reader, mention will be made of only one fact, the well-known fight between the American frigate *Chesapeake,* and the British frigate *Shannon* to which I have already referred. These two ships were almost identical in size and in the number and kinds of guns, and in the number of officers and crew, and the battle was fought on June 1, 1813, in Massachusetts Bay, under circumstances of weather and other conditions that gave no advantage to either. If material and numbers of personnel were the only factors in the fight, the fight would have continued very long and ended in a draw. Did these things occur? No, the *Chesapeake* was captured in a little less than fifteen minutes after the first gun was fired, and nearly half her crew were killed or wounded!

It would be tiresome to recount all the battles both on sea and land, in which smaller forces defeated forces numerically greater; but it may not be possible by any other means to force the fact on the attention—even sometimes of naval officers—that material vessels, guns, etc., are merely instruments, and that the work gotten out of any instrument depends not only on the instrument itself, but on the skill with which it is employed. Usually, when thinking or speaking of the power of any instrument (or means or method or organization) we mean the power of which it is capable; that is, the result which it can produce, *if used with 100 per cent of skill.* Possibly, we are subconsciously aware that we assume perfect skill; but whether we are or not, we have become so accustomed to the tacit acceptance of the phrase, "other things being equal," that we have come to forget that other things may not be equal at all; and that they certainly will not be on the day of trial, if we forget or undervalue those other things, while our antagonist does not.

Let us always remember, then, that the effective work gotten out of any means or instrument is the product of the maximum capability of the means or instrument and the skill with which it is used; that, for instance, if two fleets fight, which are numerically equal in material and personnel, but in which the skill of the personnel of the *A* fleet is twice as great as the skill of the personnel of the *B* fleet, the *A* fleet will be twice as powerful as the *B* fleet.[11]

It may be objected that it would be absurd to assume the skill of the personnel in one fleet as twice as great as that of the personnel in the other fleet, but it can easily be shown that even so great a disproportion is not impossible, provided the skill in one fleet is very great. The value of superior skill naturally becomes important where the difficulties are great. A very simple illustration is in firing a gun; for even if the skill of one marksman be greater than that of another, it will be unimportant, if the target is so large and so close that even the inferior marksman can hit it at each shot. The probability of hitting a target—so far as overs and shorts are concerned (or deviations to the left and right)—varies with the fraction a/y, where a is the half height (or width) of the target, and y is the mean error. The greater the size of the target, and the less the mean error, the greater the probability of hitting. The size of the two targets being fixed, therefore, the smaller the mean error the greater the probability of hitting. The probability of hitting, however (as can be seen by the formula), does not increase greatly with the decrease of error, except in cases

11. In the preceding paragraph Fiske first distinguishes between *forces* as an order of battle of a navy and *combat potential*, which is the value of those forces when they are organized, manned, and trained. He then takes a third step, which is best thought of as a description of the transformation of combat potential (constituted of trained forces) into *combat power* or *force*, by activating the trained forces against an enemy force. When Fiske says fleet *A*, with more skilled personnel, has twice the power of fleet *B*, he is working in the realm of outcomes when force meets force. Fiske proceeds to show why combat power must remain undefined until it is applied against an enemy.

where a/y is small, where the mean error is large relatively to the width or height of the target. For instance, if a/y is .1 in one case, and .2 in another case, the probability is practically double in the second case; whereas, if a/y is 1 in one case and 2 in another, the probability increases only 55 percent; while if it is 2 in one case and 4 in the other, the probability of hitting increases only 12 per cent.[12]

This means that if two antagonists engage, the more skilful should, and doubtless will, engage under difficult conditions, where y is considerable relatively to a; for instance, at long range. Suppose that he engages at such a range that he can make 10 per cent of hits—that is, make 90 per cent of misses; and that his misses relatively to the enemy's is as 90 to 95—so that the enemy makes 95 per cent of misses. This does not seem to be (in fact it is not) an extreme case: and yet A will hit B twice as often as B will hit A. In other words, the effective skill of A will be twice that of B.[13]

This illustrates the effect of training—because all that training in handling any instrument can do is to attain as closely as possible to the maximum output of the instrument; and as the maximum output is attained only when the instrument is handled exactly as it should be handled, and as every departure is therefore an error in handling, we see that the effect of training is merely to diminish errors.

That this illustration, drawn from gunnery, is applicable in general terms to strategy seems clear, for the reason that in

12. In other words, when the opponents fire at long range, the greater skill in marksmanship for side A will result in twice the hitting rate of side B. If the opponents fire at short range, side B is able to hit most of the time, and A's advantage in marksmanship is lost. The third case, when a/y equals either 2 or 4, is about the naval equivalent of shooting a barn door at ten paces.

13. To calibrate the reader's thinking, at the Battle of Jutland (1916) about 3 percent of major-caliber shells hit.

every strategical situation, no matter how simple or how complex, there is, and can be only one *best* thing to do; so that the statement of any strategic situation, if followed by a question as to what is the best thing to do, becomes a problem, to which the answer is—*the best thing to do.* Of course, in most strategic problems, there are so many factors almost unknown, and so many factors only imperfectly known, that we can rarely ascertain mathematically what is the best thing to do. Nevertheless, there must be a best thing to do, even if we never ascertain exactly what it is. Now in arriving at the decision as to the best thing to do, one estimates the weight of each factor and its bearing on the whole. If one estimates each factor correctly, that is, if he makes no errors in any estimate, and if he makes no error in summing up, he will make an absolutely correct decision; and any departure from correctness in decision can result from no other cause than from errors in his various estimates and in their final summation. In other words, skill in strategy is to be attained by the same process as is skill in other arts: by eliminating errors.

So, when we take the decisions of the game-board and the war problem, we must not allow ourselves to forget that there has been a tacit assumption that the numbers and the skill of the personnel have been equal on the two sides; and we must supplement our decision as to the best material to be employed by another decision as to how we shall see to it that the assumption of equality of personnel shall be realized in fact—or rather that it shall be realized in fact that our personnel shall get the maximum of effectiveness out of the material.

In designing the machine, therefore, we are confronted with the curious fact that, in general, we must design the various material parts before designing the personnel parts that are to operate them.[14]

14. You equip an army, but you man a navy.

The most obvious characteristic of the personnel parts is that the number of personnel parts shall be sufficient to operate the material parts.

To ascertain the number of personnel parts, the only means is actual trial; though naturally, if we have previously ascertained the number of men needed to operate any kind of mechanism, say a certain kind and size of gun, we can estimate quite accurately the number needed to operate a similar gun, even if it differ somewhat from the other gun. After the gun is tried, however, we may have to change our original estimate, not only because the estimate may have been in error, but because the requirement of operating the gun may have changed. For instance, the requirements of fire-control have within very recent years compelled the addition of a considerable number of men to the complements of battleships.

Now the need of supplying enough men to operate successfully any instrument or mechanism is absolute, for the reasons that the number of things to be done is fixed, and that an insufficient number of men in the ratio for instance of 9 to 8 may mean a falling off in the output of the machine much greater than in the ratio of 9 to 8. A simple illustration may be taken from the baseball game; for it is obvious that the output of a baseball team, in competition with other teams, would fall off in a much greater ratio than of 9 to 8, by leaving out one member of the nine.[15] Another illustration, or rather an analogy, may be found in machinery made of rigid metal—say a steam-engine; for the omission of almost any part in an engine would entirely stop its operation.

Not only, however, must we see that the number of person-

15. Another example of the necessary transformation from counting numbers of forces to estimating the effectiveness of those forces as Force. The transformation—the functional relationship—is nonlinear, and while the functional relationship cannot be known exactly, professional estimates can and must be made. When you want to know the penalty of playing with only eight men on the field, you don't ask a congressman's staff.

nel parts is sufficient, we must see that they are correctly divided among the various material parts; otherwise there will be too many in one place and too few in another; and while it is better to have too many men than too few, too many men prevent the attainment of the maximum effect.

The effect of having too few men, however, is not merely in limiting the effectiveness of the output of the machine; for, if carried to a considerable degree, it prevents due care of the material parts themselves, and causes those material parts to deteriorate. This deterioration may take the form of actual wasting away as by rust; but even if the deterioration does not advance so far as actual wastage, it may easily, and often does, advance to the stage where, although not evidenced by visible rust or by any other indication, so long as the mechanism is not operated at its normal rate, it declares itself very clearly as soon as the mechanism is tried in service. For this reason, all mechanics realize that it is better for every mechanism not to lie idle, but to be used considerably, though, of course, without being forced unduly.

Not only also must the personnel be sufficient in number and correctly divided, it must be organized in such manner that the personnel itself will have the characteristics of a machine, in the sense that each unit will be so placed relatively to the hope of reward and the fear of punishment, that he will do his allotted tasks industriously; that he will have the place in the organization for which his character and abilities fit him, and that he will be given such duties and exercises as will fit him more and more for his position, and more and more for advancement to positions higher.

Not only this, we must exercise foresight in the endeavor that the material parts and the personnel parts shall be ready at the same time, so that neither will have to wait for the other; and to insure the immediate availability when war breaks out, of sufficient trained personnel to man and fight effectively all the material units that we shall need to use. This raises the question: "What units shall we need?" The government itself must, of course, decide this matter; but it may be pointed out that if in any considerable war every unit we possess should not be utilized, the navy could not do as effective work as it otherwise could do. In the present war, the belligerents have not only utilized all the units that they had, they have built very many more, using the utmost possible diligence and despatch. In case we should be drawn into war with any considerable naval nation, all history and all reasoning show that we must do the same. Few considerable wars have been waged except with the greatest energy on each side; for each side knows that the scale may be turned by a trifling preponderance on one side; and that if the scale once be turned, it will be practically impossible ever to restore the balance. Every advantage gained makes one side relatively weaker to the other than it was before, and increases the chance that the same side will gain another advantage; gains and losses are cumulative in their effect. For this reason, it is essential, if we are to wage war successfully, that we start right, and send each unit immediately out to service, manned with a highly trained and skilful personnel; because that is what our foe will do.

The Germans meet the difficulty of keeping their personnel abreast of their material very wisely. They utilize the winter months, when naval operations are almost impossible, for reorganizing and rearranging their personnel; so that when spring comes, they are ready in all their ships to start the spring drilling on a systematic plan. The crews being already organized, and the scheme of drills well understood, the work of getting the recruits versed in their relatively simple tasks and the more experienced men skilled in their new positions is quickly accomplished, and the fleet is soon ready for the spring maneuvers.

The fundamental requirement of any organization of men is that it shall approach as closely as possible the characteristics of an organism, in which all the parts, though independent, are mutually dependent, each part doing its appropriate work without interfering with any other, but on the contrary assisting it. The most complex organization in the world is that of a navy, due primarily to the great variety of mechanisms in it, and secondarily to the great variety of trained bodies of men for handling those mechanisms. This variety extends from the highest posts to the lowest; and to make such varied organizations work together to a common end is one of the greatest achievements of civilized man. How it is accomplished is not clear at first view. It is not hard to see how a company of soldiers, drawn up in line, can be made to move as one body by order of the captain. But how in a battleship carrying a thousand men does the coal-passer in the fire-room do as the captain on the bridge desires? It may be objected that he does not—that the captain has no wishes regarding the doings of any coal-passer—that all the captain is concerned with is the doings of the ship as a whole. True, in a way; and yet if the various coal-passers, firemen, quartermasters, *et al.*, do not do as the captain wishes, the ship as a whole will not. The secret of the success achieved seems to lie in the knitting together of all the personnel parts by invisible wires of common understanding, analogous to the visible wires that connect the helmsman with the steering-engine. In the case of any small body of men, say the force in one fire-room, the connecting wire joining each man to the petty officer in charge of that fire-room is almost visible, because the petty officer is familiar, by experience, with the work of each man; for he has done that work himself, knows just how it should be done, and knows how to instruct each man. But the more complicated the organization is, the more invisible are the communicating wires that tie the men together, and yet the more important it is that those wires shall tie them; it is even more important, for instance, that the wires connecting the chief engineer with all his force shall operate than that the wires in any one fire-room shall operate. And yet not only are there more wires, but the wires themselves that connect the chief engineer to all the men below him, are longer and more subject to derangement, than the wires that connect the petty officer of one fire-room to the individuals under him.

The chief engineer, of course, is not tied directly to his coal-passers, but to men close to himself; close not only in actual distance, but in experience, knowledge, and sympathy; men who speak the same languages as he does, who understand what he means when he speaks, and who speak to him in ways he understands. These men immediately under him are similarly tied to their immediate subordinates by wires of knowledge, experience, and sympathy—these to their immediate subordinates, and so on.

The same statement applies to the captain in his relations with the chief engineer. The captain may not be an experienced engineer himself; but he is familiar enough with engineering, with its difficulties, its possibilities, and its aims, to converse with the chief engineer in language which both clearly understand.

The same principles seem to apply throughout the whole range of the personnel: so that, no matter how large the organization of any navy may be, there is—there must be, if good work is to be done—a network of invisible wires, uniting all together, by a strong yet flexible bond of sympathy.

And has the material of the navy no connection with this bond? Who knows! Brass and steel are said to be lifeless matter. But does any naval man believe this wholly? Does any man feel that those battleships, and cruisers, and destroyers, and submarines are lifeless which he himself—with his own eyes—has seen darting swiftly, precisely, powerfully on perfect lines and curves, changing their relative positions through complicated maneuvers without accident or mistake? Can we really believe that they take no part and feel no pride in those magnificent pageants on the ocean? From the earliest times, men have personified ships, calling a ship "he" or "she," and giving ships the names of people, and of states; and is not a ship with its crew a living thing, as much as the body of a man? The body of a man is in part composed of bones and muscles, and other parts, as truly things of matter as are the hull and engines of a ship. It is only the spirit of life that makes a man alive, and permits the members of his body, like the members of a ship, to perform their appointed tasks.

But even if this notion seems fanciful and absurd, we must admit that as surely as the mind and brain and nerves and the material elements of a man must be designed and made to work in harmony together, so surely must all the parts of any ship, and all the parts of any navy, parts of material and parts of personnel, be designed and made to work in harmony together; obedient to the controlling mind, and sympathetically indoctrinated with the wish and the will to do as that mind desires.

CHAPTER NINE

PREPARING THE ACTIVE FLEET

J OHN CLERK, of Eldin, Scotland, never went to sea, and yet he devised a scheme of naval tactics, by following which the British Admiral Rodney gained his victory over the French fleet between Dominica and Guadeloupe in April, 1782.[1] Clerk devised his system by the simple plan of thinking intently about naval actions in the large, disregarding such details as guns, rigging, masts, and weather, and concentrating on the movements of the fleets themselves, and the doings of the units of which those fleets were made. He assisted his mental processes by little models of ships, which he carried in his pockets, and which he could, and did, arrange on any convenient table, when he desired to study a problem, or to make a convert.

He was enabled by this simple and inexpensive device to

1. John Clerk of Eldin (1728–1812) was reputed to have influenced his contemporary Rodney's tactics at the Battle of the Saints near Dominica, 12 April 1782. According to S. S. Robison in *A History of Naval Tactics* (Annapolis, Md., 1942), p. 489, his *Essay on Naval Tactics* was supplied to U.S. naval ship libraries at least to the end of the nineteenth century. However, the London *Times* reviewer of *Fighting Machine* (15 February 1917), leaning on recent scholarship, said neither Rodney nor his chief of staff had been in communication with Clerk. The influence is only folklore, though Clerk's use of model fleets is not.

see the special problems of fleet tactics more clearly than he could have done by observing battles on board of any ships; for his attention in the ships would have been distracted by the exciting events occurring, by the noise and danger, and by the impossibility of seeing the whole because of the nearness of some of the parts. The amazing result was that he formed a clearer concept of naval tactics than any admiral of his time, finally overcame the natural prejudice of the British navy, and actually induced Rodney to stake on the suggestion of a non-military civilian his own reputation and the issue of a great sea fight. Furthermore, the issue was crowned with success.

Nothing could be simpler than Clerk's method. It was, of course, applied to tactics, but similar methods are now applied to strategy; for strategy and tactics, as already pointed out, are based on similar principles, and differ mainly in the fact that strategy is larger, covers more space, occupies more time, and involves a greater number of quantities.[2]

Most of the books on naval strategy go into the subject historically, and analyze naval campaigns, and also describe those measures of foresight whereby nations, notably Great Britain, have established bases all over the world and built up great naval establishments. These books lay bare the reasons

---

2. "Similar principles" could, of course, refer to the well-known Principles of War, usually about ten in number. But in general the principles of strategy were thought by most people to be more durable than the principles of tactics, and Mahan, in particular, said as much. This observer is happy to see Fiske deny the difference, for "there is a distinction between military principles—Mahan's or anyone else's—and the actions that derive from them. Tactics change, but that does not preclude the search for tactical principles, and if there are strategic principles, that does not mean that strategies do not change" (Wayne P. Hughes, Jr., *Fleet Tactics: Theory and Practice* [Annapolis, Md., 1986], p. 140). Fiske sees that new weapons have just as fundamental an effect on strategy as on tactics and says as much on the next page. And the effect of technology on both still continues.

for the large successes that good naval strategy has attained, both in peace and war, and constitute nearly all there is of the science of naval strategy.

These books and this method of treating naval strategy are valuable beyond measure; but officers find considerable difficulty sometimes in applying the principles set forth to present problems, because of the paucity of data, the remoteness in time and distance of many of the episodes described, and the consequent difficulty of making due allowance for them. Now, no study of naval strategy can be thoroughly satisfactory to a naval officer unless it assists him practically to decide what should be done in order to make the naval forces of his country, including himself, better in whatever will conduce to victory in the next war. Therefore, at the various war colleges, although the student is given books on strategy to study, the major part of the training is given by the applicatory method, an extension of Clerk's, in which the student applies his own skill to solving war problems, makes his own estimate of the situation, solves each problem in his own way (his solution being afterward criticised by the staff), and then takes part in the games in which the solutions presented are tried out. This procedure recognizes the fact that in any human art and science—say medicine, music, or navigation—it is the art and not the science by which one gets results; that the science is merely the foundation on which the art reposes, and that it is by practice of the art and not by knowledge of the science that skill is gained.

This does not mean, of course, that we do not need as much knowledge of the science of naval strategy as we can get; for the reason that the naval profession is a growing profession, which necessitates that we keep the application of the principles of its strategy abreast of the improvements of the times, especially in mechanisms; which necessitates, in turn, that we know what those principles are.

The applicatory method bears somewhat the same relation

to the method of studying books and hearing lectures that exercises in practical navigation bear to the study of the theory. There is one difference, however, as applied to strategy and navigation, which is that the science of navigation is clearly stated in precise rules and formulæ, and the problems in practical navigation are solved by assigning values to quantities like *a, b, c, d,* etc., in the formulæ, and working out the results by mathematics; whereas in strategy, no exact science exists, there are no formulæ, and even the number of assured facts and principles is small. For this reason the art of strategy is more extensive and significant relatively to its science than is the art of navigation to its science.

It is a defect of the historical system that it tends to make men do as people in the past have done—to make them work by rule. Clerk's method took no note of what had been done before, but confined itself to working out what should be done at the moment (that is, by what we now call the "applicatory method"), taking account of conditions as they are. By combining the two methods, as all war colleges do now, officers get the good results of both.

In the studies and exercises at the war colleges, note is taken of the great events that have gone by, and of the great problems now presented; by studying the historical events, and by solving war problems of the present, a certain knowledge of the science of naval strategy, and a certain skill in the art are gained. The studies and the problems naturally are of war situations.

Yet every war situation was the result of measures taken in time of peace. If these measures had been unwise on the part of one side—say Blue—in the design of certain craft, or the adoption, or failure of adoption, of certain plans, then Blue's strategic situation in the war would be more unfavorable than it would have been if the measures had been wise.

This proves that it is not only in war that strategy should be consulted; that strategy should be made to perform important services in peace as well; that strategic considerations should be the guide to all measures great and small, that not only the major operations in war, but also the minor preparations in peace, should be conducted in accordance with the principles of strategy, and conform to its requirements. By this means, and by this means only, does a system of preparation seem possible in which all shall prepare with the same end in view, and in which, therefore, the best results will be secured in the least time and with the least labor.

The naval machine having been designed, the various parts having been furnished by the administrative agencies directing personnel and material, and the consumable stores having been provided by the agencies of supply (all under the guidance and control of strategy, and in accordance with the calculations of logistics), the next step is the same as that with any other machine—to prepare the machine to do its work.

The work that strategy has to do in accomplishing the preparation is only in planning; but this planning is not limited to general planning, for it extends to planning every procedure of training and administration, no matter how great or how small. It plans the mobilization of the navy as a whole, the exercises of the fleet, the training of officers and men to insure that the plans for mobilization and fleet exercises shall be efficiently carried out, the exercises of the various craft, and of the various mechanisms of all kinds in those craft, and even the drills of the officers and men, that insure that the various craft and mechanisms shall be handled well. This does not mean that strategy concerns itself directly with the training of mess cooks and coal-passers; and it may be admitted that such training is only under strategy's general guidance. It may be admitted, also, that a considerable part of the training of men in using mechanisms is caused by the requirements of the mechanism itself; that practically the same training is needed for a water-tender in the merchant service as for a water-tender in the navy. Nevertheless, we must either declare that the training of mechanicians in the navy has no relation to the demands of preparation of the navy for war, or else admit that the training comes under the broad dominion of strategy. To admit this does not mean at all that the training of a naval radio electrician is not directed in its details almost wholly by electrical engineering requirements; it merely means that the training must be such as to fulfil the requirements of strategy, for otherwise it would have no value. No matter how well trained a man might be in radio work, his work would be useless for naval purposes, if not made useful by being adapted to naval requirements. The fact that strategy controls the training of radio electricians through the medium of electrical means is only one illustration of another important fact, which is that in all its operations strategy directs the methods by which results are to be attained, and utilizes whatever means, even technical means, are the most effective and appropriate.

The naval machine having been designed as to both personnel and material, strategy has nothing to do with the material in preparing the machine for use, because the material parts are already prepared, and it is the work of engineering to keep those material parts in a state of continual preparedness.

It must be noted, however, that the naval machine differs from most material machines in that its various parts, material as well as personnel, are continually being replaced by newer parts, and added to by parts of novel kinds. Strategy must be consulted, of course, in designing the characteristics of the newer and the novel parts; but this work properly belongs in the designing stage, and not in the preparation stage.

Strategy's work, therefore, in preparing the naval machine for work consists wholly in preparing the personnel.[3] This

---

3. Narrow though it is, this conclusion merits the attention of every strategist. It structures all that follows in the chapter.

preparing may be divided into two parts—preparing the existing fleet already mobilized and preparing the rest of the navy.

Preparing the Fleet.—The fleet itself is always ready. This does not mean that, in time of profound peace, every ship in the fleet has all its men on board, its chain hove short, and its engines ready to turn over at a moment's notice; but it does mean that this condition is always approximated in whatever degree the necessities of the moment exact. Normally, it is not necessary to keep all the men on board; but whenever, or if ever, it becomes so necessary, the men can be kept on board and everything made ready for instant use. It is perfectly correct, therefore, to say that, so far as it may be necessary, a fleet in active commission is always ready.

Training.—Before this state of readiness can be attained, however, a great deal of training has to be carried out; and this training must naturally be designed and prosecuted solely to attain this end. Unless this end be held constantly in view, and unless the methods of training be adapted to attain it, the training cannot possibly be effective. To go from any point to another point, one must proceed in the correct direction. If he proceeds in another direction, he will miss the point.

The training of the fleet naturally must be in doing the things which the fleet would have to do in war. To decide what things these will probably be, resort must be had to the teachings of history, especially the most recent history,[4] and to the teachings of the war problem, the chart maneuver, and the game-board.

The part of the personnel which it is the most important to train is, of course, the commander-in-chief himself; and no reason is apparent for supposing that his training should be conducted on principles different from those that control the

4. A point of contention. Studying recent history is a good way to prepare to fight the last war. The best insights come from taking a longer view.

training of every other person in the fleet. Men being the same in general, their qualities differing only in degree, it is logical to conclude that, if a gun-pointer or coxswain is best trained by being made first to understand the principles that underlie the correct performance of his work, and then by being given a good deal of practice in performing it, a commander-in-chief, or a captain, engineer, or gunner, can be best trained under a similar plan. Knowledge and practice have always been the most effective means of acquiring skill, and probably will continue to be the best for some time to come.

Owing to the fact that navies have been in existence for many years, the general qualifications of efficient naval officers are fairly well known; and they have always been the same in the most important particulars, though the recent coming of scientific apparatus has made available and valuable certain types of men not especially valuable before this scientific apparatus appeared.

In all navies, and equally in all armies, the qualification that has been the most important has been character. To insure, or rather to do the utmost toward insuring, proper character in its officers, all countries for many years have educated certain young men of the country to be officers in the army and navy, and they have educated young men for no other service. If knowledge were the prime requirement, special training for young men would not be needed; the various educational institutions could supply young men highly educated; and if the government were to take each year a certain number of graduates who could pass certain examinations, the educational institutions would be glad to educate young men to pass them. In securing young men of proper education and physique, little difficulty would be found. Special schools could even give sufficient instruction in military and maritime subjects to enable young men to become useful in minor positions on shipboard and in camp, after a brief experience there. In fact, for some of the positions in the army and navy, such as those in the medical corps and others, military or naval training is not needed, or exacted.

The truth of these remarks is not so obvious now as it was some years ago, and it has never been so obvious in navies as in armies; because education in the use of the numerous special appliances used in ships could be given less readily by private instruction than in the use of the simpler appliances used in armies. But even now, and even in the navy, the course given at Annapolis is usually termed a "training" rather than an education.[5]

Yet even education, educators tell us, is more a matter of training than a matter of imparting knowledge. This indicates that even for the duties of civil life, the paramount aim of educators is so to train the characters of young men as to fit them for good citizenship.

We may assume, therefore, that the primary aim of governments in preparing young men for the army and navy is to develop character along the line needed for useful work in those services.

What is that line?

Probably nine officers in ten would answer this question with the words, "the line of duty." This does not mean that officers are the only people who should be trained to follow the line of duty; but it does mean that, in military and naval schools, the training is more devoted to this than in other schools, except, of course, those schools that train young men for the priesthood or other departments of the religious life. The analogy between the clerical and the military professions in this regard has been pointed out many times; but perhaps the closeness with which the medical profession approxi-

5. Because in 1916 training predominated; but around 1959 the Naval Academy curriculum and methods of instruction were brought into the twentieth century by the superintendent, Vice Admiral Charles L. Melson, and the faculty.

mates both in its adherence to the line of duty has not been appreciated as fully as it should be.

Duty.—The reason for the predominance of the idea of duty over any other in naval training is due, of course, to a realization of the fact that more can be accomplished by officers having a strict sense of duty though otherwise lacking, than by officers having any or all the other qualifications, but lacking the sense of duty. As an extreme instance of the doubtful value of highly trained officers who lack the sense of duty, we need but to point to those traitors who, in the past, have turned their powers in the hour of need against the cause they were engaged to fight for.

One cannot pursue the path of duty when that path becomes difficult or disagreeable unless the sense of duty is so strong as to resist the temptation to leave the path. To train a man to be strong in this way, we train his character.

There are several ways in which a man is tempted to leave the line of duty; of these perhaps the most important are danger, sloth, and love of pleasure. No human being is perfectly strong along any of these lines; and some are most tempted by danger, some by sloth, and some by love of pleasure.

Sloth and the love of pleasure do not act as hinderances to efficiency in the naval profession any more than they do in other callings. There is no profession, business, or vocation, in which a man's efficiency does not depend largely on his power of resistance to the allurement of sloth and pleasure. In all walks of life, including the usual routine of the naval life, these two factors are the main stumbling-blocks to the success of any man. That is, they are the main stumbling-blocks that training can remove or lessen; the main stumbling-blocks in the way of his attaining that degree of efficiency for which his mental and physical abilities themselves would fit him. Natural abilities are not here considered; we are considering merely what training can do to develop men as they are for the naval life.

Courage.—Danger is the special influence to divert a man from duty's line that is distinctive of the army and the navy; and therefore to secure ability to overcome this influence is the distinct effort of military training. To train a young man for the army, the training naturally is directed toward minimizing the influence of one class of dangers; while to train a young man for the navy, the training must be directed toward minimizing the influence of another class. Of course training toward courage in any line develops courage in other lines; but nevertheless a naval training does not enable a man to ride a plunging cavalry horse with equanimity; nor does training as a cavalryman wholly fit a man to brave the dangers of the deep in a submarine.

Thirty years ago, the present writer showed Commander Royal Bird Bradford, U.S.N., the wonders of the U.S.S. *Atlanta*, the first ship of what Americans then called "The New Navy." When I showed Bradford the conning-tower, I remarked that many captains who had visited the *Atlanta* had said that they would not go into the conning-tower in battle. To this Bradford replied: "The captain who would not go into the conning-tower in battle would be very brave, but he'd be a d———d fool."

The obvious truth of this remark, the intimate connection which it suggested between courage and folly, and the fact often noted in life that to be brave is often to be foolish, contrasted with the fact that in all history the virtue of courage in men has been more lauded than any other virtue, suggests that a brief inquiry into the nature and influence of courage may be interesting.

The definitions of courage found in the dictionary are most unsatisfactory, except that they say that the word "courage" comes from the Latin "cor," the heart, showing that it is deemed a moral quality, rather than physical or mental.

Yet the deeds of courage that history and fiction tell have

been deeds of what we call "physical courage," in which heroes and heroines have braved death and physical suffering. Far in the background are deeds of "moral courage," though many wise men have told us that "moral courage" is a quality higher than "physical courage," and more important.

It is a little difficult to make a clear picture of courage that is physical, as distinguished from courage that is moral; or moral as distinguished from physical. Courage seems to be a quality so clearly marked as to be hardly qualifiable by any adjective except an adjective indicating degree—such as "great" or "little," but if any other adjective may be applied to it, the adjective "moral" seems to be the only one. For courage, no matter how or why displayed, is from its very essence, moral. Strictly speaking, how can there be any courage except moral courage? If a man braves death or physical suffering, the quality that enables him to brave it is certainly not physical; certainly it does not pertain to the physical body. The "first law of nature" impels him to escape or yield; and it impels him with a powerful force. If this force be not successfully resisted, the man will yield.

Now the act of resisting a temptation to escape a physical danger is due to a more or less conscious desire to preserve one's self-respect and the respect of one's fellow men; and therefore, the best way in which to train a man to be brave is to cultivate his self-respect and a desire to have the respect of his fellow men; and to foster the idea that he will lose both if he acts in a cowardly way.

Naturally, some men are more apt to be cowards as regards physical dangers than are others; and men differ greatly in this way. Men of rugged physique, dull imagination, and sluggish nerves are not so prone to fear of physical danger, especially danger far ahead in the future, as are men of delicate physique, keen imagination, and highly strung nervous system; and yet men of the latter class sometimes surpass men of the former class when the danger actually arrives—they seem to have prepared themselves for it, when men of the former class seem in a measure to be taken by surprise.

It is the attainment of physical courage, or courage to defy a threat of physical injury, that military training aims at. That it has done so successfully in the past, the history of the valiant deeds of sailors and soldiers bears superabundant witness. This courage has been brought out because it was essential. Courage is to a man what strength is to structural materials. No matter how physically strong and mentally equipped a man may be; no matter how perfectly designed and constructed an engine may be, neither the man nor the engine will "stand up to the work," unless the courage in the one case, and the strength of the materials in the other case, are adequate to the stress.

While perfect courage would enable a man to approach certain death with equanimity, all that is usually demanded of a man is that he shall dare to risk death, if need be. To do this successfully, a great assistance is a knowledge that even if things look bad, the danger is not so great as it appears. Therefore, training confronts men frequently with situations that look dangerous, but which skill and coolness can avert. In this way, the pupil becomes familiar with the face of danger, and learns that it is not so terrible as it seems. Nothing else makes a man so brave regarding a certain danger as to have met that danger successfully before. This statement must be qualified with the remark that in some cases a danger, although passed successfully, has been known to do a harm to the nervous system from which it never has recovered. This is especially the case if it was accompanied with a great and sudden noise and the evidence of great injury to others. In cases like this, the shock probably comes too abruptly to enable the man to prepare himself to receive it. The efficacy of a little preparation, even preparation lasting but a few seconds, is worthy of remark. Two theories connecting fear and trembling may be noted here: one that a person trembles because he fears; the other, and later, that trembling is automatic, and that a person fears *because he trembles.*

But the influence of fear is not only to tempt a man to turn his back on duty and seek safety in flight, for it affects him in many degrees short of this. Sometimes, in fact usually, it prevents the accurate operation of the mind in greater or less degree. Here again training comes to the rescue, by so habituating a man to do his work in a certain way (loading a gun for instance) that he will do it automatically, and yet correctly, when his mind is almost paralyzed for a time. A very few men are so constituted that danger is a stimulus to not only their physical but their mental functions; so that they never think quite so quickly and so clearly as when in great danger. Such men are born commanders.

Discussion of such an abstract thing as courage may seem out of place in a discussion of "Naval Strategy"; but while it is true that naval strategy is largely concerned with mental operations, while courage is a moral or spiritual quality, yet strategy concerns itself with the securing of all means to victory, and of these means courage is more important than any other one thing. One plan or one system of training may be better than another; but they differ only in degree, and if one plan fails another may be substituted; but if courage be found lacking, there is no substitute on earth. Now, if courage is to be inculcated by some system of training, surely it is not amiss to devote a few minutes to an analysis of the nature of courage, to seek what light we can get as to the best methods of training to employ.

Responsibility.—There is one form of courage which most men are never called upon to use, and that is willingness to take responsibility. Most men are never confronted with a situation requiring them to take it. To naval men, however, the necessity comes often, even to naval men in the lower grades; for they are often confronted with situations in which

211

they can accept or evade responsibility. That courage is needed, no one can doubt who has had experience. To accept responsibility, however, is not always best either for the individual or for the cause; often it were better to lay the responsibility on higher authority, by asking for instructions. But the same remark is true of all uses of courage; it is not always best to be brave, either for the individual or for the cause. Both the individual and the cause can often be better served by Prudence than by her big brother Courage. When, however, the conditions require courage in any form, such as willingness to accept responsibility, the man in charge of the situation at the moment must use courage, or—fail. In such cases the decision rests with the man himself. He cannot shift it to another's shoulders, even if he would. Even if he decides and acts on the advice of others, the responsibility remains with him.

From the Top Down, or from the Bottom Up?—There are two directions in which to approach the subject of training the personnel—from the top down, and from the bottom up. The latter is the easier way; is it the better?

The latter is the easier way, because it is quicker and requires less knowledge. In training a turret crew in this way, for instance, one does not have to consider much outside of the turret itself. The ammunition can be sent up and down, and the guns can be loaded, pointed, and fired with just as much quickness and accuracy as is humanly practicable, without much reference to the ship itself, the fleet, or the navy. In fact, knowledge of outside requirements hinders in some ways rather than advances training of this kind. Knowledge, for instance, of the requirements of actual battle is a distinct brake on many of the activities of mere target practice.

But while it is easier to train in this way all the various bodies of men that must be trained, it is obvious that by training them wholly without reference to the requirements of the fleet as a whole, the best result that we could expect would be a number of bodies of men, each body well trained as a unit, but the combined units not trained at all as component elements of the whole. The result would be a little like what one would expect from the efforts of an orchestra at playing a selection which the whole orchestra had never played before together, but of which each member of the orchestra had previously learned his part, and played it according to his own ideas, without consulting the orchestra leader.

By approaching the subject from the other direction, however, that is, from the top, the training of each organization within the fleet is arranged with reference to the work of the fleet as a whole, the various features of the drills of each organization being indicated by the conditions developed by that work. If this plan be carried out, a longer time will be required to drill the various bodies of men; but when it has been accomplished, those bodies will be drilled, not only as separate bodies, but as sympathetic elements of the whole.

Of course the desirability of drilling separate divisions of a fleet, and separate ships, turret crews, fire-control parties, and what-not, in accordance with the requirements of fleet work does not prevent them from drilling by themselves as often as they wish—any more than the necessity of drilling in the orchestra prevents a trombone player from practising on his instrument as much as the police will let him.

Thus the fact of keeping a fleet together does more than merely give opportunity for acquiring skill in handling the fleet itself, and in handling the various ships so that they will work together as parts of the fleet machine; because it shows each of the various smaller units within the ships themselves how to direct its training.

For this reason, the idea so often suggested of keeping the fleet normally broken up into smaller parts, those parts close enough together to unite before an enemy could strike, is most objectionable. It is impossible to keep the fleet together all the time, because of needed repairs, needed relaxation,

213

and the necessity for individual drills that enable a captain or division commander to strengthen his weak points; but nevertheless since the "mission" of training is to attain fighting efficiency in the fleet as a whole, rather than to attain fighting efficiency in the various parts; and since it can be attained only by drilling the fleet as a whole, the decision to keep the fleet united as much as practicable seems inevitably to follow. Besides, the statement cannot be successfully controverted that difficult things are usually not so well done as easy things, that drills of large organizations are more difficult than drills of small organizations, and that in every fleet the drills that are done the worst are the drills of the fleet as a whole. How could anything else be expected, when one considers how much more often, for instance, a turret crew is exercised at loading than the fleet is exercised at the difficult movement of changing the "line of bearing"?

The older officers remember that for many years we carried on drills at what we called "fleet tactics," though we knew they were only tactical drills. They were excellent in the same sense as that in which the drill of the manual of arms was excellent, or the squad exercises given to recruits. They were necessary; but beyond the elementary purpose of training in ship handling in fleet movements, they had no "end in view"; they were planned with a limited horizon, they were planned from the bottom.

General Staff.—In order to direct the drills of a fleet toward some worthy end, that end itself must be clearly seen; and in order that it may be clearly seen, it first must be discovered. The end does not exist as a bright mark in the sky, but as the answer to a difficult problem; it cannot be found by guessing or by speculating or by groping in the dark. Strategy says that the best way in which to find it is by the "estimate of the situation" method.

Owing to the fact that the commander-in-chief and all

214

his personnel are, by the nature of the conditions surrounding them, on executive duty, the working out of the end in view of any extensive drills seems the task of the Navy Department; while the task of attaining it seems to belong to the commander-in-chief. Owing to the present stage of electrical progress,[6] the Navy Department has better means of ascertaining the whole naval situation than has the commander-in-chief, and if officers (General Staff) be stationed at the department to receive and digest all the information received, and decide on the best procedure in each contingency as it arises, the Navy Department can then give the commander-in-chief the information he requires and general instructions how to proceed.

This does not mean that the department would "interfere" with the commander-in-chief, but simply that it would assist him. The area of discretion of the commander-in-chief should not be invaded; for if it be invaded, not only may orders be given without knowledge of certain facts in the commander-in-chief's possession, but the commander-in-chief will have his difficulties increased by the very people who are trying to help him. He may be forced into disobeying orders, a most disturbing thing to have to do; and he will surely be placed in a position of continuous doubt as to what is expected of him.

Of course, it must be realized that the difficulties of co-operating with a commander-in-chief at sea, by means of even the most expert General Staff, are of the highest order. It is

6. That is, radio, telegraph, and telephone. The problem Fiske sees emerging and describes in the succeeding paragraphs is one with which the U.S. Navy had no first-hand experience. But he believes the potential for interference by higher command with a commander afloat gives additional urgency for an operationally experienced staff to buffer the civilian secretary from exercising the power that "electrical progress" had placed in his hands. Despite the recently augmented power of the chairman of the Joint Chiefs of Staff, we still struggle with the problem.

hard to imagine any task more difficult. It must be accomplished, however, or else there will be danger all the time that the commander-in-chief will act as he would not act if he had all the information that the department had. This suggests at once that the proper office of the department is merely to give the commander-in-chief information and let him act on his own judgment. True in a measure; but the commander-in-chief must be given some instructions, even if they be general, for the reason that the commander-in-chief is merely an instrument for enforcing a certain policy. Clearly, he must know what the policy is, what the department desires; and the mere statement of the department's desires is of itself an order. If it is admitted that the commander-in-chief is to carry out the orders of the department, it remains merely to decide in how great detail those orders ought to be.

No general answer can be given to the question: "In what detail shall the orders be?" The general statement can be made, however, that the instructions should be confined as closely as practicable to a statement of the department's desires, and that this statement should be as clear as possible. If, for instance, the only desire of the department is that the enemy's fleet shall be defeated, no amplification of this statement is required. But if the department should desire, for reasons best known to itself, that the enemy should be defeated by the use of a certain method, then that should be stated also. Maybe it would not be wise for the department to state the method the employment of which is desired; maybe the commander-in-chief would be the best judge of the method to be employed. But maybe circumstances of governmental policy dictate the employment of a certain method, even if militarily it is not the best; and maybe also the department might prefer that method by reason of information recently received, which it does not have time to communicate in full.

Now if it is desirable for the department to give the commander-in-chief instructions, running the risk of invading his "area of discretion," and of doing other disadvantageous things, it is obvious that the department should be thoroughly equipped for doing it successfully. This means that the department should be provided not only with the most efficient radio apparatus that can be secured, manned, of course, by the most skilful operators, but also with a body of officers capable of handling that particular part of the Navy Department's work which is the concentrated essence of all its work, the actual handling of the naval forces. The usual name given to such a body of officers is "General Staff."

Such bodies of officers have been developed in navies in recent years, by a desire to take advantage of electrical appliances which greatly increase the accuracy and rapidity of comunication over long distances. In days not long ago, before communication by radio was developed, commanders on the spot were in possession of much more information about events in their vicinity, compared with the Navy Department, than they are now; and the difficulties and uncertainties of communication made it necessary to leave much more to their discretion and initiative. The President of the United States can now by telephone talk to the commander-in-chief, when he is in home waters, and every day sees some improvement in this line. This facility of communication carries with it, of course, the danger of "interfering," one of the most frequent causes of trouble in the past, in conducting the operations of both armies and fleets—a danger very real, very insidious, and very important. The very ease with which interference can be made, the trained instinct of the subordinate to follow the wishes of his superior if he can, the temptation to the superior to wield personally some military power and get some military glory, conspire to bring about interference. This is only an illustration, however, of the well-known fact that every power can be used for evil as well as for good, and

217

is not a valid argument against developing to the utmost the communication between the department and the fleet. It is, however, a very valid argument against developing it unless there be developed simultaneously some means like a "safety device" for preventing or at least discouraging its misuse.

The means devised is the General Staff; and in some countries like Germany it seems to work so well that (unless our information is incorrect) the Emperor himself does not interfere. He gives the machine a certain problem to work out, and he accepts the answer as the answer which has a greater probability of being correct than any answer he could get by other means.

Training of the Staff.—Now, if there is to be at the Navy Department a body of men who will work out and recommend what instructions should be given to the commander-in-chief, it seems obvious that that body of men should be thoroughly trained. In the German army the training of men to do this work (General Staff work) is given only to officers specially selected. Certain young officers who promise well are sent to the war college. Those who show aptitude and industry are then put tentatively into the General Staff. Those who show marked fitness in their tentative employment are then put into the General Staff, which is as truly a special corps as is our construction corps. How closely this system is followed with the General Staff in the German navy, the present writer does not know exactly; but his information is that the system in the navy is copied (though with certain modifications) after the system in the army.

How can the General Staff at the Navy Department be trained? In the same way as that in which officers at the war college are trained: by study and by solving war problems by tactical and strategical games. The training would naturally be more extended, as it would be a postgraduate course.

There is a difference to be noted between games like war

games in which the mental powers are trained, and games like billiards, in which the nerves and muscles receive practically all the training; and the difference refers mainly to the memory. Games of cards are a little like war games; and many books on games of cards have been written, expounding the principles on which they rest and giving rules to follow. These books may be said to embody a science of card-playing.

No such book on naval strategy has appeared; and the obvious reason is that only a few rules of naval strategy have been formulated. Staff training, therefore, cannot be given wholly by studying books; but possibly the scheme suggested to the department by the writer, when he was Aid for Operations, may be developed into a sort of illustrative literature, which can assist the memory.

By this scheme, a body of officers at the Navy Department would occupy their time wholly in studying war problems by devising and playing strategical and tactical games ashore and afloat. After each problem had been solved to the satisfaction of the staff, each distinctive situation in the approved solution would be photographed in as small a space as practicable, preferably on a moving-picture film. In the solution of problem 99, for instance, there might be 50 situations and therefore 50 photographs. These photographs, shown in appropriate succession, would furnish information analogous to the information imparted to a chess student by the statement of the successive moves in those games of chess that one sees sometimes in books on chess and in newspapers. Now if the film photographs were so arranged that the moves in the approved solution of, say, problem 99 could be thrown on a screen, as slowly and as quickly as desired, and if the film records of a few hundred such games could be conveniently arranged, a very wide range of situations that would probably come up in war would be portrayed; and the moves made in handling those situations would form valuable precedents for action, whenever situations approximating them should come up in war.[7]

It must be borne in mind that in actual life, our only real guide to wise action in any contingency that may arise is a memory, more or less consciously realized, of how a similar contingency has been met, successfully or unsuccessfully, in the past. Perhaps most of us do not realize that it is not so much experience that guides us as our memory of experiences. Therefore in the training of both officers and enlisted men in strategy, tactics, seamanship, gunnery, engineering, and the rest, the memory of how they, or some one else, did this well and that badly (even if the memory be hardly conscious) is the immediate agency for bringing about improvement.

Imagine now a strategical system of training for the navy, in which a body of highly trained officers at the department will continuously regulate the exercises of the fleet, guided by the revelations of the *Kriegspiel:* the commander-in-chief will

---

7. Even nowadays the lessons learned from war games and fleet exercises are usually compressed into results, conclusions, and recommendations. The results typically are in the form of a box score. But in doing these simulations of war, truly "the process is the product," and only the man who participates and studies the results profits from the richness of the play. Games are far more valuable for "how and why" than "what and when." Fiske, the scientist, had an instinct for processes and wanted to see the patterns of forces in motion. To him, outcomes were a static picture of results, and sterile; he wanted dynamic interactions. Inputs created outputs, but what went on in between? We would do well to heed his analogy of the moving chessboard, and study the openings, middle game positions, and end games of strategic situations and operational problems. Fiske believes that some "end games" will be common even though arrived at by a variety of different intervening moves.

The New York *Times* book reviewer (5 November 1916) chose to play up Fiske's idea. Underneath a seven-by-eleven-inch picture of American naval officers gaming at the Naval War College, the headline read "'MOVIES' AND 'WAR GAMES' AS AIDS TO OUR NAVY: Rear Admiral Bradley A. Fiske Advocates Combining Former With Famed Kriegspiel to Develop American Naval Strategists."

direct the activities of the main divisions of the fleet, carrying out the department's scheme; the commander of each division will regulate the activities of the units of his command in accordance with the fleet scheme; the officer in command of each unit of each division will regulate the activities of each unit in his ship, destroyer, submarine, or other craft in accordance with the division scheme; and every suborganization, in every ship, destroyer, or other craft will regulate likewise the activities of its members; so that the navy will resemble a vast and efficient organism, all the parts leagued together by a common understanding and a common purpose; mutually dependent, mutually assisting, sympathetically obedient to the controlling mind that directs them toward the "end in view." [8]

It must be obvious, however, that in order that the navy shall be like an organism, its brain (the General Staff) must not be a thing apart, but must be of it, and bound to every part by ties of sympathy and understanding. It would be possible to have a staff excellent in many ways, and yet so out of touch with the fleet and its practical requirements that co-ordination between the two would not exist. Analogous conditions are sometimes seen in people suffering from a certain class of nervous ailments; the mind seems unimpaired, but co-ordination between the brain and certain muscles is almost wholly lacking.

To prevent such a condition, therefore, the staff must be kept in touch with the fleet; and it must also permit the fleet to keep in touch with the staff, by arranging that, accompanying the system of training, there shall be a system of education which will insure that the general plan will be under-

8. Note that there is no mention of strategic and tactical doctrine. The very concept is muted in a few words like "common understanding," and below, "the system of training" and "the general plan." Now as then, the U.S. Navy vision of effective operations are those that come from "a vast and efficient organism . . . sympathetically obedient to the controlling mind."

stood throughout the fleet; and that the means undertaken to execute it will be made sufficiently clear to enable each person to receive the assistance of his own intelligence. No man can do his best work in the dark. Darkness is of itself depressing; while light, if not too intense, stimulates the activities of every living thing.

This does not mean that every mess attendant in the fleet should be put into possession of the war plans of the commander-in-chief, that he should be given any more information than he can assimilate and digest, or than he needs, to do his work the best. Just how much information to impart, and just how much to withhold are quantitative questions, which can be decided wisely by only those persons who know what their quantitative values are. This is an important matter, and should be dealt with as such by the staff itself. To get the maximum work out of every man is the aim of training; to get the maximum work that shall be effective in attaining the end in view, training must be directed by strategy, because strategy alone has a clear knowledge of what is the end in view.

Stimuli.—Some men are so slothful that exertion of any kind is abhorrent to them; but these men are few, and are very few indeed among a lot of healthy and normal men such as fill a navy. An office boy, lazy beyond belief in the work he is engaged to do, will go through the most violent exertions at a baseball game; and a farmhand who prefers a soft resting-place in the shade of an umbrageous tree to laboring in the fields will be stirred to wild enthusiasm by a horse race.

Now why are the office boy and the farmhand stimulated by these games? By the elements of competition, chance, and possible danger they bring out and the excitement thereby engendered. Training, therefore introduces these elements into drills as much as it can. Competition alone does not suffice, otherwise all men would play chess; competition and chance combined are not enough, or gentlemen would not need the danger of losing money to make card games interesting; but any game that brings in all three elements will rouse the utmost interest and activity of which a man is capable. Games involving these three elements are known by many names; one name is "poker," another name is "business," and another name is "politics." There are many other games besides, but the greatest of all is strategy.

Now in the endeavor to prepare a fleet by training, no lack of means for exciting interest will be found; in fact no other training offers so many and so great a variety of means for introducing the elements of competition, chance, and danger. The problem is how best to employ them.

To do this successfully, it must be realized, of course, that the greatest single factor in exciting interest is the personal factor, since comparatively few men can get much interested in a matter that is impersonal; a boy is more interested in watching a baseball game in which he knows some of the players than in watching a game between teams neither of which he has ever seen; and the men in any ship are more interested in the competition between their ship and some other than between any other two; feeling that *esprit de corps* by reason of which every individual in every organization personifies the organization as a living thing of which he himself is part.

Strategic Problems.—The training of the fleet, then, can best be done under the direction of a trained staff, that staff generously employing all the resources of competition, chance, and danger. The obvious way to do this is to give out to the fleet for solution a continual succession of strategic problems, which the entire fleet will be engaged in solving, and which will be the starting-point for all the drills of the fleet and in the fleet. (Some officers prefer the word "maneuver" to "problem.")

The arranging of a continual series of war problems, or maneuvers to be worked out in the fleet by "games," will call for an amount of strategical skill second only to the skill needed for operations in war, will deal with similar factors and be founded on similar principles.

Naturally, the war problems, before being sent to the fleet for solving, would be solved first by the staff, using strategical and tactical games, and other appropriate means; and inasmuch as the scheme of education and training is for the benefit of the staff itself, as well as for the benefit of the fleet, certain members of the staff would go out with the fleet to note in what ways each problem sent down was defective, in what ways good—and in what ways it could be modified with benefit. The successive situations and solutions, made first by the staff and subsequently by the fleet, can then be photographed and made part of the history of war problems, for the library of the staff.

In laying out the war problems, the staff will be guided naturally by the ends in view—first to work out solutions of strategic, logistic, and tactical situations in future wars, and second to give opportunity to the various divisions, ships, turret crews, engineers' forces, etc., for drills that will train them to meet probable contingencies in future wars.

This double end will not be so difficult of attainment as might at first sight seem, for the reason that the solution of any problem which represents a situation actually probable will automatically provide all the minor situations necessary to drill the various bodies; and the more inherently probable a situation is, the more probable will be the situations in which the various flag-officers, captains, quartermasters, engineers' forces, turret crews, etc., will find themselves.

Of course, the prime difficulty in devising realistic problems is the fact that in war our whole fleet would be employed together against an enemy fleet; and as the staff cannot supply an enemy fleet, it must either imagine an enemy fleet, divert a small part of our fleet to represent an enemy fleet, or else divide our fleet into two approximately equal parts, one "red," and one "blue."

First Scheme.—The first scheme has its usefulness in working out the actual handling of the fleet as a whole; and considering the purposes of strategy only, is the most important, though, of course, "contacts" with the enemy cannot be simulated. From the standpoint of fleet tactical drill, and the standpoint of that part of strategy which arranges for handling large tactical situations with success, it is useful, since it provides for the tactical handling of the entire fleet. This certainly is important; for if the personnel are to be so trained that the actual fleet shall be handled with maximum effectiveness in battle, training in handling that actual fleet must frequently be had; the fleet is a machine, and no machine is complete if any of its parts is lacking.

It may be objected that it is not necessary for the staff at the department to devise such training, because drills of the entire fleet can be devised and carried out by the commander-in-chief; in fact that that is what he is for. This, of course, is partly true; and it is not the idea of the author that the staff in the department should interfere with any scheme of drills that the commander-in-chief desires to devise and carry out; but it is his idea that the staff should arrange problems to be worked out by the fleet, in which the tactical handling of the fleet should be subordinate to, and carried out for, a strategic purpose.

A very simple drill would be the mere transfer of the fleet to a distant point, when in supposititious danger from an enemy, employing by day and night the scouting and screening operations that such a trip would demand. Another drill would be the massing of previously separated forces at a given place and time; still another would be the despatching of certain parts of the fleet to certain points at certain times. The problems need not be quite so simple as these, however; for they can include all the operations of a fleet under its commander-in-chief up to actual contact; the commander-in-chief being given only such information as the approximate position, speed, and course of the enemy at a given time, with orders to intercept him with his whole force; or he may be given information that the enemy has divided his force, that certain parts were at certain places going in certain directions at certain speeds at certain times, and he may be directed to intercept those supposititious parts; that is, to get such parts of his fleet as he may think best to certain places at certain times.

Of the strategic value to the staff of the practical solutions of this class of problems by the fleet, there can be little question; and the records made if kept up to date, would give data in future wars for future staffs, of what the whole fleet, and parts of it acting with the fleet, can reasonably be expected to accomplish, especially from the standpoint of logistics. And it has the advantage of dealing with only one thing; the actual handling of the actual fleet, uncomplicated by other matters, such as interference by an enemy. For the reason, however, that it leaves out of consideration the effects of scouting and of contacts with the enemy, it is incomplete.

Second Scheme.—To remedy this incompleteness, resort may be had to the device of detaching a few vessels from the fleet and making each represent a force of the enemy; one destroyer, for instance, to represent a division, four destroyers four divisions, etc. This scheme has the advantage that all the capital ships can be handled together, and that, say three-quarters of the destroyers can be handled without much artificiality on the assumption that four-fourths are so handled; while for merely strategic purposes four destroyers, properly separated, can represent four divisions of destroyers very truthfully. This scheme is useful not only strategically but tactically; for the reasons that the contacts made are actual and visible, and that all the personnel on each side are put to doing things much like those they would do in war. The scheme is extremely flexible besides; for the number of ways in which the fleet can be divided is very great, and the number of operations that can be simulated with considerable accuracy is therefore very great also. The training given to the personnel of the fleet is obviously more varied, interesting, and valuable, than in the first scheme; and the records of the solutions (games played) will form instructive documents in the offices of the staff, concerning situations which the first scheme could not bring out. These records, naturally, will not be so simple as those under the first scheme, because many factors will enter in, some of which will bring up debatable points. For when actual contact occurs, but only "constructive" hits by torpedo and gun are made, much room for difference of opinion will occur, and many decisions will be disputed.

To decide disputed questions must, of course, rest with the staff;[9] but those questions must be decided, and if correct deductions from the games are to be made, the decisions must be correct. To achieve correctness in decision the members of the staff must be highly trained. To devise and develop a good scheme of staff training, several years may be required.

Third Scheme.—The third kind of game is that in which the fleet is divided into two parts, fairly equal in each of the various elements, battleships, battle cruisers, destroyers, submarines, aircraft, etc. This scheme gives opportunity for more realistic situations than the other two, since each side operates and sees vessels and formations similar to those that it would operate and see in war; and it gives opportunity for games which combine both strategical and tactical operations and situations to a greater degree than do the other two schemes. Its only weakness is the fact that the entire fleet is

---

9. Despite the power of computer algorithms to resolve battle outcomes, it is amazing how often a human umpire is still called upon to referee disputes between the spirited competitors.

not operated as a unit; not even a large fraction, but only about one-half. Like each of the other two schemes, however, it has its distinctive field of usefulness.

Its main advantage is its realism—the fact that two powerful naval forces, each composed of all the elements of a naval force, seek each other out; or else one evades and the other seeks; and then finally they fight a fairly realistic battle; or else one successfully evades the other; or else minor actions occur between detachments, and no major result occurs; just as happens in war.

Strategically, this scheme is less valuable than the other two; tactically, more so. For the experience and the records of the staff this scheme is less valuable than the other two, but for the training of the fleet it is more so.

Of course, the division of games for staff and fleet training into three general schemes is arbitrary, and not wholly correct; for no such division really exists, and in practice it would not be observed. The thought of the writer is merely to point out that, in a general way, the schemes may be divided into three classes, and to show the convenience of doing so— or at least of recognizing that there are three general kinds of games, and that each kind has its advantages and likewise its disadvantages.

In our navy, only three strategic problems or maneuvers, devised at the department, have been worked out at sea—one in May, and one in October, 1915, and one in August, 1916: all belonged in the second category. They were devised by the General Board and the War College, as we had no staff. The solving of the problems by the commander-in-chief aroused the greatest interest not only in the fleet, but in the Navy Department, in fact, throughout the entire navy, and to a surprising degree throughout the country, especially among the people on the Atlantic coast. Discussions of the utmost value were aroused and carried on, and a degree of co-operation between the department, the War College, and the fleet, never attained before, was realized. If a routine could be devised whereby such problems could be solved by practical games, say once a month, and the results analyzed and recorded in moving-picture form by the staff in Washington, we could see our way in a few years' time to a degree of efficiency in strategy which now we cannot even picture. It would automatically indoctrinate the navy and produce a sympathetic understanding and a common aim, which would permeate the personnel and make the navy a veritable organism. It would attain the utmost attainable by any method now known.

Attention is respectfully invited to the fact that at the present time naval strategy is mainly an art; that it will probably continue so for many years; that whether a science of naval strategy will ever be formulated need not now concern us deeply, and that the art of naval strategy, like every other art, needs practice for its successful use. Naval strategy is so vague a term that most of us have got to looking on it as some mystic art, requiring a peculiar and unusual quality of mind to master; but there are many things to indicate that a high degree of skill in it can be attained by the same means as can a high degree of skill in playing—say golf: by hard work; and not only by hard work, but by doing the same thing—or similar things—repeatedly. Now most of us realize that any largely manual art, such as the technique of the piano, needs frequent repetition of muscular actions, in order to train the muscles; but few of us realize how fully this is true of mental arts, such as working arithmetical or strategical problems, though we know how easy it is to "get rusty" in navigation. Our mental muscles and whatever nerves co-ordinate them with our minds seem to need fully as much practice for their skilful use as do our physical muscles; and so to attain skill in strategy, we must practise at it. This means that all hands must practise at it—not only the staff in their secret sanctuary, not only the commander-in-chief, not only the division commanders, but, in their respective parts, the captains, the lieutenants, the ensigns, the warrant officers, the petty officers, and the youngest recruits. To get this practice, the department, through the staff, must furnish the ideas, and the commander-in-chief the tools. Then, day after day, month after month, and year after year, in port and at sea, by night and by day, the ideas assisted by the tools will be supplying a continuous stimulus to the minds of all. This stimulus, properly directed through the appropriate channels and devoted to wise purposes, will reach the mess attendant, the coal-passer, and the recruit, as well as those in positions more responsible (though not more honorable); and as the harmony of operation of the whole increases, as skill in each task increases, and as a perception of the strategic *why* for the performance of each task increases, the knowledge will be borne in on all that in useful occupation is to be found the truest happiness; that only uninterested work at any task is drudgery; that interest in work brings skill, that skill brings pleasure in exerting it; and that the greater the number of men engaged together, and the more wise the system under which they work, the greater will be the happiness of each man, and the higher the efficiency of the whole.

CHAPTER TEN

RESERVES AND SHORE STATIONS

IN THE PRECEDING chapter it was pointed out that the work of preparing the naval machine for use could be divided into two parts: preparing the existing fleet and preparing the rest of the navy.

The "rest of the navy" consists of the Navy Department itself, the naval stations, the reserve ships and men, and also the ships and men that must be brought in from civil life. As the department is the agency for preparing the naval stations, the reserves, and the men and ships brought in from civil life, it is clear that the work of preparing the department will automatically prepare the others. The work of preparing any Navy Department necessitates the preparation and execution of plans, whereby the department itself and all the rest of the navy will be able to pass instantly from a peace footing to a war footing; will be able to pass instantly from a status of leisurely handling and supplying the existing fleet by means of the offices, bureaus, and naval stations, to the status of handling with the greatest possible despatch a force which will be not only much larger, but also much less disciplined and coherent.

In time of peace a Navy Department which is properly administered for times of peace, as most Navy Departments are, can, by means of its bureaus, naval stations, offices, etc., handle the existing fleet, and also these bureaus, naval stations, offices, etc., by labors which for the most part are matters of routine. The department opens for business at a certain time in the morning and closes at a certain time in the afternoon. During office hours the various officials and their clerks fill a few busy hours with not very strenuous labor, and then depart, leaving their cares behind them. The naval stations are conducted on similar principles; and even the doings of the fleet become in a measure matters of routine. All the ordinary business of life tends to routine, in order that men may so arrange their time, that they may have regular hours for work, recreation, and sleep, and be able to make engagements for the future.

But when war breaks out, all routine is instantly abolished. The element of surprise, which each side strives to interject into its operations, is inherently a foe to routine. In a routine life, expected things occur—it is the office of routine to arrange that expected things shall occur, and at expected times; in a routine life one is always prepared to see a certain thing happen at a certain time. Surprise breaks in on all this, and makes unexpected things occur, and therefore finds men unprepared. It is the office of surprise to catch men unprepared.

Appreciating this, and appreciating the value of starting a war by achieving some great success, and of preventing the enemy from so doing, military countries in recent years have advanced more and more their preparations for war, even in time of the profoundest peace, in order that, when war breaks out, they may be prepared either to take the offensive at once, or to repel an offensive at once. With whatever forces a nation expects or desires to fight in a war, no matter whether it will begin on the offensive or begin on the defensive, the value to the nation of those forces will depend on how soon they are gotten ready. In a navy, the active fleet may be considered always ready; but the personnel and the craft of various kinds that must be added to it cannot be added to it as quickly as is desirable—because it is desirable that they should be added immediately, which is impossible.

It is not in the nature of things that they should get ready as quickly as a fleet that has been kept ready always; but it is essential that the handicap to the operations of the active fleet, due to the tardiness of its additions, should be kept as small as possible. In other words, whatever additions are to be made to the active fleet should be made as quickly as possible.

When the additions are made to the fleet (reserve ships and men, ships and men from civil life, etc.) it is clear that those ships and men should at that time be ready for effective work. If the ships are not in condition for effective work by reason of being out of order, or by reason of the ships from civil life not having been altered to suit their new requirements, or by reason of the men not being thoroughly drilled for their new tasks, considerable time will have to be lost by the necessity of getting the ships and the men into proper condition—or else warlike operations will have to be entered into while unprepared, and the classic *Chesapeake-Shannon* tragedy re-enacted.

Therefore, the endeavor must be strongly made to have ready always all the ships and men that are to be added to the fleet; the ships equipped for their duties in the fleet, and the men drilled for their future tasks.

The matter of getting ready the navy ships that are in reserve is largely a matter of getting the men to man them, as the ships themselves are kept in repair, and so in a state of readiness, materially speaking. At least this is the theory; and the successful application of the theory, when tested in practice, depends greatly on how large a proportion of the full complements has been kept on board, and on the amount and nature of the cruising which the vessels in reserve have done. The ideal conditions cannot be reached, unless the full complements have been kept on board, and the ships required to make frequent cruises. Of course, such a condition is never met in reserve ships; there would be no reason for putting ships in reserve if they were to be so handled. The more closely, however, a ship is kept in that condition of readiness, the more quickly she can be made absolutely ready in her material condition.

Unless one realizes how and why ships deteriorate in material, it is surprising to see how many faults develop, when ships in reserve, that are apparently in good condition, are put into active service. Trouble is not found, of course, with the stationary parts, like the bottoms, and sides, and decks, so much as with the moving parts, especially the parts that have to move and be steam and gas tight at the same time— the parts found mainly in the steam engineering and ordnance departments. Defects in the moving parts, especially in the joints, are not apt to be found out until they are moved, and often not until they are moved under the pressure and with the speeds required in service.

Now "in service" usually means in service in time of peace; but the service for which those ships are kept in reserve is war service, and the requirements of war service are much more rigorous than those of peace service. Objection may be made to this statement by remarking that engines turn around and guns are fired just the same in war as in peace, and that therefore the requirements are identical. True in a measure; but vessels and guns are apt to be forced more in war than in peace; and even if they were not, vessels in time of peace are gotten ready with a considerable degree of deliberation, are manned by well-trained men, and are sent to sea under circumstances which permit of gradually working up to full service requirements. But when reserve vessels are mobilized and sent into service for war, everything is done with the utmost haste; and the men, being hurriedly put on board, cannot possibly be as well trained and as ready to do skilful work as men sent on board in peace time; and when reserve vessels get to sea they may be required immediately to perform the most exacting service.

For all these reasons, it is highly desirable—it is essential to adequate preparation—that vessels should be kept in a state of material readiness that is practically perfect. Every vessel on board of which defects in material develop after she shall have been put into service, when war breaks out, will be a liability instead of an asset. She will be able to render no effective service, and she will require the expenditure of energy by officers and men, and possibly the assistance of other vessels, when their services are needed for other work.

But the problem of how to keep reserve vessels in a state of material readiness is easier than the problem of how to keep the reserve men in a state of personnel readiness, which will insure their reporting on board of the reserve ships quickly enough and with adequate training. This problem is so difficult, and its solution is so important, that in Great Britain, France, Germany, Japan, and doubtless other navies, men are compelled to go into the reserves, and to remain in for several years after completing their periods of service in the regular navy. In this way, no breaking away from the navy occurs until after reserve service has been completed, and every man who enlists remains in the navy and is subject to its discipline until his reserve period has been passed. Thus the question of the reserve is a question that has been answered in those countries, and is therefore no longer a question in them. If battleship A in any of those countries is to be mobilized, the government knows just who are to go on board and when; and knows that every man has recently served in the regular navy, has been kept in training ever since he left it, and that he is competent to perform the duties of his allotted station in battleship A.

235

The problem of getting into service the ships that are to be gotten from the merchant service is more difficult, and is perhaps of more importance; that is, it is more important to get into the service some vessels from the merchant service than some reserve ships; more important, for instance, to get colliers to serve the fleet with coal than to commission some antiquated cruisers. Naturally, the number and kinds of ships that need to be provided will depend on the nature of the war—whether, for instance, a very large force is to be sent to the other side of the world, to meet a powerful fleet there, or whether a sudden attack on our Atlantic coast is to be repelled. The difference, however, is largely numerical; so that if the plans provide for a sufficient number to take part in the distant expedition, it will be easy to get the appropriate number to meet a coast attack.

To receive an attack upon the coast, however, provision must be made for vessels and men not needed on an expedition across the seas—that is, for vessels and men that will defend the coast itself from raids and similar expeditions.

The work of preparing all that part of the naval machine which in time of peace is separate from the active fleet is purely one of logistics; it is that part of the preparation which calculates what ways and means are needed, and then supplies those ways and means. Logistics, having been told by strategy what strategy plans to do, calculates how many and what kinds of vessels, men, guns, torpedoes, fuel, food, hospital service, ammunition, etc., are needed to make possible the fulfilling of those plans; and then proceeds to provide what it has calculated must be provided.

This does not mean that strategy should hold itself aloof from logistics and make arbitrary demands upon it; for such a procedure would result in making demands that logistics could not supply; or, through an underestimate of what logistics can supply, in refraining from demanding as much as could be supplied. Logistics, of course, does provide what strategy wants, in so far as it can; but in order that satisfactory results may be obtained, the fullest co-operation between strategy and logistics is essential; and to this end frequent conferences are required between the officers representing both.

The logistic work of expanding the naval forces to a war basis may evidently be divided into two parts: the adding of vessels and other craft appropriately equipped and manned to the active fleet, and the establishment of a coast-defense force, which will be distributed along the coast and divided among the most important commercial and strategic centres.

Adding to the Fleet.—Naturally, the additions to the fleet will depend on the service for which the fleet is intended; that is, on the plans of strategy. If the navy were to be gotten ready for a definite undertaking, then the additions to carry out that undertaking could be calculated and prepared; and of course this condition does come up immediately before any war occurs. But in addition to these preparations which are to be made at the last moment (many of which cannot be made until the last moment), the staff must prepare in the leisure of profound peace for several different contingencies. Inasmuch as many of the additions will be needed, no matter with what country the war may come; and inasmuch as the same general kind of additions will be made, it is clear that there must underlie all the various plans one general plan, to which modifications must be made to adapt it to special conditions. And as, no matter whether we are to take the offensive or the defensive, no matter whether the fleet is to go far away or stay near our coast, the matter of additions to it is mainly a matter of degree (whether for instance ten extra colliers are needed or a hundred), it seems clear that the general plan should be the one demanding the greatest additions, so that the modifications to adapt it to special cases would consist merely in making subtractions from it. To carry out this plan, strategy

237

must make a sufficiently grave estimate of the situation; and logistics must make calculations to supply the most difficult demands that the estimate of the situation indicates as reasonable, and then arrange the means to provide what the calculations show. If one has provided a little more than is necessary, it is much easier to leave out something later than it is to add more, if one has not provided enough; and one's natural indolence then acts on the side of safety, since it tends to persuade one not to leave off too much; whereas in the opposite case, it tends to assure him that it is not really necessary to take the trouble to provide what it might be hard to get.

The Estimate of the Situation.—In no field of strategical work is an accurate estimate of the situation more clearly necessary than when it is to form the basis for the precise calculations of logistics. General strategical plans require a vividness of imagination and a boldness of conception that find no field for exercise in logistics; and tactics requires a quickness of decision and a forcefulness of execution that neither strategy nor logistics need; but neither strategy nor tactics calls for the mathematical exactness that logistics must have, or be of no avail. Yet there will be no use in working out the mathematically correct means to produce certain result, if the real nature of the desired result is underrated; there will be no use in working out laboriously how many ships and tons of coal and oil are needed, if the estimate of the situation, to meet which those ships and coal and oil are needed, is inadequate.

The first step, therefore, in providing for the expansion of the navy for war, is to estimate the situation correctly. The greatest difficulty in doing this arises from a species of moral cowardice, which tempts a man to underestimate its dangers, and therefore the means required to meet them. *Probably no single cause of defeat in war has been so pregnant with disaster as this failure to make a sufficiently grave estimate of the situation.* Sometimes the failure seems due more to carelessness than to cowardice; Napoleon's disastrous underestimate of the difficulties of his projected Russian campaign seems more due to carelessness than to cowardice;[1] but this may be due to a difficulty of associating cowardice with Napoleon. But is it not equally difficult to associate carelessness with Napoleon? What professional calculator, what lawyer's clerk was ever more careful than Napoleon was, when dealing with problems of war? Who was ever more attentive to details, who more industrious, who more untiring? And yet Napoleon's plans for his Russian campaign were inadequate to an amazing degree, and the inadequacy was the cause of his disaster. But whether the cause was carelessness or moral cowardice on his part, the fact remains that he did not estimate the situation with sufficient care, and make due plans to meet it.

This unwillingness to look a difficult situation in the face one can see frequently in daily life. Great difficulties seem to appall some people. They hate so much to believe a disaster possible, they fear so much to let themselves or others realize that a danger is impending, they are so afraid that other people will think them "nervous," and they shrink so from recommending measures that would cause great exertions or great expenditures, that they are very prone to believe and say that there is no especial danger, and that whatever danger there may be, can be obviated by measures that are easy and cheap to carry out.

If we yield to this feeling, we are guilty of moral cowardice, and we vitiate all the results of all our labors. We *must* make a correct estimate of the situation—or rather we must estimate the situation to be as grave as it is—or our preparations

1. Modern historians are more charitable toward Napoleon and his preparations for the invasion of Russia in 1812. True, he ran out of steam, but the distances were vast, the enemy refused battle, and the route to Moscow was bare of sustenance. Napoleon's miscalculations were strategic, not logistic. See Martin Van Creveld, *Supplying War* (Cambridge, England, 1977), pp. 61–70.

will be of no avail. If we estimate the situation too gravely, we may spend more money and time on our preparations than is quite needed, and our preparations may be more than adequate. It may be that the preparations which Prussia made before 1870 for war with France were more than adequate. In fact, it looks as if they were, in view of the extreme quickness with which she conquered France. But does any military writer condemn Prussia for having made assurance too sure?

The Value of Superadequate Preparation.—No, on the contrary. The very reasons that make adequate preparation valuable make superadequate preparation even more valuable. The reason is very clear, as is shown by the table on page 243 illustrating the progressive wasting of fighting forces, which the writer published in the *U.S. Naval Institute* in an essay called "American Naval Policy," in April, 1905.[2]

These tables grew out of an attempt to ascertain how the values of two contending forces change as the fight goes on. The offensive power of the stronger force is placed in the beginning at 1,000 in each case, and the offensive power of the weaker force at 900, 800, 700, 600, 500, 400, 300, 200, and 100. These values are, of course, wholly arbitrary, and some may say imaginary; but, as they are intended merely to show the comparative strength of the two forces, they are a logical measure, because numerical; there is always some numerical factor that expresses the comparative value of two contending forces, even though we never know what that numerical

2. I have recently been informed that Lieutenant (now Commander) J. V. Chase, U. S. N., arrived at practically the same results in 1902 by an application of the calculus; and that he submitted them to the U. S. Naval War College in a paper headed, "Sea Fights: A Mathematical Investigation of the Effect of Superiority of Force in."—B. A. F. (Author's note. Professor John Hattendorf has exhumed Chase's work from the Naval War College archives. The core of it is in Appendix C. As far as is known, this is the first publication of Chase, an honor overdue him, since his is the first mathematical representation of the "Lanchester" square law phenomenon.)

factor is. Two forces with offensive powers of 1,000 and 900 respectively may mean 1,000 men opposed to 900 men of equal average individual fighting value, commanded by officers of equal fighting ability; or it may mean 10 ships opposed to 9 like ships, manned by officers and men of equal numbers and ability; or it may mean two forces of equal strength, as regards number of men, ships, and guns, but commanded by officers whose relative ability is as 1,000 to 900. It may be objected here that it is ridiculous so to compare officers, because the ability of officers cannot be so mathematically tabulated. This, of course, is true; but the fact that we are unable so to compare officers is no reason for supposing that the abilities of officers, especially officers of high position, do not affect quantitatively the fighting value of the forces they command; and the intention in mentioning this factor is simply to show that the relative values of the forces, as indicated in these tables, are supposed to include all the factors that go to make them up.[3]

3. Note the care with which Fiske emphasizes that Table I is a representation of one Force against another: the interaction of opposing quantities of combat power. A group of one hundred soldiers pitted against ninety is the wrong mindset; one hundred identical units of fighting force opposed by ninety like enemy units is correct. At this point in the book, no one can misunderstand that Fiske thinks any attempt to quantify relative combat power is easy. We may be sure he believes best efforts to do so should be made, but for his purpose here it is not necessary. The table is pure abstraction, to show how the superior force will grow more superior with each succeeding salvo. Its value lies in showing the large proportion of combat power that will be retained by the superior side. Fiske's purpose is wholly descriptive. As for the model's predictive value, it will be as accurate as the knowledge of the initial force ratio, and the validity of the essential condition that every unit of offensive firepower may be directed freely and distributed efficiently at any enemy unit, in other words, conditions that never obtain in full. This is a good basic model of gunnery duels between battleships, and leaves plenty of room for embellishments for use by umpires in judging the outcomes of the war games of the 1920s and 1930s. But

Another convention, made in these tables, is that every fighting force is able to inflict a damage in a given time that is proportional to the force itself; that a force of 1,000, for instance, can do twice as much damage in a given time as a force of 500 can; also that a force can do an amount of damage under given conditions that is proportional to the time in which it is at work; that it can do twice as much damage in two hours, for instance, as in one hour, *provided the conditions for doing damage remain the same.* Another convention follows from these two conventions, and it is that there is a period of time in which a given force can destroy a force equal, say, to one-tenth of itself under certain conditions; that there is some period of time, for instance, in which, under given conditions, 1,000 men can disable 100 men, or 10 ships disable 1 ship, or 10 guns silence 1 gun. In the conflicts supposed to be indicated in these tables, this period is the one used. It will be plain that it is not necessary to know how long this period is, and also that it depends upon the conditions of the fight.

In Table I, it is supposed that the chance of hitting and the penetrability are the same to each contestant. In other words, it is assumed that the *effective targets* presented by the two forces are alike in the sense that, if the two targets are hit at the same instant by like projectiles, equal injuries will be done. If each contestant at a given instant fires, say a 12-inch shell, the injury done to one will be the same as that done to the other; not proportionately but quantitatively. For instance, if one force has 10 ships and the other has 9 like ships, all the ships being so far apart that a shot aimed at one ship will probably not hit another, the conditions supposed in Table I, column 2, are satisfied; the chances of hitting are identical for

a useful model must behave in a simplified way like the physical process it describes, and for modern missile warfare, another model behaves better. See Hughes, pp. 242–248.

TABLE I

		Col. 1	Col. 2	Col. 3	Col. 4	Col. 5	Col. 6	Col. 7	Col. 8	Col. 9	Col. 10
Value of offensive power	A	1000	1000	1000	1000	1000	1000	1000	1000	1000	1000
at beginning	B	1000	900	800	700	600	500	400	300	200	100
Damage done in 1st pe-	A	100	100	100	100	100	100	100	100	100	100
riod by	B	100	90	80	70	60	50	40	30	20	10
Value of offensive power	A	900	910	920	930	940	950	960	970	980	990
at end 1st period	B	900	800	700	600	500	400	300	200	100	0
Damage done in 2d pe-	A	90	91	92	93	94	95	96	97	98	..
riod by	B	90	80	70	60	50	40	30	20	10	..
Value of offensive power	A	810	830	850	870	890	910	930	950	970	..
at end 2d period	B	810	709	608	507	406	305	204	103	2	..
Damage done in 3d pe-	A	81	83	85	87	89	91	93	95	..	..
riod by	B	81	71	61	51	41	31	20	10	..	..
Value of offensive power	A	729	759	789	819	849	879	910	940	..	..
at end 3d period	B	729	626	523	420	317	214	111	8	..	..
Damage done in 4th pe-	A	73	76	79	82	85	88	91	..	..	..
riod by	B	73	63	52	42	32	21	11	..	..	..
Value of offensive power	A	656	696	737	777	817	858	899	..	..	..
at end 4th period....	B	656	550	444	338	232	126	20	..	..	..
Damage done in 5th pe-	A	65	70	74	78	82	86	..	..	..	..
riod by	B	65	55	44	34	23	13	..	..	..	..
Value of offensive power	A	591	641	693	743	794	845	..	..	..	..
at end 5th period	B	591	480	370	260	150	40	..	..	..	..
Damage done in 6th pe-	A	59	64	69	74	79	85	..	..	..	..
riod by	B	59	48	37	26	15	4	..	..	..	..
Value of offensive power	A	532	593	656	717	779	841	..	..	..	..
at end 6th period	B	532	416	301	186	71	0	..	..	..	..
Damage done in 7th pe-	A	53	59	66	72	78	..	..	..	..	..
riod by	B	53	42	30	19	7	..	..	..	..	..
Value of offensive power	A	479	551	626	698	772	..	..	..	..	..
at end 7th period	B	479	357	235	114	0	..	..	..	..	..
Damage done in 8th pe-	A	48	55	63	70	..	..	..	..	..	..
riod by	B	48	36	24	11	..	..	..	..	..	..
Value of offensive power	A	431	515	602	687	..	..	..	..	..	..
at end 8th period	B	431	302	172	44	..	..	..	..	..	..
Damage done in 9th pe-	A	43	52	60	69	..	..	..	..	..	..
riod by	B	43	30	17	4	..	..	..	..	..	..
Value of offensive power	A	388	485	585	683	..	..	..	..	..	..
at end 9th period	B	388	250	112	0	..	..	..	..	..	..
Damage done in 10th	A	39	49	59	..	..	..	..	..	..	..
period by	B	39	25	11	..	..	..	..	..	..	..
Value of offensive power	A	349	460	574	..	..	..	..	..	..	..
at end 10th period ..	B	349	201	53	..	..	..	..	..	..	..
Damage done in 11th	A	35	46	57	..	..	..	..	..	..	..
period by	B	35	20	5	..	..	..	..	..	..	..
Value of offensive power	A	314	440	569	..	..	..	..	..	..	..
at end 11th period ..	B	314	155	0	..	..	..	..	..	..	..
Damage done in 12th	A	31	44	..	..	..	..	..	..	..	..
period by	B	31	16	..	..	..	..	..	..	..	..
Value of offensive power	A	283	426	..	..	..	..	..	..	..	..
at end 12th period ..	B	283	111	..	..	..	..	..	..	..	..
				etc.							
Total damage done by .	A	717	789	800	700	600	500	400	300	200	100
	B	717	574	431	317	228	159	..	..	..	..

both contestants, and so is the damage done at every hit. Table I supposes that the chance of hitting and damaging does not change until the target is destroyed.

As the desire of the author is now to show the advantage of having a superadequate force, Table II has been calculated to show the effect of forces of different size in fighting an enemy of a known and therefore constant size.

It will be noted that if our force is superior to the enemy's in the ratio of 1,100 to 1,000, the fight will last longer than if it is superior in the ratio of 1,500 to 1,000, in the proportion of 16 to 9; and that if it is superior in the ratio of 1,100 to 1,000 the fight will last longer than if it is superior in the ratio of 2 to 1, in the proportion of 16 to 6. We also see that we should, after reducing the enemy to 0, have forces represented by 422, 1,073, and 1,683, respectively, and suffer losses represented by 678, 427, and 317, respectively.

Now the difference in fighting forces cannot be measured in units of material and personnel only, though they furnish the most accurate general guide. Two other factors of great importance enter, the factors of skill and morale. Skill is perhaps more of an active agent, and morale is perhaps more of a passive agent, like the endurance of man or the strength of material; and yet in some battles morale has been a more important factor in attaining victory than even skill. It is not vital to this discussion which is the more important; but it is vital to realize clearly that skill and morale are not to be forgotten, when we calculate how many and what kinds of material and personnel units we must provide for a war; and inasmuch as we cannot weigh morale and skill, or even be sure in most cases as to which side will possess them in the superior degree, we are forced in prudence to assume that the enemy may possess them in a superior degree, and that therefore we should secure superadequacy in units of personnel and material; not so much to win victory with the minimum of loss to ourselves, as simply to avert disaster.

TABLE II

		Col. 1	Col. 2	Col. 3
Value of offensive power at beginning	A	1100	1500	2000
	B	1000	1000	1000
Damage done in 1st period by	A	110	150	200
	B	100	100	100
Value of offensive power at end of 1st period ...	A	1000	1400	1900
	B	890	850	800
Damage done in 2d period by	A	100	140	190
	B	89	85	80
Value of offensive power at end of 2d period ...	A	911	1315	1820
	B	790	710	610
Damage done in 3d period by	A	91	131	182
	B	79	71	61
Value of offensive power at end of 3d period ...	A	832	1244	1759
	B	699	579	422
Damage done in 4th period by	A	83	124	176
	B	70	58	43
Value of offensive power at end of 4th period ...	A	762	1186	1716
	B	616	455	252
Damage done in 5th period by	A	76	119	172
	B	62	46	25
Value of offensive power at end of 5th period ...	A	700	1140	1691
	B	540	336	80
Damage done in 6th period by	A	70	114	169
	B	54	34	8
Value of offensive power at end of 6th period ...	A	646	1106	1683
	B	470	222	0
Damage done in 7th period by	A	65	110	....
	B	47	22	....
Value of offensive power at end of 7th period ...	A	599	1084	....
	B	405	112	....
Damage done in 8th period by	A	60	108	....
	B	41	11	....
Value of offensive power at end of 8th period ...	A	558	1073	....
	B	345	4	....
Damage done in 9th period by	A	56	4	....
	B	35	0	....
Value of offensive power at end of 9th period ...	A	523	1073	....
	B	289	0	....
Damage done in 10th period by	A	53	....	....
	B	29	....	....
Value of offensive power at end of 10th period ..	A	494	....	....
	B	236	....	....
Damage done in 11th period by	A	49	....	....
	B	24	....	....
Value of offensive power at end of 11th period ..	A	470	....	....
	B	187	....	....
. . . .				
Value of offensive power at end of 16th period.	A	422	....	....
	B	0	....	....

245

The present war shows us that the factors of skill and morale, while independent of each other, are closely linked together, and react upon each other. Nothing establishes a good morale more than does the knowledge of exceeding skill; and nothing promotes skill more than does an enthusiastic and firm morale.

But superadequateness of preparation has a value greater than in merely insuring victory with minimum loss to ourselves, in case war comes, because it exerts the most potent of all influences in preventing war, since it warns an enemy against attacking. At the present day, the laws of victory and defeat are so well understood, and the miseries resulting from defeat are so thoroughly realized, that no civilized country will voluntarily go to war, except for extraneous reasons, if it realizes that the chances of success are small. And as the cumulative consequences of defeats are also realized, and as no country is apt to assume that the morale and skill of its forces are measurably greater than those of a probable antagonist, no country and no alliance is apt to provoke war with a nation whose armed forces are superior in number of units of personnel and material; unless, of course, the nation is markedly inferior in morale and skill, as the Persians were to the legions of Alexander.

It is often insisted that superadequacy in armed force tends to war instead of peace, by inducing a country to make war itself; that the very principles which deter a weak country from attacking a strong country tend to make a strong country attack a weak one. There is some truth in this, of course, and history shows many cases of strong countries deliberately attacking weak ones for the purpose of conquest.

Analysis of wars, however, in which strong countries have done this, shows that as a rule, the "strong" country was one which was strong in a military sense only; and that the "weak" country was a country which was weak only militarily, but which was potentially strong in that it was possessed of wealth in land and goods. Most of the great conquests of history were made by such "strong" over such "weak" countries. Such were notably those wars by which Persia, Assyria, Egypt, Greece, Rome, and Spain gained their pre-eminence; and such were the wars by which they later fell. Such were the wars of Ghenghis Khan, Tamerlane, Mahomet, and Napoleon; such were the wars by which most tribes grew to be great nations, and by which as nations they subsequently fell. No greater cause of war has ever existed than a disproportion between countries or tribes of such a character that one was rich and weak, while the other was strong and poor. Nations are much like individuals—and not very good individuals. Highwaymen who are poor and strong organize and drill for the purpose of attacking people who are rich and weak; and while one would shrink from declaring that nations which are poor and strong do the same, it may nevertheless be stated that they have often been accused of doing so, and that some wars are explainable on that ground and on none other.

The wars of Cæsar in Gaul and Britain do not seem to fall in this category, and yet they really do; for Rome was poor in Julius Cæsar's day; and while Gaul and Britain were not rich in goods, they were rich in land, and Rome craved land.

Of course, there have been wars which were not due to deliberate attacks by poor and strong countries on rich and weak countries; wars like our wars of the Revolution, and with Mexico, our War of the Rebellion, and our Spanish War, and many others in which various nations have engaged. The causes of many wars have been so numerous and so complex that the true cause is hard to state; but it may be stated in general that wars in which countries that were both rich and strong, as Great Britain and France are now, have deliberately initiated an aggressive war are few and far apart. The reason seems to be that countries which are rich tend to become not militaristic and aggressive, but effeminate and pacific. The access of luxury, the refinements of living that the useful and the delightful arts produce, and the influence of women, tend to wean men from the hardships of military life, and to engender a distaste for the confusion, bloodshed, and "horrors" of war. For this reason, the rich countries have shown little tendency to aggression, but a very considerable tendency to invite aggression. Physical fighting among nations bears some resemblance to physical fighting among men, in that rich nations and rich men are apt to abstain from it, unless they are attacked; or unless they think they are attacked, or will be. The fact of being rich has the double influence of removing a great inducement to go to war, and of causing a distaste for it.

For all of the reasons given above, it would seem advisable when making an "estimate of the situation," in preparation for war, to estimate it as gravely as reasonable probability will permit. The tendency of human nature is to estimate it too lightly; but in matters of possible war, "madness lies that way."

This seems to mean that in preparing plans for additions to the fleet for war, we should estimate for the worst condition that is reasonably probable. In the United States, this means that we should estimate for a sudden attack by a powerful fleet on our Atlantic coast; and, as such an attack would occasion a tremendous temptation to any foe in Asia to make a simultaneous attack in the Pacific, we must estimate also for sending a large fleet at the same time on a cruise across the Pacific Ocean.

This clearly means that our estimate must include putting into the Atlantic and Pacific all the naval vessels that we have, fully manned with fully drilled crews; and adding besides all the vessels from civil life that will be needed. The vessels taken from civil life will be mostly from the merchant service, and will be for such auxiliary duties as those of hospital ships, supply ships, fuel ships, and ammunition ships, with some to do duty as scouts.

For the purposes of the United States, therefore, the office of naval strategy in planning additions to our fleet for war, is to make a grave estimate of the naval requirements in both the Atlantic and the Pacific; to divide the total actual and prospective naval force between the Atlantic and the Pacific in such a way as shall seem the wisest; to assign duties in general to each force; and then to turn over to logistics the task of making the quantitative calculations, and of performing the various acts, which will be necessary to carry out the decisions made.

Objection may be made to the phrase just used—"to divide the total force," because it is an axiom with some that one must never divide his total force; and the idea of dividing our fleet, by assigning part to the Atlantic and part to the Pacific, has been condemned by many officers, the present writer among them.

This is an illustration of how frequently phrases are used to express briefly ideas which could not be expressed fully without careful qualifications and explanations that would necessitate many words; and it shows how carefully one must be on his guard, lest he put technical phrases to unintended uses, and attach incorrect meanings to them. As a brief technical statement, we may say, "never divide your force"; but when we say this, we make a condensed statement of a principle, and expect it to be regarded as such, and not as a full statement. The full statement would be: "In the presence of an active enemy, do not so divide your force that the enemy could attack each division in detail with a superior force." Napoleon was a past master in the art of overwhelming separate portions of an enemy's force, and he understood better than any one else of his time the value of concentration. And yet a favorite plan of his was to detach a small part of his force, to hold a superior force of the enemy in check for—say a day—while he whipped another force of the enemy with his main body. He then turned and chastised the part which had been held in check by the small detachment, and prevented from coming to the relief of the force that he attacked first.

When we say, then, that strategy directs how our naval force should be divided between the Atlantic and the Pacific, this does not mean that strategy should so divide it that both divisions would be confronted with forces larger than themselves. It may mean, however, that strategy, in order that the force in one ocean shall be sufficient, may be compelled to reduce the force in the other ocean almost to zero.

Some may say that, unless we are sure that our force—say in the Atlantic—is superadequate, we ought to reduce the force in the Pacific to actual zero. Maybe contingencies might arise for which such a division would be the wisest; but usually such a condition exists that one force is so large that the addition to it of certain small units would increase the force only microscopically; whereas those small units would be of material value elsewhere—say in protecting harbors from the raids of small cruisers. Practically speaking, therefore, strategy would divide our naval force into Atlantic and Pacific fleets, but those fleets might be very unequal in size, owing to the vastly greater commercial and national interests on our Atlantic coast, and the greater remoteness of probable enemies on our Pacific coast.

In estimating the work to be done by the U.S. Atlantic fleet, three general objects suggest themselves:

1. To repel an attack made directly on our Atlantic continental coast.

2. To repel an expedition striving to establish a base in the Caribbean, preliminary to an attack on our Atlantic continental coast or on the Panama Canal.

3. To make an expedition to a distant point, to prevent the occupation of territory by a foreign government in the south Atlantic or the Pacific.

First Object.—To repel an attack made directly on the Atlantic coast, the plan must provide for getting the needed additions to the fleet with the utmost despatch. Owing to the keen appreciation by European nations of the value of secrecy and despatch, any attack contemplated by one of them on our Atlantic coast would be prepared behind the curtain, and nothing about its preparation would be allowed to be reported to the outside world until after the attacking force had actually sailed. For the force to reach our shores, not more than two weeks would be needed, even if the fleet stopped at mid-Atlantic islands to lay in fuel. It is very doubtful if the fact of stopping there would be allowed to be reported, as the commander-in-chief could easily take steps to prevent it. It is possible that merchant steamers might meet the fleet, and report the fact by radio, but it is not at all certain. A great proportion of the steamers met would willingly obey an order not to report it, or even to have their radio apparatus deranged; either because of national sympathy, or because the captain was "insulted with a very considerable bribe." The probability, therefore, would be that we should hear of the departure of the fleet from Europe, and then hear nothing more about it until it was met by our scouts.

This reasoning shows that to carry out the plans of strategy, logistics would have to provide plans and means to execute those plans, whereby our existing fleet, plus all the additions which strategy demanded, would be waiting at whatever points on the ocean strategy might indicate, before the coming enemy would reach those points. In other words, logistics must make and execute such plans that all the fleet which strategy demands will be at the selected points in less than two weeks from the time the enemy leaves the shores of Europe.

Of course, the conditions will not necessarily be such that strategy will demand that all our reserve ships, especially the oldest ships, shall go out to sea with the active fleet, ready to engage in battle. Maybe some of them will be found to be so slow and equipped with such short-range guns, that they would be an embarrassment to the commander-in-chief, instead of an assistance. Unless it is clear, however, that any ship, especially a battleship, *would be an embarrassment,* her place is clearly with the fighting fleet. The issue of the battle cannot be known in advance; and as everything will depend upon that issue, no effort and no instrument should be spared that can assist in gaining victory. And even if the older ships might not be of material assistance in the early stages of a battle, they would do no harm because they could be kept out of the way, if need be. In case either side gains a conclusive victory at once, the older ships will do neither good nor harm; but in case a decisive result is not at once attained, and both sides are severely damaged, the old ships, held in reserve, may then come in fresh and whole, like the reserve in land engagements, and add a fighting force which at that time will be most important and may be decisive.[4]

Probably some of the ships will be too old, however, to fill places of any value in the active fleet. These should be fully manned and equipped, however, for there will be many fields of usefulness for them. One field will be in assisting the land

4. Holding out second-rate warships as a reserve is a novel idea for which it is hard to think of a precedent. At Lissa (1866), the Yellow River (1894), Santiago (1898), and Tsushima (1905) all ships, strong and weak, were concentrated by both sides. Scheer incorporated his old battleships in the German battle line at Jutland (1916). When the Japanese sent their carriers into battle in 1942 in advance of the battleships, this was not because they viewed the battleships as weak, or a reserve, but because the battleships were considered to be the backbone of their force, and the carriers were in front to pave the way by taking out American air and otherwise softening up the enemy. The historical practice in naval combat is to eschew a reserve and bring all forces to action together. To put Fiske's speculation in the best light, he is attempting to develop a theory of employment for second-rate forces. No one has ever done that.

defenses, in protecting the mouths of harbors and mine-fields, in defending submarine bases, and acting as station ships in the coast-defense system.

Second Object.—To repel an enemy expedition, striving to establish a base in the Caribbean, preparation would have to be made for as prompt a mobilization as possible; for although the threat of invasion of our coast would not carry with it the idea of such early execution as would a direct attack on New York, yet the actual establishment of a base so near our shores would give such advantages to a hostile nation for a future invasion, that measures to prevent it should be undertaken with the utmost possible thoroughness and despatch; because the operation of establishing a base involves many elements of difficulty that an active defender can hinder by aeroplane attacks, etc.; whereas, after a base has once been established and equipped with appropriate defenses, attacks upon it are much less productive of results.[5]

The endeavor to establish a base and the opposing effort to

5. An invasion of the United States by a foreign power is so remote to our current thinking as to require comment. In point of fact the naval officer corps at the time took the responsibility of repelling invasion seriously. Schooled in the tradition of the Royal Navy having forestalled the invasion of the British Isles from across the English Channel for 850 years, and steeped in the memory of the burning of Washington in the War of 1812, the navy at large thought an invasion was not fanciful in spite of the fact that by 1916 the United States was a very large country. For one thing, the entire army numbered less than 100,000 and was posted all over that very large country. Absent the U.S. Navy, a few thousand men could have walked ashore unopposed at a point of the enemy's choosing. Then what? As far as the navy was concerned, then it would have failed, and the ultimate consequences were bound to be serious. Whatever his personal views, Fiske could hardly fail to address what was thought of by his fellow officers as the primary responsibility of the fleet, to be "the first line of defense." That he had considered these matters carefully is indicated by his analysis in Chapter III and the unconventional conclusion that "the primary use of our navy is to prevent a blockade."

prevent it, will offer many opportunities for excellent work on both sides. Practically all the elements of naval force will be engaged, and events on the largest possible scale may be expected. The operations will naturally be more extended both in time and distance than in the case of a direct attack upon our coast, and therefore the task of logistics will be greater. Actual battle between large forces; minor engagements among aircraft, scouts, submarines, and destroyers; attacks on the train of the invader—even conflicts on shore—will be among the probabilities.

Third Object.—To send a large expedition to carry out naval operations in far distant waters—in the south Atlantic, for instance, to prevent the extension of a monarchical government in South America, or in the western Pacific to defend our possessions there—calls for plans involving more logistical calculation and execution, but permitting a more leisurely procedure. The distances to be traversed are so great, the lack of bases is so distinct and difficult to remedy, and the impossibility of arriving in time to prevent the seizing of land by any hostile expedition is so evident, that they combine to necessitate great thoroughness of preparation and only such a measure of despatch as can be secured without endangering thoroughness. Whether the projected expedition shall include troops, the conditions at the time must dictate. Troops with their transports will much complicate and increase the difficulties of the problem, and they may or may not be needed. The critical results can be accomplished by naval operations only; since nothing can be accomplished if the naval part of the expedition fails to secure the command of the sea; and the troops cannot be landed until it has been secured, unless the fact of securing it can safely be relied on in advance. For these reasons, the troops may be held back until the command of the sea has been secured, and then sent out as an independent enterprise. This would seem the more prudent procedure in most cases, since one successful night attack on a group of transports by an active enemy might destroy it altogether.

But whether a military expedition should accompany the fleet, or follow a few hundred miles behind, or delay starting until command of the sea has been achieved, it is obvious that the logistic calculations and executive measures for sending a modern fleet to a very distant place, and sustaining it there for an indefinite period, must be of the highest order of difficulty. The difficulty will be reduced in cases where there is a great probability of being able to secure a base which would be able to receive large numbers of deep-draft ships in protected waters, to repair ships of all classes that might be wounded in battle, and to store and supply great quantities of ammunition, food, and fuel.

No expedition of such magnitude has ever yet been made— though some of the expeditions of ancient times, such as the naval expedition of Persia against Greece, B.C. 480, and the despatch of the Spanish Armada in more recent days, may have been as difficult, considering the meagerness of the material and engineering resources of those epochs.

But even if no military force accompanies the expedition, the enormous quantities of fuel, supplies, ammunition, medical stores, etc., that will be required, especially fuel; the world-wide interest that will be centred on the expedition; the international importance attaching to it; and the unspeakable necessity that the plans shall underestimate no difficulty and overlook no factor, point with a long and steady finger at the necessity of attacking this problem promptly and very seriously, and of detailing the officers and constructing the administrative machinery needed to make the calculations and to execute the measures that the calculations show to be required.

Static Defense of the Coast.—But besides the mobile fleet which is a nation's principal concern, strategy requires that for certain points on the coast, where large national and commercial interests are centred, arrangements shall be made for what may be termed a "static defense," by vessels, mine-fields, submarines, aircraft, etc.,[6] assigned as permanent parts of the defense of these points, analogous to forts on the land.[7] The naval activities of this species of defense will centre on the mine-fields which it is a great part of their duty to defend. To guard these, and to get timely information of the coming of any hostile force or raiding expedition, strategy says we must get our eyes and ears well out from the land. To do this, water craft and aircraft of various kinds are needed; and they must be not only sufficiently numerous over each area to scout the waters thoroughly, but they must be adapted to

6. Coastal forces are what Corbett calls the flotilla in *Some Principles of Maritime Strategy* (Annapolis, Md., 1988). Fiske takes a slightly wider view of what constitutes coastal forces for "static defense." Note that aircraft are an element. In the debate to come with General Billy Mitchell and other advocates of a separate air force, only the most hidebound elements of the navy argued that aircraft were not a future threat to a battlefleet. As we have seen, Fiske championed air-launched torpedoes. The navy believed that only naval aviation could do the job competently, and knew instinctively that high-altitude horizontal bombing would fail to hit maneuvering ships, and low-level horizontal bombing would be fatal to the aircraft. The navy's belief was vindicated in World War II. In the 1930s the B-17 was initially developed by the Army Air Corps to attack warships at sea at great range, but it was ineffective in the role. On the other hand, land-based aircraft could be highly effective for coastal patrol and attack, especially naval aircraft suitably trained and equipped. For a brief synopsis of a lengthy subject of great consequence, see Hughes, pp. 85–88.

7. Likening coastal forces to forts in land conflict is fitting enough, but observe that Fiske does not embrace coastal artillery in his static defense system. They are too static. He prefers the mobility of a fleet and its power to concentrate against an attack from the sea. Fiske thought fixed defenses of naval bases were another matter, however, as demonstrated in Chapter XI. The analogous problem to be thought through today is the power of land-to-sea missile systems, with their great range.

their purpose, manned by adequate and skilful crews, and organized so as to act effectively together.

The work of this patrol system is not to be restricted, however, to getting and transmitting information. Certain of the craft must be armed sufficiently to drive off hostile craft, trying to drag or countermine the defensive mine-fields; some must be able to add to the defensive mine-fields by planting mines, and some must be able to pilot friendly ships through the defensive mine-fields; others still must be able to countermine, drag, and sweep for any offensive mines that the enemy may plant.

Vessels for this patrol work do not have to be very large; in fact, for much of the work in the mine-fields, it were better if they were small, by reason of the ability of small vessels to turn in restricted spaces.

It would seem that for the patrol service, the vessels of the Revenue Marine and Lighthouse Service (coast guard) are ideally adapted; but, of course, there are only a few in total. These would have to be supplemented by small craft of many kinds, such as tugs, fast motor-boats, fishing-boats, and trawlers. To find men competent to man such vessels and do the kind of work required would not be so difficult as to get men competent to man the more distinctive fighting ships. Good merchant sailors, fishermen, and tugboat men would fit into the work with considerable ease, and in quite a short time. Strategy declares, however, that a coast guard may be needed a very short time after war breaks out; and that the vessels and the men, with all the necessary equipment and all the necessary organization and training, should be put into actual operation beforehand.

Not only the fleet, however, but all the bureaus and offices of the Navy Department, all the navy-yards, and all the radio stations, recruiting stations, hydrographic offices, training stations, and agencies for securing information from foreign countries, will have to pass instantly from a peace basis to a war basis. To do these things quickly and correctly many preliminaries must be arranged; but if the General Staff prepares good plans beforehand, arranges measures which will insure that the plans shall be promptly carried out, and holds a few mobilization drills to test them, the various bureaus and offices in the department can do the rest. If the fires have all been lighted, the engine gotten ready, and the boilers filled in time, the engineer may open the throttle confidently, when the critical time arrives, for the engine will surely do its part.

But if the proper plans have not been made and executed, the sudden outbreak of war, in which any country becomes involved with a powerful naval country, will create confusion on a scale larger than any that the world has ever seen, and compared with which pandemonium would be a Quaker meeting. A realization of facts will come to that country, and especially to the naval authorities, that will overwhelm them with the consciousness of their inability to meet the crisis marching toward them with swift but unhurried tread— confident, determined, inescapable. Fear of national danger and the sense of shame, hopelessness and helplessness will combine to produce psychological effects so keen that even panic will be possible. Officers in high places at sea and on shore will send telegrams of inquiry and suggestion; civilians in public and private station will do the same. No fitting answers can be given, because there will be no time for reflection and deliberation. The fact that it would be impossible to get the various additions to the fleet and the patrol services ready in time, and the consciousness that it would be useless to do any less, will tend to bring on a desperate resolve to accept the situation and let the enemy do his worst. The actual result, however, will probably be like the result of similar situations in the past; that is, some course of action will be hastily decided on, not in the reasoned-out belief that it can accomplish much, but with the feeling that action of any kind will relieve the nervous tension of the public by giving an outlet for mental and physical exertion and will, besides, lend itself to self-encouragement, and create a feeling that proper and effective measures are being taken.

Such conditions, though on a much smaller scale, are familiar to naval officers and are suggested by the supposititious order "somebody do something"; and we frequently see people placed in situations in which they do not know what to do, and so they do—not nothing, but anything; though it would often be wiser to do nothing than to do the thing they do do. Many of the inane remarks that people make are due to their finding themselves in situations in which they do not know what to say, but in which they feel impelled to say "something."

Now what kind of "something" would be done under the stimulus of the outbreak of a war for which a country had not laid its plans? Can any worse situation be imagined—except the situation that would follow when the enemy arrived? The parable of the wise and foolish virgins suggests the situation, both in the foolishness of the unpreparedness and in the despair when the consequent disaster is seen approaching.

In nearly all navies and armies, until the recent enormous increase in all kinds of material took place, the work of getting a navy ready for war in personnel and material was comparatively simple. This does not mean that it was easier then than now; because the facilities for construction, transportation, communication, and accounting were much less than now; but it does mean that the actual number of articles to be handled was much less, and the number of kinds of articles was also much less; and it also means that the various mechanical improvements, while they have facilitated construction, transportation, communication, and accounting, have done so for every nation; so that none of the competing navies have had their labors expedited or made less. On the contrary, the very means devised and developed for expediting work is of the nature of an instrument; and in order to use that instrument successfully, one has to study it and practise with it; so that the necessity for studying and practising with the instrument has added a new and difficult procedure to those before existing.

Fifty years ago the various mechanisms of naval warfare were few, and those few simple. In our Navy Department the work of supplying those mechanisms was divided among several bureaus, and each bureau was given the duty and the accompanying power of supplying its particular quota. The rapid multiplication, during the past fifty years, of new mechanisms, and new kinds of mechanisms; the increased expense of those mechanisms compared with that of former mechanisms; the increased size and power of vessels, guns, and engines; the increased size and complexity of the utilities in navy-yards for handling them; the necessity for providing and using means and methods for despatching the resulting "business" speedily, and for guarding against mistakes in handling the multiplicity of details—the increase, in brief, in the number, size, and kinds of things that have to be done in preparation, has brought about not only more labor in doing those things by the various bureaus assigned to do them, but has brought about even more imperiously the demand for means whereby the central authority shall be assured that each bureau is doing its work. And it has brought about more imperiously still a demand that a clear conception shall be formed first of what must be done, and second of the maximum time that can be allowed for doing it.[8]

8. Most of this chapter has dealt with operational planning, including operational logistics. These are belabored by Fiske because he knows the magnitude of the effort required is unappreciated, especially by the secretary of the navy and his civilian advisers. In the succeeding four paragraphs he shifts focus and discusses the need for closer cooperation between technologists who develop the means of war and operators who use it, a need that still exists and is receiving a good deal of attention at present. Fiske

Clearly, the forming of a correct conception should not be expected of men not trained to form it; clearly, for instance, mere knowledge of electricity and mere skill in using electrical instruments cannot enable a man to devise radio apparatus for naval use; a certain amount of knowledge of purely naval and nautical matters is needed in addition. Clearly, the concept as to the kind of performance to be required of radio apparatus is not to be expected of a mere technician, but is to be expected of a strategist—and equally the ability to design, construct, and supply the apparatus is not to be expected of a strategist, but it is to be expected of a technician.

A like remark may be made concerning any mechanism— say a gun, a torpedo, or an instrument, or a vessel of any kind. The strategist, by studying the requirements of probable war, concludes that a certain kind of thing is needed; and the technician supplies it, or does so to the best of his ability.

The statement thus far made indicates a division of work into two sharply defined departments; and, theoretically, such a division does exist. This does not mean, however, that the strategist and the technician should work independently of each other. Such a procedure would result in the strategist demanding things the technician could not supply, and in the technician supplying things the strategist did not want, under a mistaken impression as to what the strategist wanted. The

will refer to the customers who operate the fleet as "strategists," and he is being consistent with his definition of strategy (page 135). He would communicate more effectively if "operational art" or campaign planning were available to him, for it is fleet operators and operations with which he deals. Fiske's predictable solution is to add the burden of communicating technological needs to the long list of responsibilities of the General Staff. Taking the office either of the Chief of Naval Operations or the Joint Chiefs of Staff as the modern equivalent of his General Staff, we know now that the solution to the problem is not so pat: marrying technological opportunity with operational requirements is a challenge that is still with all navies, and entails more than Fiske's straight-forward solution.

fullest and most intimate understanding and co-operation must exist between the strategist and the technician, as it must equally between the architect and the builder of a house.

From an appreciation of such facts as these, every great Navy Department, except that of the United States, has developed a General Staff, which studies what should be done to prepare for passing from a state of peace to a state of war; which informs the minister at the head of the department what things should be done, and is given power to provide that the various bureaus and offices shall be able to do them when war breaks. This is the scheme which all the navy departments, except the American, have devised, to meet the sudden and violent shock of the outbreak of a modern war. *No other means has yet been devised,* and no other means is even forecast.

The means is extremely simple in principle, but complex beyond the reach of an ordinary imagination in detail. It consists simply in writing down a digest of all the various things that are to be done, dividing the task of doing them among the various bureaus and offices that are authorized by law to do them, and then seeing that the bureaus shall be able to do them in the time allowed.

The best way of ascertaining if the bureaus are able to do them is to mobilize—to put into commission and send out to sea all the craft that will be needed, fully equipped with a trained personnel and with a well-conditioned material; and then direct the commander-in-chief to solve a definite strategic problem—say to defend the coast against a hypothetical enemy fleet—the solution including tactical games by day and night.

Before attempting the solution of a strategic problem by an entire naval force, however, it is usual to hold mobilization exercises of a character less complete, in the same way that any course of training begins with drills that are easy and progresses to drills that are difficult. The simplest of all the preparative drills—if drills they correctly can be called—is the periodical reporting, once a month, or once a quarter, by each bureau and office, of its state of readiness; the report to be in such detail as experience shows to be the best.

In the days when each bureau's preparation consisted of comparatively few things to do, the chief of that bureau could be relied on to do the things required to be done by his bureau; and his oral assurance to the secretary that—say all the ships had enough ammunition, or that adequate provision had been made for coal, or that there were enough enlisted men—would fulfil all requirements. But in the past fifty years, the requirements have increased a hundredfold, while the human mind has remained just as it was. So it has seemed necessary to institute a system of periodical preparation reports, to examine them carefully, and to use all possible vigilance, lest any item be forgotten or any work done by two bureaus that ought to be done by only one.

Who should examine the reports? Naturally the same persons as decide what should be done. The same studies and deliberations that fit a person to decide what is needed, fit him to inspect the product that is offered to supply the need; not only to see if it comes up to the specifications, but also to decide whether or not any observed omission is really important; to decide whether, in view of certain practical difficulties, the specifications may be modified; and also to decide whether certain improvements suggested by any bureau should or should not be adopted.

This procedure may seem to put the strategy officers "over" the technical officers, to put a lieutenant-commander on the General Staff "over" a rear admiral who is chief of bureau; but such an idea seems hardly justified. In any well-designed organization relative degrees of official superiority are functions of rank, and of nothing else; superiority in rank must, of course, be recognized, for the reason that when on duty together the junior must obey the senior. But even this superiority is purely official; it is a matter of position, and not a matter of honor. All the honor that is connected with any position is not by reason of the position itself, but by reason of the honorable service which a man must have rendered in order to attain it, and which he must continue to render in order to maintain it. So, in a Navy Department, the General Staff officers cannot be "over" the bureau officers, unless by law or regulation certain of the staff are made to rank over certain bureau officers. A procedure like this would seem to be unnecessary, except in the case of the chief of staff himself, who might, for the purpose of prompt administration, be placed by law over the bureau chiefs.[9]

The importance of the question, however, does not rest on a personal basis, but a national basis. It makes no difference to the nation whether Smith is put above Jones, or Jones above Smith; and in all discussions of national matters it is essential to bear in mind clearly not only that national questions must not be obscured by the interjection of the personal element, but also that great vigilance is needed to prevent it. For the reason that questions of the salaries of government officials have been settled in advance, questions of personal prestige and authority are more apt to intrude themselves among them than among men in civil life, whose main object is to "make a living"—and as good a living as they can. In the long struggle that has gone on in the United States Navy Department between the advocates and the opponents of a General Staff, the personal element has clouded the question—perhaps more than any other element. Not only in the department itself, but in Congress, the question of how much personal "power" the General Staff would have has been dis-

9. Fiske is answering one of the objections raised by opponents of the General Staff at the time. Today the dilemma is solved by letting the staff officer on the CNO's staff speak "by direction" of the CNO, allowing plenty of room for a bureau chief to escalate the level of discussion if the "lieutenant commander on the General Staff" has gotten out of line.

cussed interminably—as though the personal element were of any importance whatever.

Such an attitude toward "power" is not remarkable when held by civilians, but it is remarkable when held by men who have had a military or naval training. Of course, there is an instinct in all men to crave power; but it is not recognized as an instinct wholly worthy. It is associated in most men's minds with a desire for material possessions, such as money or political position, and not with such aspirations as a desire for honor. In other words, a strong desire for wealth or power, while natural and pardonable, is considered a little sordid; while a desire for honor, or for opportunity to do good service, is held to be commendable. So, when public officials, either military or civilian, condemn a measure because it will give somebody "power," the reason given seems to be incomplete, unless a further reason is given which states the harm that would be done by conferring the "power."

Military and naval men exercise "power" from the beginning of their careers until their careers are closed; and they exercise it under the sane and restraining influence of responsibility; without which influence, the exercise of power is unjustifiable, and under which influence the exercise of power is a burden—and oftentimes a heavy one. That men trained as military men are trained, should aspire to power for power's own sake, is a little hard to understand—unless it be confessed that the person desiring the power appreciates its pleasing features more than its responsibilities, and regards its duties more lightly than its glories. Few men, even those who shoulder responsibility the most courageously, desire responsibility for its own sake—and so the fact of a man ardently desiring "power" seems a good reason for withholding power from him.

And what is "power," in the sense in which officials, both military and civilian, use the word? Is it ability to do good service, or is it ability to bestow favors in order that favors may be received, to give orders to others coupled with authority to enforce obedience, or to take revenge for injuries received or fancied? Of course, "power" is ability to do all these things, good and bad. But if a man desires power simply to do good service, and if he holds a highly conscientious view of the accompanying duties and responsibilities, will he crave "power" as much as some men seem to do?

It seems fundamental, then, that any strategic plan for preparing the Navy Department for war should be framed with a strong endeavor to leave out the personal element, and should regard national usefulness only. If this be done successfully, and if good selections be made of the personnel to do it, it will be found that the members of the personnel will think no more about their "power" than does an officer of the deck while handling a battleship in fleet formation during his four hours on the bridge.

In preparing the department for war, one would be in danger of being overwhelmed by the enormousness and the complexity of the task, unless he bore in mind continuously that *it is only when we get into details that any matter becomes complex;* and therefore that if we can get a clear idea of the whole subject, the principles that underlie it, and the major divisions into which it naturally is divided, we can then make those divisions and afterward subdivide those divisions, and later divide the subdivisions; so that the whole subject will seem to fall apart as a fowl does under the hands of a skilful carver. The divisions and subdivisions of the subject having been made, the remaining task, while onerous, will be largely a matter of copying and of filling in blank forms.

As all navy departments have means regulated by law such that the actual executive work of recruiting, constructing, and supplying the necessary personnel and material shall be done by certain bureaus and offices, strategy does not need executive power, except for forcing the bureaus and offices to do the necessary work—should such forcing become necessary. Strategy being the art of being a general (*strategos*), one cannot conceive of it as bereft of executive power, since we cannot conceive of a general exercising generalship without having executive power. It is true that strategy occupies itself mainly with planning—but so does a general; and it is also true that strategy itself does not make the soldiers march, but neither does a general; it is the colonels and captains and corporals who make the soldiers march. The general plans the campaign and arranges the marches, the halts, the bivouacs, provisions, ammunition, etc., through his logistical officers, and they give the executive officers general instructions as to how to carry out the general's plans.

Strategy without executive functions would be like a mind that could think, but was imprisoned in a body which was paralyzed.

Of course, strategy should have executive functions for the purposes of strategy only; under the guidance of policy and to execute policy's behests. Policy is the employer, and strategy the employee.

267

CHAPTER ELEVEN

NAVAL BASES

THE NATURE of naval operations necessitates the expenditure of fuel, ammunition, and supplies; wear and tear of machinery; fatigue of personnel; and a gradual fouling of the bottoms of the ships. In case actual battles mark the operations, the expenditure of stored-up energy of all kinds is very great indeed, and includes not only damage done to personnel and material by the various agencies of destruction, but actual loss of vessels.

To furnish the means of supplying and replenishing the stored-up energy required for naval operations is the office of naval bases.[1]

A naval base capable of doing this for a large fleet must be a very great establishment. In such a naval base, one must be able to build, dock, and repair vessels of all kinds, and the

1. That a base contains stored-up energy (the capacity to do work) need not be taken as a simile if combat is defined to be the accomplishment of military work, and we allow the transfer of the stored-up (potential) energy from base to fighting ship or aircraft. The units of work are an interesting problem, but the notion of combat force applied over a distance ought to be retained if military energy and work are to have any meaning. Even if we regard stored-up energy as pure simile it is handy. If the Japanese had thought like Fiske, they might have hit the fuel and ammunition dumps at Pearl Harbor, rendering the surviving fleet incapable of recharging its battery after its internal energy was expended, and hence impotent until the potential energy of the base was restored.

mechanisms needed in those vessels; anchor a large fleet in safety behind adequate military and naval protection; supply enough fuel, ammunition, and supplies for all purposes, and accommodate large reserves of material and personnel. Inasmuch as a naval base is purely a means for expending energy for military purposes, and has no other cause for its existence, it is clear that it cannot be self-supporting. For this reason it is highly desirable that a naval base shall be near a great city, especially if that city be a large commercial and manufacturing centre.

It is true that many large naval bases, such as Malta and Gibraltar are not near great cities; and it is true that most large naval bases have no facilities for building ships. But it is also true that few large naval bases fulfil all the requirements of a perfect naval base; in fact it is true that none do.

The most obvious requirement of a naval base is a large sheet of sheltered water, in which colliers and oil-carriers may lie and give coal and oil to fighting craft, and in which those fighting craft may lie tranquilly at anchor, and carry on the simple and yet necessary repairs and adjustments to machinery that every cruising vessel needs at intervals. Without the ability to fuel and repair, no fleet could continue long at work, any more than a man could do so, without food and the repairs which nature carries on in sleep. The coming of oil fuel and the consequent ease of fuelling, the practicability even of fuelling in moderate weather when actually at sea, subtract partially one of the reasons for naval bases; but they leave the other reasons still existent, especially the reasons connected with machinery repairs. The principal repair, and the one most difficult to furnish, is that given by docking in suitable docks. The size and expense of docks capable of carrying dreadnaughts and battle cruisers are so great, and their vulnerability to fire from ships and from aircraft is so extreme, that the matter of drydocks is perhaps the most troublesome single matter connected with a naval base.

The necessity of anchorage areas for submarines is a requirement of naval bases that has only recently been felt; and the present war shows a still newer requirement in suitable grounds for aircraft. The speed of aircraft, however, is so great that little delay or embarrassment would result if the camp for aircraft were not at the base itself. Instead of the camp being on Culebra, for instance, it might well be on Puerto Rico. The extreme delicacy of aircraft, however, and the necessity for quick attention in case of injuries, especially injuries to the engine, demand a suitable base even more imperiously than do ships and other rugged things.

That the vessels anchored in the base should be protected from the fire of ships at sea and from guns on neighboring shores is clear. Therefore, even if a base be hidden from the sea and far from it as is the harbor of Santiago, it must be protected by guns, or mines, or both; the guns being nearer to the enemy than are the ships in the waters of the base. An island having high bluffs, where large guns can be installed, and approached by gradually shoaling waters in which mines can be anchored, with deeper water outside in which submarines can operate, is desirable from this point of view.

Ability to store and protect large quantities of provisions is essential, and especially in the case of ammunition and high explosives. For storing the latter, a hilly terrain has advantages, since tunnels can be run horizontally into hills, where explosives can lie safe from attack, even attack from aircraft dropping bombs above them.

Naturally, the country that has led the world in the matter of naval bases is Great Britain; and the world at large has hardly yet risen to a realization of the enduring work that she has been quietly doing for two hundred years, in establishing and fortifying commodious resting-places for her war-ships and merchant ships in all the seas. While other nations have been devoting themselves to arranging and developing the interiors of their countries, Great Britain has searched all the oceans, has explored all the coasts, has established colonies and trading stations everywhere, and formed a network of intimate commercial relations which covers the world and radiates from London. To protect her commercial stations and her merchant ships from unfair dealings in time of peace, and from capture in time of war, and to threaten all rivals with defeat should they resort to war, Great Britain has built up the greatest navy in the world. And as this navy pervades the world, and as her merchant ships dot every sea and display Great Britain's ensign in every port, Great Britain has not failed to provide for their safety and support a series of naval stations that belt the globe.

Bases are of many kinds, and may be divided into many classes. An evident ground for division is that of locality in relation to the home country. Looked at from this point of view, we may divide naval bases into two classes, home bases and distant bases.

Home Bases.—A home base is, as its name implies, a base situated in the home country. The most usual type of the home naval base is the navy-yard, though few navy-yards can meet all the requirements of a naval base. The New York navy-yard, for instance, which is our most important yard, lacks three of the most vital attributes of a naval base, in that it has no means for receiving and protecting a large fleet, it cannot be approached by large ships except at high tide, and it could not receive a seriously injured battleship at any time, because the channel leading to it is too shallow.

Home bases that approach perfection were evidenced after the battle off the Skagerrak;[2] for the wounded ships of both sides took refuge after the battle in protected bases, where they were repaired and refitted, and resupplied with fighting men and fuel. These bases seem to have been so located, so protected, and so equipped, as to do exactly what bases are

2. The Battle of Jutland, May 1916.

271

desired to do; they were "bases of operations" in the best sense. The fleets of the opposing sides started from those bases as nearly ready as human means and foresight could devise, returned to them for refreshment after the operations had been concluded, and, during the operations, were based upon those bases. If the bases of either fleet had been improperly located, or inadequately protected or equipped, that fleet would not have been so completely ready for battle as, in fact, it was; and it could not have gone to its base for shelter and repairs so quickly and so surely as, in fact, it did. Many illustrations can be found in history of the necessity for naval bases; but the illustration given by this battle of May 31 is of itself so perfect and convincing, that it seems hardly necessary or even desirable to bring forward any others.

The fact of the nearness to each other of the bases of the two contending fleets—the nearness of Germany and Great Britain in other words—coupled with the nearness of the battle itself to the bases, and the fact that both fleets retired shortly afterward to the bases, bring out in clear relief the efficacy of bases; but nevertheless their efficacy would have been even more strongly shown if the battle had been near to the bases of the more powerful fleet, but far from the bases of the other fleet—as was the case at the battle, near Tsushima, in the Japan Sea.

Of course the weaker fleet in the North Sea battle would not have been drawn into battle under such conditions, because it would not have had a safe refuge to retreat to. It was the proximity of an adequate naval base, that could be approached through protected waters only, which justified the weaker fleet in dashing out and taking advantage of what seemed to be an opportunity. Similarly, if the Russian fleet in the Japan Sea had had a base near by, from which it had issued ready in all ways, and to which it could have retired as soon as the battle began to go against it, the Russian disaster might not have occurred, and full command of the sea by the

Japanese might have been prevented. But there being no base or harbor of refuge, disaster succeeded disaster in a cumulative fashion, and the Russian fleet was annihilated in deep water.

If a naval base were lacking to the more powerful fleet, as was the case in the battle of Manila, the effect would in many cases be but slight—as at Manila. If, however, the more powerful fleet were badly injured, the absence of a base would be keenly felt and might entail disaster in the future, even though the more powerful fleet were actually victorious. The Japanese fleet was practically victorious at the battle of August 10, near Port Arthur; but if it had not been able to refit and repair at a naval base, it would have met the Russian fleet later with much less probability of success.

Mahan states that the three main requirements in a naval base are position, resources, and strength;[3] and of these he considers that position is the most important; largely because resources and strength can be artificially supplied, while position is the gift of nature, and cannot be moved or changed.

Mahan's arguments seem to suggest that the bases he had in mind were bases distant from home, not home bases; since reference is continually made by him to the distance and direction of bases from important strategic points of actual or possible enemies.

His arguments do not seem to apply with equal force to home bases, for the reason that home bases are intended primarily as bases from which operations are to start; secondarily as bases to which fleets may return, and only remotely as bases during operations; whereas, distant bases are intended as points from which operations may continually be carried on, during the actual prosecution of a war. The position of a home base, for instance, as referred to any enemy's coasts or

3. In *Naval Strategy Compared and Contrasted with Principles and Practice of Military Operations on Land* (Boston, Mass., 1911).

bases, is relatively unimportant, compared with its ability to fit out a fleet; while, on the other hand, the position of distant bases, such as Hong-Kong, Malta, or Gibraltar, relatively to the coasts of an enemy, is vital in the extreme. It is the positions of these three bases that make them so valuable to their holders; placed at points of less strategic value, the importance of those bases would be strategically less.

Home bases are valuable mainly by reason of their resources. This does not mean that position is an unimportant factor; it does not mean, for instance, that a naval base would be valuable if situated in the Adirondack Mountains, no matter how great resources it might have. It does mean, however, that the "position" that is important for a home base is the position that the base holds relatively to large home commercial centres and to the open sea. New York, for instance, could be made an excellent naval base, mainly because of the enormous resources that it has and its nearness to the ocean. Philadelphia, likewise, could be made valuable, though Philadelphia's position relatively to deep water is far from good. "Position," as used in this sense, is different from the "position" meant by Mahan, who used the word in its strategic sense. The position of Philadelphia relatively to deep water could be changed by simply deepening the channel of the Delaware; but no human power could change the strategic position of Malta or Gibraltar.

Yet for even home bases, position, resources, and strength must be combined to get a satisfactory result; the "position" not being related to foreign naval bases, however, but to large industrial establishments, mainly in order that working men of various classes may be secured when needed. The requirements of work on naval craft are so discontinuous that steady employment can be provided for comparatively few men only; so that a sort of reservoir is needed, close at hand, which can be drawn up when men are needed, and into which men can be put back, whenever the need for them has ceased.

And the same commercial and industrial conditions that assure a supply of skilled workers, assure a supply of provisions and all kinds of material as well.

Distant Bases.—Distant bases have two fields of usefulness which are distinct, though one implies the other; one field being merely that of supplying a fleet and offering a refuge in distress, and the other field being that of contributing thereby to offensive and defensive operations. No matter in which light we regard a distant naval base, it is clear that position, resources, and strength must be the principal factors; but as soon as we concentrate our attention on the operations that may be based upon it, we come to realize how strong a factor position, that is strategic position, is. The base itself is an inert collection of inert materials; these materials can be useful to the operations of a fleet that bases on it; but if the fleet is operating in the Pacific, a base in the Atlantic is not immediately valuable to it, no matter what strength and resources the base may have.

The functions of a home base are therefore those that the name "home" implies; to start the fleet out on its mission, to receive it on its return, and to offer rest, refuge, and succor in times of accident and distress.

The functions of a distant base concern more nearly the operations of a prolonged campaign. A distant base is more difficult to construct as a rule; largely because the fact of its distance renders engineering operations difficult and because the very excellence of its position as an outpost makes it vulnerable to direct attack and often to a concentration of attacks coming from different directions.

If naval operations are to be conducted at considerable distances from home, say in the Caribbean Sea, distant bases are necessary, since without them, the fleet will operate under a serious handicap. Under some conditions, a fleet operating in the Caribbean without a base there, against an enemy that had established a satisfactory base, might have its normal fighting efficiency reduced 50 per cent, or even more. A fleet is not a motionless fort, whose strength lies only in its ability to fire guns and withstand punishment; a fleet is a very live personality, whose ability to fight well—like a pugilist's—depends largely on its ability to move quickly and accurately, and to think quickly and accurately. The best pugilists are not usually the strongest men, though physical strength is an important factor; the best pugilists are men who are quick as well as strong, who see an advantage or a danger quickly, and whose eyes, nerves, and muscles act together swiftly and harmoniously. A modern fleet, filled with high-grade machinery of all kinds, manned by highly trained men to operate it, and commanded by officers fit to be intrusted with such responsibilities, is a highly developed and sensitive organism—and, like all highly developed and sensitive organisms, exists in a state of what may be called "unstable equilibrium." As pointed out in previous pages, the high skill needed to perform well any very difficult task can be gained only by great practice in overcoming difficulties and eliminating errors of many kinds; and when the difficulties are manifold and great, a comparatively small increase or decrease in the overcoming of them makes a great difference in the results attained.[4] An interesting though possibly not very correct analogy is to be seen in the case of a polished surface; for we readily note that the more highly polished the surface is, the more easily it is sullied. Another analogy may be found in the performance of a great pianist or violinist; for a very small failure in his skill for even an instant will produce a painful feeling that could

4. Again we see Fiske's insistence that combat force is a highly nonlinear function of all its components. The logic is the same as on p. 190. In battle the expert operates at the edge of his performance envelope and, it is hoped, beyond the edge of his enemy's. To use a fresh analogy, a sprinter who is consistent in peaking his training just before a race and is a fraction of a second faster than the second-best man's peak performance will never lose. But his margin of success is a split second, and his advantage fragile.

not be produced by a much greater failure in an ordinary performer. Another analogy is to be found in the case of a ship that is going at the upper limit of her speed; for a very minor failure of any part of her machinery will produce a much greater slowing than it would if her speed were slower.

Perhaps apologies are in order for dwelling so long on what may seem to some an academic question, but it does not seem to the writer to be academic at all. Certainly, the "condition" of a pugilist, or a fleet, about to fight, is not an academic consideration; and if it is not, no matter which affects this condition can rightfully be considered academic. The whole usefulness of bases is due to their ability to put fleets into good fighting condition and to maintain them in it; and it seems a very proper and useful thing to note that the more highly trained a fleet is, and the more highly organized the various appliances the fleet contains, the more difference results from a falling off in the condition of its personnel and material.

This shows the advantage of having a base as close to the place where a fight is going to happen as may be possible. This does not mean, of course, that a fleet should remain for long periods within its base; because a fleet, like any other practiser of any art, needs constant practice. It merely means that the closer the base is to the scene of the operations or the actual battle, the better "tuned up" the personnel and material will be. It also means that this consideration is of the highest practical importance.

Advanced Bases.—The extreme desirability of having a base near the scene of operations, even if the base be only temporarily held, has led to the use of what are called "advanced bases." An excellent and modern illustration of an advanced base is the base which the Japanese established at the Elliot Islands about sixty miles from Port Arthur, which the Japanese were besieging. The Russian fleet could issue from their base at Port Arthur whenever the Russians wished, and return to it at will. While inside, until the Japanese had landed and attacked them from the land side, the Russians could make their preparations in security and leisure, and then go out. The Japanese fleet, on the other hand, until they had established their base, were forced to remain under way at sea, and to accept action at the will of the Russians; so that, although Port Arthur was besieged, the advantages of the offensive, to some extent, resided with the Russians. The establishment of the base did not, of course, change the situation wholly; but it permitted a very considerable relaxation of vigilance and mental strain on the part of the Japanese, and a considerable easement of the motive power of their ships. Naturally, the Japanese made arrangements whereby their heavy ships could remain in comparative tranquillity near the base, while destroyers and scouts of various kinds kept touch with Port Arthur, and notified the base by wireless of any probable sortie by the Russian fleet.

The temporary advanced base at the Elliot Islands[5] was, as temporary advanced bases always must be, quite incomplete in every way as compared with the permanent bases at home. It fulfilled its mission, however, and was in fact as good a base as really was required. The strategic ability of the Japanese was indicated quite early in the war by the promptness and skill with which they established this base.

Of course, all advanced bases are distant bases, but the words usually imply temporariness, as does in fact the word "advance." An instance of an advanced base that has been far from temporary is the island of Jamaica, and another is the island of Bermuda; another is Malta, and still another is Gibraltar. These bases form stepping-stones, by which Great Britain's navy may go by easy stages from one position to

5. Coastal islands seventy-five miles east of Port Arthur, now the Li-changshan Liedao.

another, stopping at a base when desired, or going beyond it without stopping, secure in the knowledge that the base is "under her lee" in case of accident or distress.

Viewed from the standpoint of operations in an actual war, the strategic value of a certain position for a base is important, no matter whether the operations are offensive or defensive; and the same factors that make a position good for defensive operations make it good for offensive operations also. For instance, if we wish to send a fleet on a hostile expedition to a distant point, it is well to have a base on a salient as far out as practicable from the coast, in order that the fleet may be able to start, full of fuel and supplies, from a place near the distant point; and equally, if we are to receive an attack upon the coast, it is well to have a base far out, in order to embarrass the transit of the enemy toward our coast, by the threat—first against his flank, and later against his rear and his communications. Naval bases looked at from this point of view resemble those forts that European nations place along their frontiers.

It is true that any base placed at a salient has the weakness of all salients, in that fire can be concentrated on it from several directions; and a naval base has the added disadvantage of a more difficult withdrawal, if attacked by an overwhelming force, and a longer line of communications that has to be protected. But this weakness all distant bases have, from the fact that they are distant; and, naturally, the more distant they are, the more difficult it is to support them, because the longer are their lines of communications.

Distant naval bases, therefore, are vulnerable in a high degree; they are vulnerable both to direct attack and to an attack on their lines of communications; and the factors that help a base in one way injure it in another. If a naval base is placed on a rock, or a rugged little island that holds nothing else, and on which a hostile army could not land, it is very safe from land attack; whereas, if it is placed on a large and fertile island, on which an invading army could easily land, it is extremely vulnerable to land attack. But, on the other hand, the naval base on the inaccessible island could be starved out by simply breaking its lines of communications, while the naval base on the large and fertile island might be able to survive indefinitely, even though the communications were wholly ruptured.

The establishment of any permanent distant naval base is a matter of great expense, even if the natural conditions are favorable. But favorable conditions have rarely existed; and the expense of establishing such bases as Malta, Gibraltar, and Heligoland has been tremendous. An important consideration has been the fact that, unless the base were made so strong that it could not be taken, it might be better not to attempt to fortify it, on the theory that it would be better to let a poor naval base fall into the hands of the enemy than a good one. To this reasoning, the answer is usually made that no base can be made absolutely impregnable, and that sufficient defense will be provided if it makes the task and cost of capturing the base greater than the base is worth. This means simply that the more valuable the base is, the more money should be spent in defending it; and that *it is worse than useless to defend it by any means that is obviously too small, in proportion to its value.*

It often happens that the places that have the best position are weak in strength and resources; a notable instance is Gibraltar, another is Culebra,[6] and the most notable of all is Guam. None of these places is fortunate in either resources or natural strength, though Gibraltar was strong for the artillery of the time when the base was established there. In fact, it is hard to think of any place that combines in itself the three

6. American island twenty miles east of Puerto Rico, now used by the U.S. Navy for target practice.

advantages of a fine strategical position, large resources, and great strength. The three attributes seem almost incompatible; for how can a base far distant from its home be well placed with reference to attacking the lines of communication of any enemy intending to attack the home coast, and yet have its own lines of communications safe? How can it have a sheet of water, just deep enough but not too deep to anchor a large fleet in, with all of its auxiliaries extensive enough to accommodate all the vessels and far enough from the sea to be safe from gun-fire, and yet be on an island so small and so rugged, that an enemy could not land troops near the base and capture it from the land side, as the Japanese captured Port Arthur? The natural strategic advantages of a large and sheltered sheet of water seem to entail the disadvantages of a large island, or a continent.

There seems only one way in which to solve the problem of where and how to establish a permanent naval base at a distant point, and that is the way in which the world's preceptor—Great Britain—has solved it; and the solution is to select a place that has already the advantage of position, and then add to it the artificial advantages of resources and military strength.[7]

This brief statement makes the matter seem a little too simple; and so it will have to be modified by adding that the mere fact of a place having a fine position is not quite sufficient, because the place must be of such a character that it is capable of having resources and strength added to it; a sharp pinnacle rock in the middle of the Mediterranean, for instance, might have a fine strategic position, and yet be unavailable as a naval base. Even here, however, we must pause

---

7. The British fleet's wartime base at Scapa Flow, with its peculiar advantages and disadvantages, might have been mentioned. Though its location in the Orkneys was just off Great Britain, it had the austerity of an advanced base.

to note that energy and will could do much toward making even a pinnacle rock a naval base; for we see the gigantic fortress of Heligoland erected on what was little but a shoal; and we see the diminutive water areas of Malta and Gibraltar made to hold in safety the war-ships of the greatest navy in the world.

Despite the paramount importance of strategic position, we must not forget that a naval base should have sufficient military strength to be able to hold out for a long time against hostile operations, as many bases, notably Gibraltar and Port Arthur, have done, without the assistance of the fleet. The German base at Kiao-chau[8] held out for more than two months in 1914, without any external aid. During all the time of siege, even if surrender is ultimately to occur, the enemy's forces are prevented from being utilized elsewhere. This condition was clearly shown during the siege of Port Arthur, because the large force of Japanese troops required to conduct the siege were urgently needed in Manchuria—to which region they were sent as soon as Port Arthur fell.

From this point of view, naval bases again look much like fortresses on the land; fortresses like Metz and Strasburg, that had to be subdued before an enemy could safely pass them.[9]

Strategic Position of Distant Bases.—Since the strategic position of an outlying naval base is the principal factor that

8. The German protectorate facing the Yellow Sea of which Tsing Tao (modern Qingdao) is the principal port.

9. The attention given advanced bases highlights one of the unheralded and underappreciated accomplishments of U.S. naval logistics in 1944: the mobile advanced bases established directly on the heels of the Third and Fifth Fleets during their swift advance across the Pacific. The present navy is so adept at maintaining its presence remote from the U.S. that the next section will seem like second nature to most naval officers. Still, Fiske's tight exposition is apt in most respects, after new considerations of vulnerability to air and missile attack are factored in. That Fiske does not wholly ignore the role of aircraft will be seen on p. 291, and we

goes to make its value, it may be well to consider what elements make a strategic position good.

To make the problem clear, let us take a concrete case, that of our own country, and consider what elements would constitute a good strategic position for a naval base of the United States, leaving out of consideration for the moment any questions of resources and military strength.

In the case of a war with a nation that had only one naval home base, it is clear that the best position for our distant base would be one as close to the enemy's base as possible; because, if placed there, our fleet, if it were the more powerful, could do more to injure the enemy's fleet, or prevent its going out, than if placed at any point more distant from the enemy's base; and if it were less powerful, it could do more to cut the enemy's communications, because it could attack them at or near their source.

A poor position would be one far away from both countries, and far away from the line joining them. In the case of a war between this country and Norway, for instance, a very poor position for a naval base would be a spot near—say Juan Fernandez—in the south Pacific.

In case the enemy country has two home bases of equal importance, the best position for our base clearly would be one equidistant from them, and as near to each as practicable. If the distance from our base to a point half-way between the two bases is shorter than is the distance to it from either base, then a fleet at our base could probably prevent the junction of two forces issuing from those two bases— assuming, of course, that we had a proper system of scouting. Our fleet would be able to operate on what are often called "interior lines"—a technical expression that has great efficacy in confusing a simple matter. It is also assumed that our

---

may easily forgive his crystal ball for not anticipating their full potential fifty years later.

fleet is considerably stronger than either of the two separated enemy forces; otherwise our case would be hopeless.

If the two home bases of the enemy are unequal in importance, it would seem that our base should be nearer to the important base than to the other. More strictly speaking, it should be nearer to the base from which the larger force may be expected to come out.

If the enemy country has three or more bases from which parts of a fleet may be expected to come out, the question seems a little more complex; but nevertheless, since the first duty of our fleet would probably be to prevent junctions or a junction, of the separated parts of the enemy's fleet, the best position for our home base would be at a point about equally distant from them all, and as close to them as possible. In the wars between Great Britain and France in the early part of the nineteenth century, the base of the British fleet for operations on the western and northern coasts of France was as close to the enemy home bases as practicable—though the base was England itself. For operations on France's southern coast, the base was at Gibraltar, or some Mediterranean island.

That any country should be able to hold a distant base close to the home base of a possible naval enemy might seem impossible, if we did not know that Great Britain holds Bermuda and Jamaica near to our own coast, and Hong-Kong actually inside of China, all far away from Britain; besides Malta and Gibraltar in the Mediterranean, nearer to the coasts of sometime enemies than to her own.[10] That the United States should own a base far from her own coasts, and near those of other countries, might seem improbable, were it not for the fact that Guam is such a base, and is so situated. It is true that Guam is not strictly a naval base, because it is not

10. As well as the modern American naval base at Guantanamo Bay, Cuba.

so equipped or fortified; but we are thinking now of position only.

In case the enemy country has several home bases, and it is impossible to have our distant base so near to them as to prevent the junction of parts of a fleet issuing from them, the value of the base is less than it otherwise would be.

In this case, which is the one in which our country is actually concerned, because of its great distance from other countries, its value becomes merely the usual value attaching to a naval base; and the fact that the entire enemy fleet can operate as a unit, that it can divide into separate forces at will near its own shores, or send out detachments to prey on the long line of communications stretching from our distant base to that base's home, necessitates that the base be fortified in the strongest possible way, and provided with large amounts of supplies. Its principal function in war would be to shorten the long trip that our vessels would have to make without refreshment, and therefore the length of their lines of communications, and to enable our vessels to arrive in enemy's waters in better condition of readiness for battle than would otherwise be the case.

We have thus far considered the best position for an advanced naval base, in the case of operations against one country only.

It seems clear that, if we are to consider operations against two countries separately, and at different times, we should be led to conclude that the case of each country should be decided individually; in the case of wars with Norway and Portugal, for instance, the best places for our two bases would be as close to the home bases of those countries as possible; and even in the case of fighting two simultaneously, the conclusion would be the same, if the two countries were in widely different directions from us—as are Switzerland and China. If we consider the case of war against two contiguous coun-

285

tries simultaneously, however, it would seem better to have one base, situated similarly toward the home bases of the two countries as toward two different home bases in one country— since the two countries would be, in effect, allies; and their fleets would act in reality like separated portions of one fleet.

As the United States possesses no island on the Atlantic side which is nearer to foreign countries than to our own, and as our interests for the immediate future lie mostly on the Atlantic side, it may be well now to apply the general principles just considered to the question of where is a naval base most urgently needed under actual conditions.

Imagining a war between us and some one European naval Power, and imagining a war also between us and two or three allied European naval Powers, and realizing the length of our Atlantic and Gulf coasts, extending from Maine to Panama, a glance at the map shows us that, apart from the home naval bases on our continental coasts, the position on American soil which is the closest to European bases is on the little island of Culebra, which occupies a salient in the northeastern end of the Caribbean Sea.[11]

The only reason an enemy would have for entering the Caribbean would be an intention to attack the Panama Canal region, or an intention to establish an advanced base, from which he could conduct more or less deliberate siege of our Atlantic coast and cities. In either case, our fleet would be seriously handicapped if it had no adequate base in the Caribbean; because its line of communications north would be exposed to the enemy's operations at all times; and seriously wounded American ships would have little chance of getting repairs; little chance even of making successfully the long trip to Norfolk or New York.

11. The acquisition by the United States of the island of Saint Thomas [Virgin Islands], about 20 miles east of Culebra, if accomplished, will extend the salient just so much farther toward Europe. (Author's note.)

In case the enemy fleet should start from Europe fully prepared in every way, we should be in ignorance of its intended destination; and as the enemy fleet would be stronger than ours (otherwise it would not start) it would doubtless be able to destroy our undefended station at Guantanamo, seize some suitable place in the West Indies, say the Bay of Samana,[12] and then establish a base there, unless we had first seized and fortified all suitable localities; and the United States would then find itself in the anomalous position of being confronted near its own coasts with an enemy fleet well based for war, while her own fleet would not be based at all. Not only would the enemy fleet be superior in power, but it would possess the strategical advantage, though far from its own shores. The situation, therefore, about a month after the foreign fleet left Europe, would be that the Caribbean Sea would contain a hostile fleet which was not only superior to ours in power, but was securely resting on a base; while ours had no base south of Norfolk, the other side of Hatteras. Our fleet would be in a position similar to that of the Russian fleet when it rushed to its destruction in Tsushima Straits, though not in so great a degree; because it would have had more recent docking and refitting in our home ports, and the personnel would be fresher.

In case, however, we had a naval base strongly fortified and thoroughly equipped, at a salient in the Caribbean region, say at Culebra, and if our fleet were based upon it, a hostile fleet, even if it were considerably superior to our own, would hesitate to pass it and enter the Caribbean, by reason of the continuous threat that the fleet would exert on its communications. Even if the hostile fleet should pass Culebra, and establish a base farther on, an American force based on Culebra would continue to exert this threat on the communications between the hostile base and its mother country.

12. On the northeast coast of the island of Hispaniola, about midway between Guantanamo to the west and San Juan, Puerto Rico, to the east.

An American base—say at Guantanamo—would be very effective in embarrassing hostile operations *west* of Guantanamo, because it would be on the flank of the line of communications extending from Europe; but it would be comparatively ineffective in embarrassing operations east of it, since the hostile line of communications would be protected from it by the interposition of its own main body; this interposition necessitating the despatch of defending forces around that main body. The coming hostile force would push before it all resistance, and leave the sea free for the passage of its auxiliaries and supplies. A defending force, operating from Guantanamo, in endeavoring to prevent a hostile fleet from establishing a base to the *eastward* of it, would act much less effectively than a force operating from Culebra. Not only would the force from Guantanamo have to pass around the main body to attack the train; it would again have to pass around the main body to get back to Guantanamo; whereas a force operating from Culebra could make a direct attack upon the enemy's train, and then a direct retreat to Culebra.

This comparison assumes, as has been said, that the matter of resources and strength are not in question; that is, that they are equal in our two supposed bases. But, as in practice they would not be equal, the practical point to consider is how much strength and resources can compensate for inferiority of position, and how much position must be insisted on.

Of course, no correct quantitative answer can be given, except by accident. The problem, unfortunately, cannot be solved by mathematics, for the simple reason that no quantitative values can be assigned to the various factors, and because no mathematical formula now exists that expresses their relations to each other. It may be pointed out, however, that if a position be good, strength and resources can be artificially supplied; and that the cost of doing this, even on a tremendous scale, is relatively small compared to the cost of the fleet which the base will support, and in distress protect.

In other words, we may be able to form an estimate of the relative values of bases, say at Guantanamo and Culebra, even if we cannot ascribe arithmetical values to each, and compare arithmetically those arithmetical values. If, for instance, we see that a fleet costing $500,000,000, would, if it operated from a base at Culebra, be 10 per cent more effective than if it operated from Guantanamo, and that it would cost $20,000,000 more to make a strong base there than to make an equally strong one at Guantanamo, we should conclude that, since 10 per cent of $500,000,000 is $50,000,000, it would be wise to spend that $20,000,000, even if we had to forego the building of one battleship.[13]

We should come to the same conclusion, if we realized that no matter what their comparative values might be, a base at one place would not meet our necessities, and a base at the other place would. If a base at Guantanamo would not meet our necessities in case of an invasion of the Caribbean by a naval fleet superior to ours, then it seems idle to discuss the value of Guantanamo relative to some other place, no matter how good the position of Guantanamo may be, and no matter how nearly it may approximate to adequacy. There is no real usefulness in having a naval base anywhere, unless that naval base can accomplish the purpose for which it is desired. A naval base is desired for purposes of war, and for no other purpose whatever; and to decide on a position for a base without keeping this fact clearly in view, is to act on an under-

13. With characteristic boldness Fiske tries a comparison of incommensurables by the methods of systems analysis. But he falters: the $20 million increased marginal cost of the base at Culebra provides a fixed asset. The foregone battleship is a mobile asset, veritably a liquid asset. The $50 million marginal value of the Culebra base is only worth the $20 million cost for a specific scenario, defense of the Caribbean. If that strategic situation is not sufficiently dominant, then build the battleship for its flexibility, and forgo the tempting increment of static combat power offered by the Culebra base.

estimate of the situation, the folly of which has been pointed out in previous pages.

We may conclude, then, that in deciding on the place for a distant permanent naval base, on which the operations of a whole fleet are to base for war, we should select the best site available, even if military strength and resources may have to be added to it artificially—unless in the case of any site considered the difficulties of adding them are insuperable.

The last sentence may seem like shirking the whole question, because it does not state what "insuperable" means; so it may be well to add that in modern days few engineering difficulties are insuperable, as the existence of the fortress at Heligoland shows. If the submarine and the mine did not exist, the difficulties would be greater than they actually are; because guns alone, no matter how carefully mounted and protected, could hardly be expected to keep off indefinitely the attack of a heavy fleet, or even to save from injury the fighting and auxiliary vessels anchored in its waters. But the submarine and mine combine to keep fighting ships at distances greater than those over which ship's guns can fire, and reduce the amount of fortification required on shore.

One of the principal sources of expense in establishing bases at some points would be that of dredging out harbors sufficiently extensive, while harbors sufficiently extensive are provided already by nature in such localities as Samana. But, as pointed out before, harbors on large islands can be taken from the land side, as was Port Arthur; and adequate protection from land attack is, in many cases, almost impossible if the enemy has command of the sea, as a superior hostile fleet would have in the Caribbean; while the hills and waters of Culebra and Vieques Sound [14] could long defy not only actual invasion, but any fleet attack.

14. Encompassed by Culebra, Vieques Island, and the east coast of Puerto Rico, and adjacent to the present naval station, Roosevelt Roads.

This brings us face to face with the fact that it may be less expensive to establish and protect a naval base situated on a little island, even if an artificial harbor has to be constructed, than to establish and protect a base on a large island, even if the base on the large island has a large natural harbor and can be more easily defended against bombardment from the sea. It would be cheaper, for instance, to protect a base on Culebra than one at Guantanamo, or even Samana, if the enemy commanded the sea; and cheaper to protect a base on the forbidding rocks of Polillo[15] or Guam than on the large and fertile island of Luzon, with its extensive gulfs and bays, in many of which a fleet in command of the sea could land its force; because protecting a base on a large island would require covering a very large area, and perhaps a long extent of coast.

Aircraft may exercise an important influence on the choice of the position of a base, perhaps in the direction of choosing a base on a large island rather than on a small one; since the great speed of aircraft tends to lessen the importance of having the base out a great distance from home—so far as purposes of scouting are concerned. It seems probable also that aircraft will soon be recognized as inherently adapted to preventing the landing of hostile troops, by dropping bombs on the troops, while they are in process of disembarkation, while proceeding in small boats to the shore, and while in the act of landing on the beach, with their guns, ammunition, supplies, horses, and impedimenta of various kinds.

Co-operating Bases.—Discussion of the relative values of positions for bases, say in the Caribbean, should not blind our eyes to the fact, however, that no nation is prevented from establishing as many bases as it needs, wherever its flag

15. The Polillo Islands are off Luzon's east coast, on the latitude of Manila. Their citizens and the Guamanians would be astonished to learn they live on forbidding rocks.

may float; that the United States, for instance, is not debarred from establishing permanent naval bases at both Guantanamo and Culebra, should such a procedure seem desirable. The fact that each locality has advantages that the other does not have, suggests the idea that two bases, placed in those localities, would form a powerful combination. In fact, the great value of the position of Culebra being its distance toward the enemy, which necessitates a great distance away from our continental coast, and a long line of communications from that coast suggest an intermediate base as a support and stepping-stone. Analogous cases are seen in all the countries of Europe, in the fortresses that are behind their boundary-lines—the fortresses existing less as individuals than as supporting members of a comprehensive scheme.

Two bases, one at Guantanamo and one at Culebra, would in time of war in the Caribbean, add a value to our fleet that might make the difference between defeat and victory. The effective work that a fleet can do is a function of the material condition of the ships themselves, and of the physical and mental condition of the personnel that man them. Fighting is the most strenuous work that men can do; it calls for the last ounce of strength, the last effort of the intellect, the last struggle of the will; it searches out every physical imperfection in men, in ships, in engines, in joints, in valves. Surprise has sometimes been expressed at the quickness with which the Japanese defeated the Russians at Tsushima; but would any one express surprise if a pugilist, fresh from rest, quickly defeated another pugilist who, exhausted from long travelling, staggered hopelessly into the ring? And how would the betting be before a football match, if it were known that one of the teams would enjoy a rest of twenty-four hours before the game, whereas the other team would walk from the railroad to the ball grounds after a trip across the continent?[16]

16. Damage to—even defeat of—a carrier battle group is a contingency that is part and parcel of the U.S. Navy's forward strategy. Likely or not, it

These analogies may seem forced—but are they? A living animal requires hours of rest and refreshment, in order that the tissues expended in action may be repaired by the internal mechanism of the body, and the food consumed be supplied from some external source. A fleet is in exactly the same category, even when operating in times of peace: and in time of war it needs, in addition, a station in which injuries may be repaired—a station analogous to that of the hospital for wounded men.

In the Caribbean it would seem necessary to successful operations, therefore, to have two bases, one say at Guantanamo and one at Culebra; the one at Culebra to be the principal base, and the one at Guantanamo the auxiliary. Culebra, by reason of the great work to be accomplished, and the engineering difficulties to be encountered, cannot be gotten ready for several years. Reliance, meanwhile, will have to be placed on Guantanamo; and as the coming of any war is not usually very long foretold, the urgency of fortifying Guantanamo stands out in clear relief.

The mutual relations of Guantanamo and Culebra are much like the mutual relations of Pearl Harbor in Hawaii and Guam—and so are the joint relations of each pair to the mother country. Culebra and Guam are the potential bases of the United States farthest away from the coast in the Atlantic and the Pacific respectively; and the nearest to countries in Europe and Asia with any one of which, of course, war will be always possible, and sometimes probable. Each is a small and rugged island, admitting of tremendous military strengthening by guns, fortifications, mines, and submarines, but connected to the motherland by a long line of communications. The line of communications of Culebra would, of course, be safer than that of Guam, because it is shorter than would be

warrants thorough planning. Preparation for damage repair proximate to the scene of action is mere prudence inherent in the strategy.

the line of an enemy attacking it; whereas, the line of communications of Guam would be longer. Guantanamo and Pearl Harbor are both stations about half-way from the home country to Culebra and Guam respectively; and though greater danger to our vital and commercial interests exists in the Atlantic than in the Pacific, Pearl Harbor has been fortified, and Guantanamo has not—and neither has Culebra. This sentence is not intended as a criticism of the government for fortifying Pearl Harbor. The Hawaiian Islands occupy the most valuable strategic position in the Pacific, and Pearl Harbor is the most important strategic place in the Hawaiian Islands; and it ought to have been strengthened many years ago, and to a greater degree even than is contemplated now. But the sentence is intended as a protest against our continued inertness in failing to establish any suitable naval bases whatever, especially in the Caribbean.

Distant Base in the Philippines.—The difficulty of finding suitable positions for bases is exemplified in the Philippines, for no suitable island is to be found there except some that are within the archipelago itself; and these are so placed that, to reach them, our fleet would have to go through long reaches of water, ideally suited for destroyer and submarine attack. A possible exception is the island of Polillo, twenty miles east of the eastern coast of Luzon; and in many ways Polillo seems ideal. The practical difficulties are so great, however, the status of the islands in our national policy is so ill defined, and the futility of strengthening it, unless Guam be adequately strengthened also, is so apparent, that the question has been hardly even mooted. Polillo made impregnable, with Guam defenseless, supported by an undefended line of communications several thousand miles long to the main country, would in case of war with an active Asiatic power be reduced to the zero of effectiveness in whatever was the length of time in which its accumulated stores would be exhausted.

This sentence may be modified by saying that the time

might be lengthened by the occasional arrival of supply ships and colliers that might come by way of the Mediterranean, or the Cape of Good Hope, or any other route which approached the Philippines from the southward; and it is possible that, in the unfortunate event of a war between us and some Asiatic power, our relations with European countries might be such as to make the use by us of such routes feasible and safe. In view, however, of the conditions of island possession in the Pacific as they actually are, and because of the rapid and abrupt changes that characterize international relations, the probability of being able to use such routes seems too small to receive grave consideration.

Other Bases in the Pacific.—The Pacific Ocean is so vast, and the interests of the United States there will some day be so great, that the question of establishing naval bases, in addition to bases at Pearl Harbor, the Philippines, and Guam, will soon demand attention. The localities that are the most obvious are the Panama Canal Zone and the Samoan Islands in the south, and the Aleutian Islands in the north. A moderately far-seeing policy regarding the Pacific, and a moderately far-seeing strategy for carrying out the policy, would dictate the establishment and adequate protection of bases in both the southern and the northern regions; so that our fleet could operate without undue handicap over the long distances required. The same principles that govern the selection of positions and the establishment of bases in the Atlantic apply in the Pacific; the same requirements that a base shall be near where the fleet will conduct its operations—no matter whether those operations be offensive or defensive, no matter whether they concern direct attack or a threat against communications.

In view of the great value of naval bases, one may be pardoned perhaps for a feeling of surprise that the United States has no real naval base, home or distant. Our large navy-yards are our nearest approximation to real bases. The yards at

Norfolk and Bremerton seem to combine the three factors of position, strength, and resources better than do any other stations; though both are surpassed in resources by New York, Philadelphia, and Boston. Bremerton has the greatest natural military strength of all our stations; in fact, it is naturally very strong indeed, because of the length and nature of the waterway leading to it from the sea and the ease with which it could be denied. Norfolk is fortunate in its nearness to Chesapeake Bay and Lynn Haven Roads, and the ease with which the entrance to the Chesapeake from seaward could be defended; but the fact that it is only 18 miles from the Atlantic coast-line makes it more vulnerable than Bremerton to the attack of troops landed by an enemy fleet. The yard at Mare Island, near San Francisco, is faultily placed as regards deep water; but dredging could rectify this. The Panama Canal Zone has great facilities for repairs, docking, and supplies; but it must be adequately fortified in order to be a trustworthy base in the case of operations in its vicinity.

New York, by reason of its enormous wealth of every kind, its steamer terminals, and its excessively vulnerable position, within gunshot of ships out in the deep water (a position without parallel in the large cities of the world) must, of course, be protected. The cheapest way to protect it is to do so locally, by means of fortifications, and other shore defenses. The only other means would be by a fleet permanently kept near New York, a measure that would be expensive beyond reason.

In case the enemy should inform us that he would reach the vicinity of New York at a certain time, and in case he should fulfil his promise, the fact that New York was properly strengthened would not be very important; since our fleet would go there, and the whole war would be settled by one "stand-up fight." But wars are not so conducted and never have been. From the oldest times till now, and even among savage tribes, finesse has always been employed, in addition to actual force—more perhaps by the weaker than by the stronger side, but very considerably also by the stronger. A coming enemy would endeavor to keep his objective a close secret, and even to mislead us; so that our fleet would have to take a position out at sea, perhaps far away, which would leave our bases open to attack by the enemy fleet or at least exposed to raids.

The most effective local defense of a naval base is a combination of mine-fields and heavy guns, which also give protection to which the wounded vessels can retire, as the German vessels did after the North Sea battle. Unless such protection be provided, swift destroyers can complete the work that guns began, as the Japanese destroyers did, after the artillery battle at Tsushima.

In addition to their value in defending navy-yards from raids, and in giving wounded ships a refuge, the military strengthening of home bases, if such home bases are wisely placed near large commercial centres, prevents actual destruction of those commercial centres themselves, in case an attack is made upon them, either in the absence of the defending fleet, or after that fleet may have been destroyed. The line of engineering advance during recent years, although it has greatly increased the offensive power of warships, has increased even more greatly the defensive power of land works. For this reason, it is perfectly possible to defend successfully almost any land position against attack by ships; and it is so easy, that not to do so, is, in the case of large commercial centres, a neglectfulness of the extremest character.

One important reason, therefore, for placing a permanent home base near a large commercial centre is the fact that the fortification of one is also the fortification of the other.

Assuming that New York is to be defended locally, we can state at once that the New York naval station can easily be made to be a permanent naval base of the highest order, and of the most efficient type. In fact, it can be made into a naval

base better than any other now in the world, because of the
large sheets of water tributary to it in New York Bay, Hudson
River, and Long Island Sound; the proximity of the sea; the
untold resources in money, supplies, and men that it could on
demand produce, and the ease with which it could be defended. To make such a base, it would be necessary to fortify
the vicinity of Coney Island and the entrances from the ocean
to the Lower Bay, and Long Island Sound; to deepen the channel to the navy-yard, and to make clear and safe the waterway
from the East River to Long Island Sound. It would be necessary also to enlarge the navy-yard; and to this end, to buy
back the land adjoining it, which the government most un-
wisely sold to private parties about twenty-five years ago.

Owing to the position of Block Island,[17] relatively to the
lines of communication of a hostile force coming from Europe to attack our eastern coast, and because of the sheltered
waters held within it, suitable for small craft, the advisability
of establishing a small naval base there is apparent. With a
suitable base there and another on Martha's Vineyard, and
the present canal from Massachusetts Bay to Buzzards Bay
sufficiently enlarged, the whole coast from Boston to New
York, including Narragansett Bay, could be made to form one
naval base which would have three exits. Our own ships could
pass from one point to another, and concentrate at will near
Sandy Hook, Block Island, or Massachusetts Bay; and, which
is equally important, the establishment of an enemy base near
New York would be made almost, if not quite, impossible.

In case of an attack on our eastern coast, made directly
from Europe, which could be accomplished easily during the
calm months of the summer, the degree of efficiency shown by
the bases at Norfolk, Philadelphia, New York, and Boston

17. Located just east of Montauk Point, Long Island. New London and
Narragansett Bay serve Fiske's purpose better than Block Island.

would influence vitally the condition in which our fleet would go to battle. Owing to the traditional policy, or rather lack of policy of the United States, and the consequent unreadiness of our preparations, we may reasonably assume that war will find us in such a condition that the utmost haste will be necessary to get our whole naval force out to sea in time to prevent the enemy from making an actual bombardment of our shores. We have no reason to suppose that the ships actually cruising in our active fleet will not be ready; we have every reason to believe that they will be ready. But it is inconceivable that we should not try to oppose such an attack with all the naval force that we could muster; which means that we should try to send out many ships from our home bases to join the active fleet at sea.

The ease with which the passage of an enemy's fleet up the Delaware or Chesapeake could be prevented, in case any means of national defense whatever be attempted, compared with the difficulty of defending New York, and combined with the greater damage that an enemy could inflict on New York, mark the vicinity of New York as the probable objective of any determined naval attack upon our coast; no matter whether that attack be made directly from Europe, or indirectly from Europe by way of the Caribbean. To meet such an attack, various parts of the fleet would have to issue from their bases; even parts of the active fleet would probably have had to go to their home ports for some needed repairs or supplies. The first thought of an attacking fleet would naturally be to prevent our ships from getting out, as it was the thought of Nelson and other British commanders to prevent the issuing of forces from the ports of France. But in view of the great distance from Europe to our coast, and the impossibility of preventing the knowledge reaching us of the departure of the fleet (unless indeed all the power of Europe combined to prevent it), it seems probable that no such issuing

299

could be prevented, and that a very considerable American force would have time to take its station out at sea, prepared to meet the coming foe.

The home bases if properly prepared would exert a powerful effect on a battle near them by equipping the fleet adequately and promptly, and also by preventing a possible defeat from becoming a disaster, by receiving wounded ships before they sank. The wounded ships of the enemy, on the other hand, would have no base near by, and only those inconsiderably injured could probably be gotten home.

CHAPTER TWELVE

OPERATING THE MACHINE

THE NAVAL MACHINE, including the various vessels of all kinds, the bases and the personnel, having been designed, put together, and prepared for its appointed task of conducting war, and the appointed task having at last been laid upon it, how shall the machine be operated—how shall it be made successfully to perform its task?

In order to answer this correctly, we must first see clearly what is its task.

War.—War may be said to be the act of two nations or two sets of nations, by means of which each tries to get its way by physical force. The peaceful methods of diplomacy having been exhausted, arguments and threats having been tried in vain, both parties resort to the oldest and yet the latest court, the same court as that to which resort the lions of the desert, the big and little fishes of the sea, the fowls of the air, and even the blades of grass that battle for the sunshine.

The vastness of the issue decided by war, the fact that from its decision there is no appeal, the greatness of the forces that nations can produce, the length of experience of war extending through 8,000 wars, and during more than three thousand years of recorded history, the enormous literature of the subject, and the fact that more brain power, energy, and character have been devoted to war than to any other fruit of

301

man's endeavor—combine to give to the conduct of war an importance that no other subject can possess.

The thing that each side brings forward against the other side is force; "that which moves or tends to move matter."[1] In all ages, it has been directed primarily against the physical bodies of individual men, threatening each individual man with suffering and death. It appeals to the primal instinct of men, self-preservation, and is the *ultima ratio regum,* the last argument of kings—and not only of kings, but of all other living things as well.

The first feeling aroused by the threat against life, or physical well-being, is fear; and, therefore, the first force with which to oppose the threat is a force of the same spiritual nature as fear, but opposite in direction. This force is called in the English language "courage." Without courage every man and every nation would be at the mercy of every man or nation that made a threat against it. The inherent necessity for courage is thus apparent; and the reason is therefore apparent, for the fact that in every nation and tribe physical courage has been esteemed the greatest virtue in a man. In Latin, we know, the word *virtus* meant courage, and also virtue— showing that the Romans held the two qualities to be identical or similar.

In discussing the operations of war, little is usually said of courage. The reason, however, is not that its value is unrecognized, but that its existence is assumed; in the same way as that in which all the other faculties among the men are assumed, such as physical health, ability to march, etc. Move-

---

1. Fiske sees two forces each trying to move the other. He does not make the mistake, so common in military literature, of confusing forces, the ships and aircraft that are the raw materials, with force, the raw materials put into action against an opposing force. Clearly he believes that "force" is real and tangible, and not mere metaphor, except in that the poverty of language compels us to borrow back a term that physical science has coopted and defined for its own purposes.

ments to inspire fear, however, actions to break down the morale, are of frequent use; because, if the morale of the opposing side is broken down, its power of resistance is destroyed.

In the operations, therefore, of two contending parties, force is opposed by force. If the forces on both sides could be concentrated at a single point, and exerted in opposite directions, the result would be decided in an instant. Such an arrangement has never yet been brought about; though fairly close approximations have been made, when two parties have selected two champions who have fought for them—the victory going by agreement to the side whose champion became the victor.

Barring such rare occasions, contests in war have usually been between two forces spread over considerable areas of land or water; and the contest has usually been decided by the defeat of one of the two. If in any individual combat, all the forces possessed by both sides had been engaged, and if either force had been annihilated, the entire war between the two parties would have been decided. This was nearly the case in the naval battle off Tsushima between the Russian and Japanese fleets—and the treaty of peace was signed soon after. Usually, however, neither party to the quarrel has had all its forces on the field in any one battle, and neither force in the battle has been annihilated. Usually, only partial forces have been engaged, and only partial victories have been won; with the result that wars between contending nations have usually consisted of a series of battles, with intervals of rest between.

If two opposing forces in any battle were exactly equal in fighting power, neither side in any battle would gain a victory, the two sides would inflict identical amounts of damage on each other, and the two sides would end the battle still equal in force. At rare intervals, such conditions have been approximated; but usually one side has had more fighting power than the other, and has inflicted more damage of various kinds than it has received, with the result that it attained an advantage more or less important over the other, and with the further result that the original disproportion between the two forces was increased.[2] The increase may not necessarily have been due to a greater number of killed and wounded or even to a greater loss of material, such as guns or ships; there may have been no increase in inequality in either of these ways, for the increase in inequality may have consisted in the fact that the weaker force was driven to a position less advantageous to it for conducting operations in the future. But whatever the nature of the advantage gained by the stronger side, the result has been that the weaker side has come out of the battle relatively weaker than it was before.

For this reason, it is highly desirable to each side to win each battle. This does not mean that the loss of any one battle by either party to a war means that the party losing that battle will necessarily lose the war; for many battles may be fought by such small portions of the whole nations' forces, or be lost by such small margins that the loss of one battle, or even several battles, may be retrieved; in fact, in few wars have the victories been all on one side. It does mean, however, that each lost battle is a backward step; and that for this reason the effort must be that no battle shall be lost.[3]

2. The only instance in which Fiske allows confusion between the two senses of force to enter in. The hazard is so extreme that "combat power" is solid coin for forces in action. Here and in his other works Fiske refers to fighting power as the thing that military forces dispense in combat.

3. Because in this and the preceding paragraph Fiske's discussion is entirely qualitative, it is easy to miss how great he believes the disproportion will be between the winner's losses and the loser's. Doubtless he has in mind the quantities exhibited in Table I on page 243. Very shortly, on pages 314–316, he will return to a quantitative appraisal. Fiske's belief in the winner's advantage was widely held. In strategic games conducted at the Naval War College during the 1920s, some simple rules for battle outcomes were often applied (on the assumption that no one could anticipate the results in detail). When the force ratio was 4:3 the superior force won, but

Strategy and Tactics.—Now, to win battles, two things combine, strategy and tactics. The strategy of each side tries to arrange matters so that the forces on its side shall enter each battle with the greatest chance of victory; tactics tries to handle the forces with which it enters a battle in such a way that its side shall gain the victory. Strategy prepares for battles; tactics fights them.[4]

The tactics of any battle must be in the hands of the commanders-in-chief on both sides. Any other arrangement is inconceivable; but the strategy controlling the series of battles in any war cannot now be committed to them solely; though it was usually committed to them until lately. In the days when Alexander went to war, or even when Napoleon and Nelson went to war, twenty-one centuries later, no telegraph by sea and land made swift communication possible; and the commanders on the spot were the only ones in possession of enough information about the contending forces to decide what measures should be taken. Even in those days, however, the capitals of the countries engaged in war, by reason of their knowledge of what was passing in the way of policy, exerted an influence on the strategy of the forces on both sea and

---

was incapable of carrying out any major operations for the duration of the game. When the force ratio was 3:2, the smaller force lost half its strength, no harm to the winner, and when the ratio was 2:1, the inferior force was removed from the game. See Francis J. McHugh, *Fundamentals of War Gaming*, 3rd edition (Newport, R.I., 1966), pp. 4-28 and 4-29. Contrast that with ground combat, in which the attacker against a prepared position is usually thought to require a 2:1 advantage just to achieve parity.

4. The relationship of strategy and tactics is as well said as it could be in Fiske's day. Some would now say
- Strategy defines aims
- Operational art offers the opportunity of victory
- Tactics strives to gain the victory

With Fiske we must always read strategy as encompassing both the plan of operations and the operations preparatory to battle. A nice touch, typical of Fiske's care with words, is to avoid saying tactics will win the battle.

land; Cæsar, for instance, was embarrassed in many of his operations by the Roman Senate, and it was for this reason that he crossed the Rubicon and passed from Gaul into Italy. When William I and Napoleon III went to war in 1870, however, Von Moltke had foreseen the effects of the telegraph and of rapid-mail communications, in giving to the headquarters of the army information of a much greater scope and reliability than had previously been the case, and had established a General Staff which had elaborated plans whereby not only would the commanders-in-chief in the field have the assistance of information compiled at headquarters, but whereby the general nature of the operations of a war, especially those operations at the outset on which the future conduct of the war would largely depend, would be decided and laid down in advance and during times of peace. The reason for the rapid victory of the Prussians over the French in 1870 was that the Prussians were better prepared in almost every way; especially in the most important thing—the war plans.

Now, these war plans could not, of course, be of such a kind that they would foresee every contingency and prescribe the conduct to be followed, so that a commander in the field could turn to page 221 of volume 755, and get directions as to what he ought to do; nor could they furnish the chief of staff, Von Moltke, with printed recommendations which he should offer to the King. In other words, the war plans could be only plans and, like all plans for future action, could be only tentative, and capable of being modified by events as they should come to pass. They were only plans of preparation, not plans of operation.

Yet there were plans of preparation for operations, plans prepared in accordance with the principles of strategy, and based on information as to the enemy's resources, skill, point of view, and probable intentions. They formed the general guide for future operations.

Since 1870, the invention and practical development of the wireless telegraph, and especially its development for use over very great distances, has modified the relations of commanders on the spot to home headquarters, and especially of naval commanders to their navy departments. The wireless telegraph, under circumstances in which it operates successfully, annihilates distance so far as communication is concerned, though it does not annihilate distance so far as transportation is concerned. It improves the sending and receiving of news and instructions, both for the commander at sea and for his department at home; but it does it more effectively for the department than for the man at sea, because of the superior facilities for large and numerous apparatus that shore stations have, and their greater freedom from interruptions of all kinds.

This condition tends to place the strategical handling of all the naval machine, including the active fleet itself, more in the hands of the department or admiralty, and less in the hands of the commander-in-chief: and this tendency is confirmed by the superior means for discussion and reflection, and for trial by war games, that exist in admiralties, compared with those that exist in ships.

The general result is to limit the commander-in-chief more and more in strategical matters: to confine his work more and more to tactics.

Such a condition seems reasonable in many ways. The government decides on a policy, and tells the Navy Department to carry it out, employing the executive offices and bureaus to that end, under the guidance of strategy. Strategy devotes itself during peace to designing and preparing the naval machine, and in war to operating it, utilizing both in war and peace the bureaus and offices and the fleet itself. And in the same way as that in which the bureaus and offices perform the calculations and executive functions of logistics, for furnish-

307

ing the necessary material of all kinds, the fleet performs those of tactics. From this point of view, strategy plans and guides all the acts of navies, delegating one part of the practical work needed to carry out those plans to logistics, and the other part to tactics.

Operating the naval machine in war means practically operating the active fleet in such a way as to cause victories to occur, to cause the fleet to enter each battle under as favorable conditions as practicable, and to operate the other activities of the navy in such a way that the fleet will be efficiently and promptly supplied with all its needs. Strategy employs tactics and logistics to bring these things to pass; but this does not mean that strategy stands apart and simply gives logistics and tactics tasks to do. The three agencies are too mutually dependent for any such procedure and require for their successful working, both individually and together, the most thorough mutual understanding and support.[5]

Flanking, T-ing, etc.—It being a fact that no nation can put a force upon the sea that is concentrated at one point; it being a fact that every naval force must be spread over a considerable area and made up of various parts, and that the efficacy of the various parts in exerting force upon a definite enemy depends on the unity of action of the various parts, it results that the most effective way in which to attack any naval force is not to attack all the parts at once, thus enabling all to reply, but to attack the force in such a way that all the parts cannot reply. If we attack a ship for instance, that can fire 10 guns on a broadside and only 4 guns ahead, it is clear that we can do

5. Because he had only recently relinquished his duties as aid for operations, Fiske was acutely aware of the interrelationship of strategy, logistics, and tactics, and for the need to specify the responsibilities of all the players in the actual conduct of operations. At the time (1913–1915) he was deeply involved in the navy's movements in the Caribbean, especially during President Wilson's actions to suppress Huerta, the self-proclaimed dictator of Mexico.

better by attacking from ahead than from either side. Similarly, if 10 ships are in a column, steaming one behind the other, each ship being able to fire 10 guns from either side and only 4 ahead, the 10 ships can fire 100 guns on either side and only 4 ahead; and therefore it would be better to attack the column from ahead (to "T" it), than to attack it from either side.

It is curious to note how widely this simple illustration can be made to apply to both strategy and tactics; how the effort of each is to dispose our force so toward the enemy's force that we can use our weapons more effectively than he can use his. An extreme illustration might be made by imagining 1,000 soldiers standing in line and unable to face except to the front; in which case it is clear that, no matter how perfectly they might be armed, or how quickly and accurately they could fire, one man standing on the flank, or behind them, could kill one soldier after the other, until all the 1,000 were killed, and be in no danger himself.

In case of attacking a ship or a column of ships from ahead, or of attacking a line of soldiers on the flank, the effectiveness of the method of attack lies in the fact that a number of the weapons that are present in the force attacked cannot be used in reply.

Concentration and Isolation.—The value of "concentration" is often insisted on, but the author desires to call attention to a misunderstanding on this point, to which he called attention in an essay in 1905.[6] To the author, it seems that concentration is a means and not an end, and that the end is what he called "isolation" in the essay. If a man concentrates his mind on any subject, the advantage he gains is that he prevents other subjects from obstructing the application of his mental powers to that subject; he pushes to one side and

6. "American Naval Policy," pages 49–50. Although Fiske prefers "isolation" as the best term, no one else seems to have difficulty applying "concentration" in the right way.

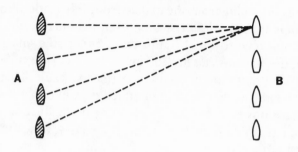

Figure 1

isolates all other subjects. In this particular activity it does not matter whether we call his act "concentration" or "isolation," because the whole operation goes on inside of his own skull, and concentration on one subject automatically produces isolation or elimination of all others. But when concentration is attempted on external objects, the case is very different, for concentration may not produce isolation at all. For instance, if 4 ships in column *A* concentrate their fire on the leading ship in column *B*, the other 3 ships in column *B* are not isolated, and can fire on the ships of column 1, even more effectively than if column *A* was not concentrated on the leading ship of *B*, because they are undisturbed by being fired at. If, however, the 4 ships of *A* "flank" or "T" the ships of column *B*, as shown in Fig. 2, and concentrate on the leader of *B*, they thereby isolate the other ships, and practically nullify their ability to fire at *A*.

Figure 2

This effect is approximated by an approximate "T-ing" or "flanking,"

310

such as is shown in Fig. 3; because the average distance from the ships of *A* to the leading ship in *B* is less than the average distance from the ships in *B* to any ship in *A;* and because the direction of fire from each ship in *A* is more nearly abeam than is the direction of

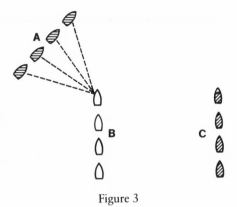

Figure 3

fire from the ships of *B*. These positions are very difficult to gain, even if *A's* speed is considerably greater than *B's;* since all *B* has to do to prevent it is to head to the right, unless shoals or other dangers such as enemy battleships, *C,* are on that side, co-operating with *A*.

An interesting position is that shown in Fig. 4, which may be assumed by *A*, either for flight, or to get the advantage in torpedo fire. The advantage is that the *A* ships are running away from torpedoes fired by *B*, while *B* is running into torpedoes fired by *A*. This advantage is not great if the distance between *A* and *B* is so little that *B's* torpedoes can reach *A*.

But if *A* is able to make this distance equal to the entire range over which *B's* torpedoes can run, or near it, *B's* torpedoes cannot reach *A* at all.

A similar advantage, though in a modified degree, is that shown as possessed by *A* in Fig. 5. Due to the direction of movement of the *A* and *B* fleets, it is easier for *A's* torpedoes to reach *B*, than for *B's* torpedoes to reach *A*.

Positions of advantage are usually

Figure 4

311

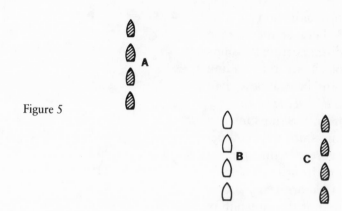

Figure 5

gained by superior speed. One of the main reasons for the development of the battle cruiser has been the fact that her high speed and great offensive power enable her to gain positions of advantage and utilize them. The *A* positions shown in the figures are attainable by battle cruisers against battleships, and are very effective.

A procedure analogous to that of flanking is one in which part of a force is attacked when it is separated from the rest of the force, and cannot be supported by it—in that some of the weapons of one force cannot be used. The effect is similar in the two cases, but the events leading up to the two conditions may be quite different.

In the former case, that of being flanked, or T'd, the force caught at a disadvantage was together, and was able to operate effectively as one force against a force located in a given direction; but was attacked by a force located in another direction; while in the latter case, the force was divided, and one part was caught, while distant from and entirely unsupported by the other part. The former condition is more likely to result from tactical operations, and the latter from strategical operations—and yet, especially in land operations, the flanking of one force may be brought about by the carefully

312

planned strategical combinations of the other force; and catching one part of the enemy's force unsupported by the other parts may take place during the tactical maneuvers of an actual or a simulated battle.

In naval operations, the catching of separated parts of an enemy's force is a more frequent attempt and accomplishment than is that of getting a position where a column of ships can be attacked from ahead or astern. It seldom happens, with the great number of vessels of all kinds which compose a modern fleet, that it is practicable to keep the various parts together, or that it would be desirable to do so. The closest approximation to keeping a large naval force together, is keeping them in column; because in that formation, the ships can be made simply to "follow the leader" without signal, and act like one long, flexible body. But the vessels of a modern fleet would make a column many miles long—a column of 20 battleships alone would be 5 miles long, and the addition of the various cruisers, destroyers, and other vessels, would make a column so long that it would be unwieldy; and if its ends were attacked, the other vessels could not come to their relief. Besides, the duties of battleships, battle cruisers, scouts, destroyers, and submarines, are distinct—with the result that as in land operations, bodies of the various types operate separately and apart from those of other types.

Not only, also, do the various types operate separately, but often the necessities of a case demand that a certain number—say of battleships—be sent away from the main body on some mission; or that a certain number of destroyers be sent away from the main body of destroyers.[7]

7. Here and in the succeeding paragraphs Fiske echoes Clausewitz and all the best strategists in pointing out the folly of blind conformance with the principle of concentration. The principle requires intelligent application, which is the rub. Clausewitz's rule is "A great many unsound reasons for dividing one's forces [can be avoided] . . . as soon as concentration of forces is recognized as the norm, and every separation and split as an ex-

Any such diversion entails a danger that is sometimes great, and sometimes small; but such diversions and risks cannot be avoided, and should not be avoided when they are necessary, any more than a man should avoid going out of doors, though that act always entails some danger. Suppose, for instance, that in the operations of a war carried on in the Caribbean, the Navy Department should get trustworthy information that the enemy had detailed 3 battle cruisers to speed north and bombard New York. The department would probably have to detach a force from the fleet and send it north, to prevent the bombardment. Yet not only would the force so sent be in danger until it returned of an attack by a superior force, but the main body from which it was detached would be thereby weakened; furthermore, the information might have been incorrect—it might have been originated and given out by the enemy, in the hope that it would cause such a diversion of force.

Every operation in war entails a risk more or less great; and if no risks were to be taken, it would be better not to go to war. It is true that some wars have been undertaken in which the preponderance of force was so great that there was very little doubt of the actual outcome, and very little risk taken by one of the two parties. Such wars, however, have been very few; and they were hardly wars in the usual sense, any more than the beating of a little boy by a big boy could properly be called a "fight."

Reference may again be made here to Table I on the next page, which shows the way in which fights between unequal forces proceed, and the advantage of fighting the separated parts of an enemy rather than the united force. We can see this clearly if we note that if two forces each aggregating 1,000 were in each other's vicinity, and if the entire force A

---

ception that has to be justified" (*On War*, edited and translated by Michael Howard and Peter Paret, Princeton, 1976, p. 204).

TABLE I

		Col. 1	Col. 2	Col. 3	Col. 4	Col. 5	Col. 6	Col. 7	Col. 8	Col. 9	Col. 10
Value of offensive power	A	1000	1000	1000	1000	1000	1000	1000	1000	1000	1000
at beginning	B	1000	900	800	700	600	500	400	300	200	100
Damage done in 1st pe-	A	100	100	100	100	100	100	100	100	100	100
riod by	B	100	90	80	70	60	50	40	30	20	10
Value of offensive power	A	900	910	920	930	940	950	960	970	980	990
at end 1st period ...	B	900	800	700	600	500	400	300	200	100	0
Damage done in 2d pe-	A	90	91	92	93	94	95	96	97	98	..
riod by	B	90	80	70	60	50	40	30	20	10	..
Value of offensive power	A	810	830	850	870	890	910	930	950	970	..
at end 2d period	B	810	709	608	507	406	305	204	103	2	..
Damage done in 3d pe-	A	81	83	85	87	89	91	93	95	..	..
riod by	B	81	71	61	51	41	31	20	10	..	..
Value of offensive power	A	729	759	789	819	849	879	910	940	..	..
at end 3d period	B	729	626	523	420	317	214	111	8	..	..
Damage done in 4th pe-	A	73	76	79	82	85	88	91	..	..	..
riod by	B	73	63	52	42	32	21	11	..	..	..
Value of offensive power	A	656	696	737	777	817	858	899	..	..	..
at end 4th period ...	B	656	550	444	338	232	126	20	..	..	..
Damage done in 5th pe-	A	65	70	74	78	82	86	..	..	..	..
riod by	B	65	55	44	34	23	13	..	..	..	..
Value of offensive power	A	591	641	693	743	794	845	..	..	..	..
at end 5th period ...	B	591	480	370	260	150	40	..	..	..	..
Damage done in 6th pe-	A	59	64	69	74	79	85	..	..	..	..
riod by	B	59	48	37	26	15	4	..	..	..	..
Value of offensive power	A	532	593	656	717	779	841	..	..	..	..
at end 6th period ...	B	532	416	301	186	71	0	..	..	..	..
Damage done in 7th pe-	A	53	59	66	72	78	..	..	..	..	..
riod by	B	53	42	30	19	7	..	..	..	..	..
Value of offensive power	A	479	551	626	698	772	..	..	..	..	..
at end 7th period ...	B	479	357	235	114	0	..	..	..	..	..
Damage done in 8th pe-	A	48	55	63	70	..	..	..	..	..	..
riod by	B	48	36	24	11	..	..	..	..	..	..
Value of offensive power	A	431	515	602	687	..	..	..	..	..	..
at end 8th period ...	B	431	302	172	44	..	..	..	..	..	..
Damage done in 9th pe-	A	43	52	60	69	..	..	..	..	..	..
riod by	B	43	30	17	4	..	..	..	..	..	..
Value of offensive power	A	388	485	585	683	..	..	..	..	..	..
at end 9th period ...	B	388	250	112	0	..	..	..	..	..	..
Damage done in 10th	A	39	49	59	..	..	..	..	..	..	..
period by	B	39	25	11	..	..	..	..	..	..	..
Value of offensive power	A	349	460	574	..	..	..	..	..	..	..
at end 10th period ..	B	349	201	53	..	..	..	..	..	..	..
Damage done in 11th	A	35	46	57	..	..	..	..	..	..	..
period by	B	35	20	5	..	..	..	..	..	..	..
Value of offensive power	A	314	440	569	..	..	..	..	..	..	..
at end 11th period ..	B	314	155	0	..	..	..	..	..	..	..
Damage done in 12th	A	31	44	..	..	..	..	..	..	..	..
period by	B	31	16	..	..	..	..	..	..	..	..
Value of offensive power	A	283	426	..	..	..	..	..	..	..	..
at end 12th period ..	B	283	111	..	..	..	..	..	..	..	..
					etc.						
Total damage done by .	A	717	789	800	700	600	500	400	300	200	100
	B	717	574	431	317	228	159	..	..	..	..

315

was able to engage half of B, or 500, it would whip half of B, and have 841 remaining, with which to engage the other half (500) of B. Reference to column 3 at the end of the third period in this table shows also that if a force of 789 engages a force of 523, it will have 569 left, after the other has been reduced to zero. So, a force of 1,000 that engages two forces of 500 separately, will have more than 500 left, after the others have both been reduced to zero: whereas, if it engages both when they are united, both sides will be gradually reduced to zero, remaining equal all the time.[8]

It is interesting to note how this simple fact is the key to most of the operations of strategy and tactics; how—the mechanical tools in the way of ships and guns and torpedoes having been supplied—the key to their successful use is simply to take advantage of all opportunities of isolating one part of the enemy's force from the rest, and then attacking one of the parts with a force superior to it. Opportunities lacking, one must, of course, try to create opportunities by inducing the enemy to detach some part of his force, under circumstances such that you can attack it, or the weakened main body, with a superior force. Naturally, one must try to prevent a similar procedure by the enemy.[9]

This does not mean that the sole effort of naval operations

8. Although Table I seems to the modern analyst to be a labored way to show the effect of what was known at the time as the "N-square law," it has the advantage of tracing for the layman step by step exactly how a small advantage in force accumulates over time and becomes a greater and greater advantage. Fiske devotes much space to different variations of it in "American Naval Policy." As we saw earlier, he intends the quantities to be proxies for *force*, not forces. That the N-square effect was real was common coin among officers of the battleship era, based on instinct and empirical evidence. The mathematics simply expressed the belief quantitatively.

9. The contemporaneous naval battles of World War I in the North Sea were all manifestations of these two sentences. The Germans and British both used deception to try to ensnare an inferior force with a superior one, and both sides fled the scene when they smelled a trap.

is finesse in either strategy or tactics; sometimes the sole effort is to force a pitched battle by the side that feels superior, and to avoid a pitched battle by the side that feels inferior. Before the actual inferiority or superiority has been ascertained, however, the strategy of each commander is to bring about a situation in which his force shall have the advantage. The advantage having been gained and recognized (or an advantage existing and being recognized), strategy insists on forcing a battle, for the reason that *every contest weakens the loser more than it does the winner.*

This does not mean that it is always wise to engage a weaker force that is temporarily separated from its main body. It is readily understandable, for instance, that it would be unwise in two cases:

1. A case in which the weaker force were so little weaker, and were part of a force so much larger than the total of the smaller force, that the gain as between the two forces actually engaged would not be great enough to compensate for the loss entailed. For instance, a reference to Table I shows that an *A* force of 1,000 engaging a *B* force of 800 would have 569 left when *B* was reduced to zero. This is impressive: but if the *B* force of 800 were part of a total *B* force of 2,000, in other words if there were another *B* force of 1,200 near at hand, *A* would have 569 left with which to oppose 1,200, a proportion little less advantageous than the proportion he started with—1,000 to 2,000.[10]

2. A case by which the *B* force may have divided with the express purpose of luring *A* to attack; arrangements having

10. Side *A* is outnumbered 2:1 (2,000 versus 1,000) at the outset. After defeating 800 of *B*, Side *A* is outnumbered 2.1:1 (1,200 versus 569). If the Lanchester Square Law is assumed, which is the equivalent of saying that fire is continuous instead of in discrete salvoes, then side *A* will have a force of 600 (not 569) remaining after the first engagement and (computationally speaking) Side *A* will be outnumbered for the second engagement by exactly 2:1.

TABLE III

		Col. 1	Col. 2	Col. 3
Value of offensive power at beginning	A	970	569	841
	B	800	200	500
Damage done in 1st period by	A	97	57	84
	B	80	20	50
Value of offensive power at end 1st period ...	A	890	549	791
	B	703	143	416
Damage done in 2d period by	A	89	55	79
	B	70	14	42
Value of offensive power at end 2d period ...	A	820	535	749
	B	614	88	337
Damage done in 3d period by	A	82	54	75
	B	61	9	34
Value of offensive power at end 3d period ...	A	759	526	715
	B	532	32	262
Damage done in 4th period by	A	76	53	72
	B	53	3	26
Value of offensive power at end 4th period ...	A	706	523	689
	B	456	0	190
Damage done in 5th period by	A	71	....	69
	B	46	....	19
Value of offensive power at end 5th period ...	A	660	....	670
	B	385	....	121
Damage done in 6th period by	A	66	....	67
	B	39	....	12
Value of offensive power at end 6th period ...	A	621	....	658
	B	319	....	54
Damage done in 7th period by	A	62	....	66
	B	32	....	5
Value of offensive power at end 7th period ...	A	589	....	653
	B	257	....	0
Damage done in 8th period by	A	59	....	....
	B	26	....	....
Value of offensive power at end 8th period ...	A	563	....	....
	B	198	....	....
Damage done in 9th period by	A	56	....	....
	B	20	....	....
Value of offensive power at end 9th period ...	A	543	....	....
	B	142	....	....
Damage done in 10th period by	A	54	....	....
	B	14	....	....
Value of offensive power at end 10th period ..	A	529	....	....
	B	88	....	....
Damage done in 11th period by	A	53	....	....
	B	9	....	....
Value of offensive power at end 11th period ..	A	520	....	....
	B	35	....	....
Damage done in 12th period by	A	52	....	....
	B	4	....	....
Value of offensive power at end 12th period.	A	516	....	....
	B	0	....	....

been made whereby the inferior B force would simply hold the A force until the whole B force could come to its assistance; arrangements having been also made that this would be accomplished before the detached part of B should get very badly damaged.

Attention is invited to Table III, which is a continuation of Table I. It represents what would happen if a force of 1,000 should fight separately two forces, one of 800 and the other of 200. In column 1, A is supposed to have engaged the 200 first, and so to have become reduced to 970, and to engage 800 afterward. In column 2, A is supposed to have engaged 800 first, thereby becoming reduced to 569, and then to engage the 200 force. The table indicates that it makes no difference whether A engages the stronger or the weaker force first.[11]

Column 3 shows that a force of 841, the part remaining after a force of 1,000 had annihilated a force of 500, would have 653 left after annihilating a second force of 500. Taken in connection with columns I and 2, this indicates that it is easier to defeat two separated *equal* forces than two separated *unequal* forces of the same aggregate value; that the weakest way in which to divide a force is into *equal* parts.[12] This fact is mathematically demonstrated by Mr. F. W. Lanchester in a recent book called "Air Craft in Warfare."[13]

11. Fiske quite appropriately disregards the trivial difference between 516 (column 1) and 523 (column 2). If he had done the computation using the Lanchester square law, then the results would have been identical (566 in both instances). That Fiske was aware of the Lanchester format is evident from the next paragraph of the text.

12. On the evidence this was a truth the U.S. Navy knew and took to heart. Throughout most of the 1920s and 1930s, when it was necessary to maintain fleets in the Atlantic and the Pacific, one or the other was kept as small as strategic interests were thought to permit, and the main force concentrated in the other.

13. Frederick W. Lanchester's article "Aircraft in Warfare, the Dawn of the Fourth Arm: The Principle of Concentration" first appeared in 1914 in the British journal *Engineering*. It is reprinted in James R. Newman, *The*

The main advantage of superior speed in naval operations is the ability it gives to secure tactical positions of advantage, and to make desirable strategic dispositions;[14] ability, for instance, to T or flank an enemy force, and to prevent the enemy from T-ing or flanking; also to catch separated parts of an enemy fleet before they can unite, while retaining the ability to divide one's own force without undue risk. For these purposes, speed is an element of the highest value; but the high price that it costs in gun power or armor protection—or both—and the fact that speed cannot always be counted on by reason of possible engine breakdowns and foul bottoms, result in giving the warships a lower speed than otherwise they would have.[15]

Owing to the fact that, for any given horse-power put into a ship, the speed attainable increases with her length; and

World of Mathematics, Volume IV (New York, 1956), pp. 2138–2157. Lanchester was a notable engineer and in 1900 produced one of the earliest automobiles. He also had the intellectual curiosity characteristic of a scientist, with interests ranging over aerodynamics, economics, fiscal policies, military science, and the theory of relativity. It is ironic that Lanchester applied his mathematics to aerial combat, where it has turned out to be less suitable than for naval or ground combat.

14. This is a deep-seated verity that should not be passed over lightly. Tactically, speed's hope is to secure advantageous positions, but in modern war speed has tended to be transferred to weapons (missiles and aircraft), so the advantage of new and greater fleet speed has been hard to demonstrate. Strategically, high sustained speed from nuclear power has proven its value.

15. These wise words are a change in tone from a scarcely qualified exuberance for speed expressed by Fiske in his 1905 prize essay. For further insight as to his mature (1912) views on speed, see Appendix A: "Fleet Tactics," paragraphs 40 to 51. Fleet command had had a sobering effect. American naval thinking was the most conservative toward speed of any of the major naval powers. The U.S. battle line that operated between the world wars comprised ships authorized between 1909 and 1916, all with a designed speed of a mere 20.5 to 21 knots. The U.S. Navy opted for heavy armament, heavy armor, and slow speed.

owing to the further fact that the weight that any ship can carry increases more rapidly than the displacement (weight of the ship complete), the best combination of gun power, armor protection, and speed is attainable in the largest ship. In other words, the larger the ship, the more power it can carry in proportion to its size, and the more quickly that power can be placed where it can do the most good.[16]

Strategic Operations.—These may be divided into two classes, offensive and defensive. The two classes are distinct; and yet there is no sharp dividing-line between them any more than there is between two contiguous colors in the spectrum. Defensive operations of the kind described by a popular interpretation of the word "defense" would be operations limited to warding off or escaping the enemy's attack, and would be just as efficacious as the passive warding off of the blows of fists. Such a defense can never succeed, for the reason that the recipient is reduced progressively in power of resistance as the attacks follow each other, while the attacker remains in unimpaired vigor, except for the gently depressing influence of fatigue. Reference to Table I will render this point clear, if we make the progressive reductions of the power of one contestant, and no reductions of the power of the other contestant.

Defensive operations, therefore, include "hitting back"; that is, a certain measure of offensive operations, intended to weaken the ability of the enemy to do damage. In fact, no operations are more aggressively offensive, or more productive of damage to the enemy's personnel and material, than operations that are carried on in order to defend something.

16. Then as now, certain congressmen deplored the growth in the size of capital ships. A few years earlier they had inflicted their preference for numbers of battleships over size on a protesting navy. Today, the argument for large carriers centers on the ability to operate large, high-performance aircraft, but the essence of Fiske's argument for size is also still a factor, namely economies of scale.

321

No animal is so aggressively belligerent as a female "defending" her young.

Offensive and defensive operations are nevertheless quite different, especially in two particulars, one being the use of the initiative or attack, and the other the distance to the home. In offensive operations, the attack is made; in defensive operations, the attack is resisted; and even if the resistance takes an aggressive character, and drives the original attacker back to the place he started from, yet the side which has made the original attack has carried on offensive operations, and the other side defensive. Offensive operations are, as a rule, carried on farther from home than defensive operations. If A is carrying on offensive operations against B, A is usually farther away from his home than B is from his home. We see from this that the offensive has the advantage of the initiative, of making an attack for which the enemy may be unprepared, and has the disadvantage of being far from its home bases; whereas the defensive has the disadvantage of not knowing when or where or whence an attack is to come, and the advantage of the support of various kinds given by home bases. In other words, the offensive has the advantage except in so far as it is impaired by unfavorable conditions.

For this reason, every military nation at the outset of war desires to be able to assume the offensive; and only refrains from the offensive from motives of prudence or because, in a particular case, the distance between the adversaries is so great, that the lack of bases would be of greater weight than the advantage of the initiative—or because the situations of the contending parties would be such that the side accepting the defensive rôle and staying near home, might be able to carry on aggressive attacks better than could the other. An illustration of a mistake in taking the offensive, and the wisdom of the other side in accepting the defensive, may be seen in Napoleon's expedition against Russia; for the Russians were able to repel his attack completely, and then to assume a terrible offensive against his retreating, disorganized, and starving army. Another illustration was the expedition made by a weak Spanish fleet under Cervera to the Caribbean in 1898.[17] Another illustration was that of the Russians in the war of 1904; the practical disadvantages under which the Russian fleet operated at Tsushima were too great to be balanced by the advantage of the attack; especially as the situation was such that the Japanese were able to foretell with enough accuracy for practical purposes the place where the attack would be delivered, and the time.

Operations on the sea, like operations on the land, consist in opposing force to force, in making thrusts and making parries. If two men or two ships contend in a duel, or if two parallel columns—say of ten ships each—are drawn up abreast each other, the result will depend mainly on the hitting and enduring powers of the combatants; the conditions of the "stand-up fight" are realized, and there is little opportunity for strategy to exert itself.

But if any country—say the United States—finds herself involved in war with—say a powerful naval Power or Powers of Europe, and the realization of the fact comes with the suddenness that characterized the coming of war in August, 1914, and we hear the same day that a fleet of battleships, battle cruisers, destroyers, submarines, aircraft, and auxiliaries has left the enemy's country, followed by a fleet of transports carrying troops—there will be immediate need for strategy of the most skilful kind; and this need will continue until either the United States or her enemy has been made to acknowledge herself beaten, and to sue for peace.

As such a war will be mainly naval, and as naval wars are characterized by great concentration of force, by each side

---

17. A lapse by Fiske. It could hardly be called a Spanish "mistake in taking the offensive," for not to have done so would have been to concede the American purpose in Cuba.

getting practically all its naval force into the contest, by each side staking its all on the issue of perhaps a single battle (as the Russians and Japanese did at Tsushima) one fleet or the other will be practically annihilated, and its country will be exposed naked to the enemy.

The first effort on hearing of the departure of the hostile fleet will be, of course, to get our fleet out to sea, reinforced as much as practicable, by our reserve ships; and to get the coast-guard on their patrol stations. As we should not know the destination of the enemy, we should either have to assume a destination and send our fleet to that place (leaving the other places undefended) or else send our fleet out to sea to some position from which it would despatch scouts in different directions to intercept the enemy, in order that our fleet might meet it and prevent its farther advance.

Of course, the latter procedure could not be carried out reasonably, unless we had a great enough number of trained scouts to make the interception of the enemy fleet probable; because otherwise the probabilities would be that an enemy having the battle cruisers and scouts that European navies have, would succeed in evading our fleet and landing a force upon our shores; and it could not be carried out reasonably either, if we knew that our fleet was markedly inferior to the coming fleet; because to send out our fleet to meet a much more powerful one in actual battle would be to commit national suicide by the most expeditious method.

In case the departure of the enemy fleet occurred in the stormy months of the winter, we might feel warranted in guessing that its immediate destination was the Caribbean; yet if our fleet were in the Caribbean at the time, and if our coast lacked shore defenses as at present, we might argue that the enemy would take the opportunity to make a direct descent upon our coast, seize a base—say on the eastern end of Long Island—and march directly on New York. It would be very difficult to plan the development of a line of scouts in such a way that the scouts would intercept an attack directed at some unknown point between Boston and the West Indies, perhaps in the southern part of the West Indies—say Margarita Island.[18] In fact, it would be impossible; with the result that, unless we intercepted it by simple good luck, the enemy would succeed in landing a force on our eastern coast, or else in the seizing of a base in the West Indies or the southern part of the Caribbean Sea.

Either one of these acts, successfully performed by an enemy, would give him an advantage; that is, it would make his position relatively to ours better than it was before.[19] It would have the same effect, therefore, as winning a battle; in fact it would constitute the winning of a battle—not a physical battle but a strategic battle.

It may be objected that, unless we knew our fleet to be more powerful it would be wiser and more comfortable for all concerned to withdraw our ships to the shelter of their bases, and let the enemy do his worst—on the theory that he could not do anything else so ruinous to us as to sink our fleet.

There is of course considerable reasonableness in this point of view; and strategy declares the unwisdom of engaging in battles that are sure to be lost. It must be remembered, however, that the coming fleet will operate at a considerable strategic disadvantage, owing to the necessity for guarding the "train" of auxiliary ships that will come with it, holding fuel and supplies of various kinds; that this handicap will offset a considerable advantage in offensive strength; and that the handicap will be still greater if the enemy fleet have near it a flotilla of transports carrying troops. It must be remembered also that in all probability, we should not have detailed information as to the number of vessels coming, and should not really know whether it was superior to ours or not; though

18. Off the coast of Venezuela.
19. The advantage he speaks of is an advanced base.

we should be justified in assuming that the coming fleet believed itself to be superior to ours in actual fighting power. Absence of trustworthy information on such points is usual in warfare, and is one of the elements that is the most difficult to handle. The Navy Department would be more able to form a correct estimate on this point than the commander-in-chief until such time as our scouts might come into absolute contact with the enemy's main body; but, until then, all that the department and fleet would know would be that a large hostile force had left Europe. They would not know its size or destination.

Clearly, the first thing we should need would be information. To get this after war has broken out, the only means is scouts.

Scouting and Screening.[20]—Scouts are needed by every navy; but they are most needed by a navy that has a very long coast-line to protect. If the great commercial centres and the positions that an enemy would desire for advanced bases along the coast, have local defenses adequate to keep off a hostile fleet for, say, two weeks, the urgency of scouts is not quite so absolute; since, even if the hostile fleet evades our scouts and our fleet, and reaches our shores, our fleet will have two weeks in which to get to the place attacked. But if the coast is not only long but also unguarded by shore defenses, the urgency is of the highest order.

20. This is clean, contemporary (World War I) usage of the terms *scouting* and *screening*. Scouts detect and track the enemy. Screens prevent the enemy from doing the same. The scouting force serves both functions simultaneously. In 1916 a scouting force was a major component of the fleet, and had extensive tactics of its own. These are admirably sketched for a lay reader (and who now among us is not a lay reader regarding the tactics of 1916?) in the section that follows. In current usage "screening" is a mishmash of searching and shooting activities, and often very much a part of the main fleet action itself. Scouting and screening are, if possible, more prominent than when Fiske wrote. Fiske's elemental discourse briefly illustrates the best of the conventional thinking of his day.

If we knew our fleet to be the weaker, but if we did not believe it to be so much the weaker as to force it to seek safety in flight, our natural plan would be that of Napoleon's in Italy in 1797—to keep our force together, and to hurl it against detached parts of the enemy's force, whenever possible. This plan might not be difficult of execution, if the enemy were accompanied by his train of auxiliary and supply ships; since such ships are vulnerable to almost any kind of attack, have almost no means of defense whatever, and therefore require that a part of the fighting force of the main body be detached to guard them. Whether the enemy would have his train quite close to him, or a day's steaming behind, say 240 miles, we should not, of course, know.

How could we ascertain?

If the enemy came along with no scouts ahead, and if we happened to have some scouts located along his line of advance, these scouts faster than his ships, and so heavily armed as not to fear to venture near, our scouts might proceed along the flank of the enemy in daylight, pass along his rear, go entirely around him, and then report to our commander-in-chief by wireless telegraph exactly what craft of all kinds comprised the force, what formation they were in, the direction in which they were steaming, and the speed. Such information would be highly appreciated by our commander-in-chief, as it would enable him to decide what he had better do. If, for instance, the scouts reported that the enemy fleet were steaming at a speed of 10 knots an hour, and that the train was proceeding behind the fighting fleet without any guards of any kind around them, our commander-in-chief might decide to keep just out of sight until after dark, and then rush in with all his force of heavy ships and torpedo craft, and destroy the train entirely.

But suppose the enemy fleet should advance with a "screen" consisting of a line 10 miles long of, say, 50 destroyers, 50 miles ahead of the main body; followed by a line of, say, 10 battle cruisers, 25 miles behind the destroyers; and with destroyers and battle cruisers on each flank—say, 20 miles distant from the main body.[21] How could our scouts find out anything whatever about the size, composition, and formation of the enemy—even of his speed and direction of advance? The purpose of the "screen" is to prevent our ascertaining these things; and each individual part of the screen will do its best to carry out that purpose. All the vessels of the screen and of the main body will be equipped with wireless-telegraph apparatus and a secret code, by means of which instant communication will be continuously held, the purport of which cannot be understood by our ships. Any endeavor of any of our scouts to "penetrate the screen" will be instantly met by the screen itself, out of sight of the enemy's main body; and the screen cannot be penetrated in the daytime, unless we can defeat those members of the screen that try to hold us off. Now, inasmuch as all the considerable naval Powers of Europe have many battle cruisers, and we have no battle cruisers whatever, and no scouts of any kind, except three inefficient ones (the *Birmingham, Chester,* and *Salem*) the degree of success that we should have penetrating the screen in the daytime can be estimated by any lawyer, merchant, or schoolboy.

The laws of successful scouting and of the use of "search curves" have been worked out mathematically, and they are used to find an enemy of which one has certain information; but they are also used by the enemy to avoid being found, and they aid the enemy that is sought almost as much as they aid the seeker. And the sought has the advantage that the use of force, if force can be employed, breaks up the application of the mathematics of the seeker.

21. This is a potent scouting-screening force indeed, even by the standards of the British Grand Fleet and the German High Seas Fleet in 1916 at Jutland.

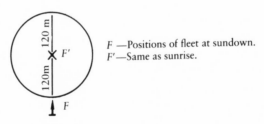

F —Positions of fleet at sundown.
F'—Same as sunrise.

Figure 6

It is true that two main bodies of two fleets may stumble against each other in the night-time, or in a fog or heavy mist.[22] To prevent this possible occurrence, or to prevent a night attack by destroyers, no sure means has yet been found except examination before dark of a very large area around the fleet that is sought; but the area is too great for a search rigid enough to give complete security, and will probably be so until swift aircraft can scout over long distances at sea. Accepting for the minute the convention that the main body of each side goes at the cruising speed of 10 knots, and that darkness lasts 12 hours, each side will go 120 miles in darkness; and if the two main bodies happen to be going directly toward each other they will approach 240 miles in the darkness of one night. Therefore, a coming fleet, in order to feel entirely safe, would in daylight have to inspect by its scouts a circle of 120 miles radius. To insure safety against destroyer

22. Despite two formidable scouting forces (or perhaps because they performed their opposing screening functions so well), at Jutland the German fleet was completely surprised by the British, and the British fleet had only just completed its shift from cruising formation to battle formation when the two main forces collided. Visibility was poor and rapidly got worse as the evening twilight deepened, not from fog or mist but from the gun and stack smoke of 250 ships.

attack, the area would have to be much greater on account of the greater speed of destroyers.[23]

Unless our defending fleet knew with reasonable sureness, however, the location, speed, and direction of motion of the coming fleet, so that it could make its dispositions for attack, it would hardly desire to meet the enemy at night, unless it were confident that it would meet the train and not the main fleet or the destroyers. Night attacks, both on sea and land, are desirable, if the attacker can inflict surprise on the attacked, and not be surprised himself. In the darkness a flotilla of destroyers may make an attack on the various vulnerable colliers and supply vessels of a fleet, or even on the main body, and achieve a marked success, because that is the rôle they are trained to play. But the tremendous power and accuracy of battleships cannot be utilized or made available in darkness; and therefore a commander-in-chief, anxious to defeat by superior skill a coming fleet larger than his own, would hardly throw away all chance of using skill by risking his main body in a night encounter. Every operation planned by strategy is supposed to result from the "decision" which follows the estimate of the situation; even if in some simple or urgent cases, the decision is not laboriously worked out, but is almost unconscious and even automatic. Now, it is hardly conceivable that any estimate of the situation would be followed by a decision to go ahead and trust to luck, except in very desperate circumstances. In such circumstances, when hope is almost gone, a desperate blow, even in the dark, may save a situation—as a lucky hand at cards may redeem a gambler's fortune at even the last moment. But strategy is

23. In the diagram, the circle bounds all starting positions from which an enemy force traveling at 10 knots might reach point F'. Fiske might have used a more sophisticated diagram with a scouting line ahead, incorporating what we now call the limiting lines of (enemy) approach. This would have shown that there was no threat (from a 10-knot enemy) in the rear semicircle of a force itself moving at 10 knots.

opposed to taking desperate measures; and pugilists and even gamblers recognize the fact that when a man becomes "desperate," his judgment is bad, and his chances of success are almost zero.[24]

While it is possible, therefore, that the main bodies of hostile fleets may come together in the night, we may assume that it will not be as part of any planned operations, and therefore not within the scope of this discussion; and that any combat which may result will be one in which strategy will play no part, and in which even tactics will yield first place to chance.

But while our defending fleet will have to base most of its decisions on guesses, the coming fleet, on the other hand, having accepted the strategical disadvantage of leaving its base far in rear, will advance with all the advantage of the offensive, especially in knowing where it intends to go and what it desires to do. Coming over on a definite mission it will have been able to know what preparations to make; and as the naval Powers of Europe understand the need of co-ordination between policy and strategy, the fleet will doubtless have had time to make those preparations; it will not have started, in fact, and war will not have been declared, until all those preparations have been made.

We may assume that the coming fleet will come across with all possible precautions for protecting itself against detection

24. The above paragraph nicely encapsulates U.S. and Japanese tactical planning in the 1930s. The American navy sought a long-range daylight gunnery duel between opposing battle lines, and drilled for such a duel so assiduously that its thinking was straitjacketed. During the night surface ship battles of 1942, such tactics of columns and guns fell victim to Japanese tactics exploiting their superior torpedoes. The Japanese, who expected to be outnumbered because of the inferiority imposed on them by the Washington Treaty of 1922 and knew the American preference for daylight action, took the gamble as Fiske describes it, and trained for night action at close range, in such a way that the torpedo, not the gun, became the weapon of decision. If the U.S. Navy had not had superior radar and

by the defender's scouts, and therefore against an unexpected attack, by night or by day. It cannot receive an unexpected attack unless surprised; and how can it be surprised, if it has more scouts, faster scouts, and more powerfully armed scouts than the defending fleet has?

The possession of the more powerful scouts, however, will be valuable to the enemy, not only for forming a screen as a protection against enemy scouts, but also for scouting and thereby getting information for itself. A numerous squadron of scouts of different kinds, sent out ahead and on each flank would see any of our scouts that saw them; and the scouts that were the more powerful would force the weaker scouts back to the arms of their own main body, toward which the more powerful scouts would, of course, advance. The weaker scouts, therefore, would have no value whatever as a screen, save in retarding the advance of the stronger scouts, and in delaying their getting information.

If the coming fleet is more powerful than the defending fleet, and has a more numerous and powerful scouting force, it will, therefore, be able to push back the defending fleet, whether an actual battle occurs or not; and it will be able to bring over, also, a large invading force in transports if its fighting superiority be great enough. Furthermore, if we have not fortified and protected the places which the enemy would wish to seize and use as advanced naval bases, the enemy will be able to seize them, and will doubtless do so.

Of course, this is so obvious as to seem hardly worth declaring; and yet some people hesitate even to admit it, and thereby they assume a passive condition of moral cowardice; for they know that a strong force has always overcome a weaker force that opposed it in war; and that it always will

---

learned how to exploit it tactically, the Japanese might have won even more of those deadly battles.

do so, until force ceases to be force. They know that force is that which moves, or tends to move, matter; and that the greater the force, the more surely it will move matter, or anything that opposes it.

If, however, we establish naval bases near our valuable commercial and strategic ports, both on our coast and in the Caribbean, and if we fortify them so that an enemy could not take them quickly, the condition of the enemy fleet will be much less happy; because it will have to remain out on the ocean, where fuelling and repairing are very difficult, and where it will be exposed, day and night, especially at night, to attack by destroyers and submarines; and in case necessity demands the occasional division of the force, it must beware of attacks on the separated portions of the fleet. The condition of a large fleet under way on an enemy's coast is one requiring much patience and endurance, and one in which the number of vessels is liable to be continuously reduced by the guerilla warfare of the defenders.

In the case of our attempting offensive operations against the distant coast of an enemy, we would be in the same position as a foreign enemy would be in when attacking our coast, in that our chances of success would be excellent if our fleet were considerably superior to the defending fleet in fighting power, and in the number and strength of scouts, and if the enemy coast possessed numerous undefended bays and islands which we could seize as bases. But even if the superiority of our fleet in fighting power and scouts was considerably greater than the enemy's our ultimate success would be doubtful, if the enemy's coast and islands were so protected by guns and mines and submarines that we could not get a base near the scene of operations. It is true that the British were able to maintain blockades of the French coast during many weary months without any base nearer than England— a place far away to ships whose only motive power was sails;

but destroyers and submarines and mines did not then exist, and these agencies are much more valuable to the defender than to the blockader who has no base at hand.[25]

Our operations without a base on a distant enemy coast would be apt to degenerate into warding off a continual series of more or less minor attacks by the minor craft of the defender. The commander of our fleet would be constrained to keep his fighting force pretty close together, thus restricting his initiative; lest the entire enemy fleet catch a detached part out of supporting distance of the main body, and annihilate it with little loss to themselves. We could probably shut off most of the enemy's sea-borne commerce; and the war would become one of endurance between our fleet, on the one hand, and the economic forces and the morale of the enemy country on the other hand.

In the case of operations carried on far away from the bases of both fleets, operations like those that the French and British carried on in the West Indies, the commanders-in-chief will naturally be much less directed by the admiralties at home than will a commander-in-chief operating near home; and the strategical advantage, as affected by the proximity of

25. Fiske forgoes the opportunity to illustrate his point by citing Britain's distant blockade of Germany in the war then under way in Europe. More serious is his failure to mention the German U-boat campaign, which at least by the time of his second edition was the most serious aspect of the naval war. Was it the dead hand of Mahan gripping American naval thought, or was it that the navy as a fighting machine to win command of the seas in decisive battle was too important an abstraction to be communicated and understood to allow deflection by some passing concern with commerce protection? Fiske, who was representative of the very best of naval officer thinking and who in most ways was broader and more pragmatic than any of the strategic theorists, inadvertently exposes how a faulty theoretical foundation crumbles like sand when put to the test of a real-world campaign against shipping. After getting as close to the truth as to say the U.S. Navy's ultimate purpose is to prevent an enemy blockade, he then passes by the U-boat threat without a murmur.

bases, and by the possession of the better chance for the initiative, will be reduced to its minimum.

Of course, the victory will go to the more powerful force; but so many factors go to make up power, that it may be difficult to determine which is the more powerful, until after victory itself shall have decided it. Supposing the skill to be equal on both sides, the victory will go to the side that possesses the most numerous and powerful vessels of all kinds. But unless there is a very great disproportion, it may be difficult to determine which side has the more powerful ships, even though we may know which side has the more numerous. It is extremely difficult to compare even two single warships because we do not know the relative values of their factors. Suppose two ships, for instance, to be equal in all ways, except that one ship has ten 14-inch guns, and the other has twelve 12-inch guns of higher initial velocity. Which is the more powerful ship? Suppose one ship has more armor, another more speed. Formulæ designed to assign numerical values to fighting ships have been laboriously worked out, notably by Constructor Otto Kretschmer of the German navy; but the results cannot be accepted as anything except very able approximations. Furthermore, if ship *A* could whip ship *B* under some conditions, *B* could whip *A* under other conditions. An extreme illustration would be battleship *A* engaged with submarine *B* at close quarters; *B* being on the surface in one case, and submerged in the other case.[26]

26. Fiske at his analytical best. Force (or fighting power, if you wish) can be assessed only when the opponent and the circumstances of battle are known. We make assessments in advance because not to make them is worse folly than to make them and take them at face value. What places Fiske a cut above the rest is found at the close of the paragraph. It is a bit of early systems analysis. Effectiveness indices fail because effectiveness depends on circumstances. Fighting force can only be computed when the enemy is specified. Whether we are dealing with analysis, war gaming, or operations at sea, we either have force against force or we have nothing but

Aircraft.—The influence of aircraft on naval operations is to be very great indeed, but in directions and by amounts that it would not be wise to attempt to predict. The most obvious influence will be in distant scouting, for which the great speed of aircraft will make them peculiarly adapted, as was demonstrated in the battle near the Skagerrak.[27] It is the belief of the author, however, that the time is close at hand when aeroplanes and dirigibles of large size will be capable of offensive operations of the highest order, including the launching of automobile torpedoes of the Whitehead type.

Skill.—The question of skill bears a relation to the question of the material power directed by it that is very vital, but very elusive. If, for instance, ship *C*, firing ten 12-inch guns on a side, fights ship *D*, firing five like guns on a side, the advantage would seem to be with *C;* but it would not be if each gun on *D* made three hits, while each gun on *C* made one hit; a relative performance not at all impossible or unprecedented. Similarly, if the head of the admiralty of the *E* fleet were a very skilful strategist, and the head of the admiralty of the *F* fleet were not, and if the various admirals, captains, lieutenants, engineers, and gunners of the *E* fleet were highly skilled, and those of the *F* fleet were not, the *E* fleet might be victorious, even if materially it were much the smaller in material and personnel. In case the head of the admiralty of the *E* fleet were the more skilful, while the officers of the *F* fleet were, on the average, more skilful than those of the *E* fleet, it would be impossible to weigh the difference between them; but as a rough statement, it may be said that if the head of the admiralty of either fleet is more skilful than the other, his

---

combat potential. Potential exists in and of itself, but the effective force of one side by itself cannot be defined.

27. The Battle of Jutland. But Fiske exaggerates the contribution of aerial scouting in that battle.

officers will probably be more skilful than the officers of the other; so pervasive is the influence of the chief.

The effectiveness of modern ships and guns and engines and torpedoes, when used with perfect skill, is so great that we tend unconsciously to assume the perfect skill, and think of naval power in terms of material units only.[28] Yet daily life is full of reminders that when two men or two bodies of men contend, the result depends in large though varying measure on their relative degrees of skill.

Whenever one thinks of using skill, he includes in his thought the thing in the handling of which the skill is employed. One can hardly conceive of using skill except in handling something of the general nature of an instrument, even if the skill is employed in handling something which is not usually called an instrument. For instance, if a man handles an organization with the intent thereby to produce a certain result, the organization is the instrument whereby he attempts to produce the result.

If a man exercises perfect skill, he achieves with his instrument 100 per cent of its possible effect. If he exercises imperfect skill, he achieves a smaller percentage of its possible effect.

To analyze the effectiveness of skill, let us coin the phrase, "effective skill,"[29] and agree that, if a man produces 100 per

28. A point of view shared by this commentator. One of the latter-day concerns of operations analysts has been the often unstated assumption that equipment will work as intended and be employed in the best way. Perhaps this is the unconscious result of analysts' search for "optimal" solutions and their penchant for optimization algorithms. But naval leaders, the best of whom carry in their makeup a Can Do attitude, are victims of the same way of thinking, and Fiske tells us here that this is nothing new.

29. The concept of effective skill is very powerful, and typical of Fiske's practical genius. For example, if we applied effective skill to C^3, we would do away with the overused and misleading notion that C^3 is a "force multiplier." The more practical approach is to think of its absence as a force degrader. Fiske's pragmatism leads him beyond where most naval officers

cent of the possible, his effective skill is 100 per cent, and, in general, that a man's effective skill in using any instrument is expressed by the percentage he achieves of what the instrument can accomplish; that, for instance, if a gun is fired at a given range under given conditions, and 10 per cent hits are made in a given time, then the effective skill employed is 10 per cent.

From this standpoint we see that imperfect skill is largely concerned with errors. If a man uses, say, a gun, with perfect skill, he commits no error in handling the gun; and the smaller the sum total of errors which he commits in handling the gun, the greater his effective skill and the greater the number of hits.

The word "errors," as here used, does not simply mean errors of commission, but means errors of omission as well. If a man, in firing a gun, fails to press the button or trigger when his sights are on, he makes an error just as truly as the man does who presses the button or trigger when the sights are not on.

Suppose that, in firing a gun, under given conditions of range, etc., the effective skill employed is 10 per cent. This means that 10 per cent of hits are made. But it means another thing equally important—it means that 90 per cent of misses are made. To what are these misses due? Clearly they are due to errors made, not necessarily by the man who fires the gun, but by all the people concerned. If the correct sight-bar range were given to the gun, and if the gun were correctly laid and the pointer pressed the button at precisely the right instant, the shot would hit the target, practically speaking. But, in actual practice, the range-finder makes an error, the spotter

stop. He is convinced not only that skill is important, but that its value can and must be quantified because its influence is so great. Fiske first published "The Effectiveness of Skill" very much as you see it here in the U.S. Naval Institute *Proceedings,* January–February 1915, pp. 67–70.

makes an error, the plotting-room makes an error, the sight-setter makes an error, and the gun-pointer makes an error. The sum total of all of these errors results in 90 per cent of misses.

Suppose that by careful training these errors are reduced in the relation of 9 to 8, so that instead of there being 90 per cent of misses there are only 80 per cent. This does not seem a very difficult thing for training to accomplish, but note the result: the hits are increased from 10 per cent to 20 per cent. In other words, by a decrease in errors in the relation of 9 to 8, the effective skill and the hits are doubled.[30]

Conversely, if the errors increased in the ratio of 9 to 10, the misses would increase from 90 per cent to 100 per cent, and the hits would be reduced from 10 per cent to 0.

Suppose now that the conditions are so very difficult that only 1 per cent of hits is made, or 99 per cent of misses, and that by training the misses are reduced from 99 per cent to 98 per cent. Clearly, by a decrease of errors of hardly more than 1 per cent the effective skill and the hits are doubled.[31]

Conversely, if the errors increased in the ratio of 99 to 100, the misses would increase from 99 per cent to 100 per cent, and the hits would be reduced from 1 per cent to 0.

But suppose that the conditions are so easy that 90 per cent of hits are made and only 10 per cent of misses. Clearly, if the

30. Fiske had fought at Manila Bay—indeed, his role there was to observe gunnery effectiveness—so he well knew how miserable shooting could be. That was the battle in which Dewey hauled clear at one point because of an inaccurate report that his ships were almost out of ammunition. Some in the modern navy are prone to think that missile guidance systems will improve these low-hit probabilities. This thinking does not take into account the human being's ability to adapt and survive.

31. These percentages are not absurd. At Jutland, where the two fleets had rather sophisticated fire control, the fraction of hits was around 3 per cent, a little more by the Germans, a little less by the British. In the Spanish-American War the battle ranges were shorter but the percentage of hits was even worse.

errors were divided by 10, so that only 1 per cent of misses was made, instead of 10 per cent, the number of hits would increase only 9 per cent, from 90 per cent to 99 per cent.

Of course, this is merely an arithmetical way of expressing the ancient truths that skill becomes more and more important as the difficulties of handling an instrument increase; and that, no matter how effective an instrument may be when used with perfect skill, the actual result obtained in practice is only the product of its possible performance and the effective skill with which it is used.

Applying this idea to naval matters, we see why the very maximum of skill is required in our war mechanisms and war organizations, in their almost infinite variety and complexity.[32] The war mechanisms and war organizations of the military nations are capable of enormous results, but only when they are used with enormous skill. There are no other instruments or organizations that need so much skill to handle them, because of the difficulties attending their use and the issues at stake. Their development has been a process long and painful. On no other things has so much money been spent; to perfect no other things have so many lives been sacrificed; on no other things, excepting possibly religion, have so many books been written; to no other things has the strenuous exertion of so many minds been devoted; in operating no other things has such a combination of talent and genius and power of will and spirit been employed.

A battleship is an instrument requiring skill to handle well, considered both as a mechanism and as an organization. Its effective handling calls for skill not only on the part of the

32. It is amazing that so little is made of this: machines will always seem to be handled badly and perform poorly in combat because they must be operated at the outer limits of their capabilities. Skill is magnified in importance as difficulties are compounded. The handful of fighting men who reach the upper limits of skill have done, and will continue to do, a disproportionate share of the damage to the enemy.

captain, but on the part of all hands. The finest dreadnaught is ineffective if manned by an ineffective crew. The number and complexity of the mechanisms on board are so great as to stagger the imagination; and the circumstances of modern warfare are so difficult that, as between two forces evenly matched as to material, a comparatively slight advantage in errors made will turn the scale in favor of the more skilful. A difference in errors, for instance, in the relation of 9 to 8, under the conditions mentioned above, between two fleets having an equal number of similar ships, would give one side twice as many hits as the other in any given length of time.

In March, 1905, the writer published an essay in the *Proceedings of the U.S. Naval Institute* called "American Naval Policy," in which the effect of initial superiority in gun-fire was shown in tables. One table showed that an initial advantage of only 10 per cent secured an overwhelming victory by an accumulative effect. Now a difference of 10 per cent in hits, under conditions in which the hits were about 10 per cent of the maximum, would mean, roughly speaking, the difference between 10 hits and 9 hits in a given length of time, or a difference between 90 misses and 91 misses; a difference in errors made of a little more than 1 per cent.[33]

33. U.S. Naval Institute *Proceedings*, January (not March) 1905, p. 20, Table II, Column 2. Fiske assumes two forces, each with a fighting strength of 1,000. Force A's effectiveness per salvo is at the rate of 10 percent of its remaining strength (thus one hundred units of B will be taken out with A's first salvo) but B's effectiveness is only 9 percent (worth ninety units of A for B's first salvo). Fiske's laborious calculation shows that after twelve salvoes A has 362 units left and B has 232.

Lanchester approached this problem by assigning different coefficients of effectiveness to the numerically identical forces, A and B. Using Lanchester's method is much easier and faster. We find A has 385 units left when B is reduced to 232, slightly higher because the attrition is continuous. When B is eliminated, A will have only 316 units (32 percent) remaining. Moreover the battle will continue for a much longer time. But Fiske makes the essential point: under "square law" conditions (operative in

The conclusion to be drawn is too obvious to be stated. Perhaps the conclusion is not broadly new; but possibly the idea is new that so small a difference in errors made will, under conditions of sufficient difficulty, produce such a tremendous difference in results.

Now, a division is more complex and more difficult to handle perfectly than is a battleship; a squadron more so than a division; a fleet more so than a squadron; a navy more so than a fleet.

Necessity for Knowledge of the Naval Machine.—There is no machine or tool so simple that knowledge of it is not needed in order to use it skilfully. This does not mean that intimate knowledge of the details of construction of a machine is necessary in order to operate it; it does not mean, for instance, that a sharpshooter must have a profound knowledge of the metallurgy of the metal of which his gun is mainly made, or of the laws of chemistry and physics that apply to powder, or of the laws of ballistics that govern the flight of the bullet to its target. But it does mean that any skilful handler of any machine must know how to use it; that a sharpshooter, for instance, must know how to use his machine—the gun.

Of course, a sharpshooter's skill is exercised in operating under very limited conditions, the conditions of shooting; and it does not include necessarily the maintenance of his gun in good condition. The operating of some machines, however, includes the maintenance of those machines; and a simple illustration is that of operating an automobile. An automobile is constructed to be operated at considerable distances from home; and a man whose knowledge and skill were limited to steering, stopping, starting, and backing the car—who had no

---

these discussions), combat effectiveness is proportional to the square of the number of forces but only in direct proportion (i.e., linearly) with the individual effectiveness of each unit. That is why the advantage of superiority, measured in the difference in the number of survivors, was not as striking for superior gunnery effectiveness as it was for superior numerical force.

knowledge of its details of construction and could not repair a trifling injury—would have very little value as a chauffeur.

A like remark might truthfully be made about the operation of any complex machine; and the more complex the machine, the more aptly the remark would apply. The chief engineer of any electric plant, of any municipal water-works, of any railroad, of any steamship must have the most profound and intimate knowledge of the details of construction and the method of operation of the machine committed to his charge. Recognition of this fact by the engineering profession is so complete and perfect as to be almost unconscious; and no man whose reasoning faculties had been trained by the exact methods of engineering could forget it for a moment. The whole structure of that noble science rests on facts that have been demonstrated to be facts, and the art rests on actions springing from those facts; and neither the science nor the art would now exist, if machines created by engineering skill had been committed to the charge of men unskilled.

It is obvious that the more complicated in construction any machine is, the more time and study are needed to understand it fully; and that the more complicated its method of operation is, the more practice is needed in order to attain skill in operating it.

The more simple the method of operation, the more closely a machine approaches automatism; but even automatic machines are automatic only in so far as their internal mechanisms are concerned; and the fact of their being automatic does not eliminate the necessity for skill in using them. An automatic gun, for instance, no matter how perfectly automatically it discharges bullets, may be fired at an advancing enemy skilfully or unskilfully, effectively or ineffectively.[34]

34. This entire section on the knowledge of his machine required of a naval officer seems as relevant and carefully said now as when it was written. Artificial intelligence is a subject currently under much discussion. This observer recalls a lecturer at the Naval Postgraduate School who startled

In operating some machines, such as a soldier's rifle, or a billiard cue, the number of mental, nervous, and muscular operations is apparently very few; yet every physician knows that the number is very great indeed, and the operations extremely complex—complex beyond the knowledge of the psychologist, physicist, chemist, and biologist. The operation of more complex mechanisms, such as automobiles, seems to be more difficult, because the operator has more different kinds of things to do. Yet that it is really more difficult may be doubted for two reasons; one being that each single operation is of a more simple nature, and the other reason being that we know that a much higher degree of skill is possessed by a great billiardist than by an automobile chauffeur. Of course, the reason of this may be that competition among billardists has been much more keen than among chauffeurs; but even if this be true, it reminds us that *the difficulty of operating any machine depends on the degree of skill exacted.* It also reminds us that, if a machine is to be operated in competition with another machine, the skill of the operator should be as great as it can be made.

The steaming competitions that have been carried on in our navy for several years are examples on a large scale of competitive trials of skill in operating machines. These machines are very powerful, very complex, very important; and that supreme skill shall be used in operating them is very important too. For this reason, every man in the engineering department of every ship, from the chief engineer himself to the youngest coal-passer, is made to pass an examination of some kind, in order that no man may be put into any position for

---

his audience by saying the artificial intelligence required in a machine that performs simple physical acts like throwing and lifting are on the whole more difficult to emulate than many mental processes. Evidently Fiske would have been less surprised at his remarks than most other laymen in the field of AI.

which he is unfit, and no man advanced to any position until he has shown himself qualified for it, both by performance in the grade from which he seeks to rise, and by passing a professional examination as to the duties in the grade to which he desires to rise.

The same principles apply to all machines; and the common sense of mankind appreciates them, even if the machines are of the human type. A captain of a company of soldiers, in all armies and in all times, has been trained to handle a specific human machine; so has the captain of a football team, so has the rector of a church. The training that each person receives gives him such a subconscious sense of the weights and uses of the various parts of the machine, that he handles them almost automatically—and not only automatically but instantly. The captain on the bridge, when an emergency confronts him, gives the appropriate order instantly.

Now the word "machine" conveys to the minds of most of us the image of an engine made of metal, the parts of which are moved by some force, such as the expansive force of steam. But machines were in use long before the steam-engine came, and one of the earliest known to man was man himself—the most perfect machine known to him now, and one of the most complicated and misused; for who of us does not know of some human machine of the most excellent type, that has been ruined by the ignorance or negligence of the man to whose care it was committed?

A machine is in its essence an aggregation of many parts, so related to each other and to some external influence, that the parts can be made to operate together, to attain some desired end or object. From this point of view, which the author believes to be correct, a baseball team is a machine, so is a political party, so is any organization.

Before the days of civilization, machines were few in type; but as civilization progressed, the necessity for organizations of many kinds grew up, and organizations of many kinds appeared. Then the necessity for knowledge of how to operate those organizations brought about certain professions, first that of the military, second that of the priesthood, and later those of the law, medicine, engineering, etc. As time has gone on, the preparation required for these professions, especially the progressive professions, has become increasingly difficult and increasingly demanded; and the members of the professions have become increasingly strict in their requirements of candidates for membership.

Now the profession that is the most strict of all, that demands the greatest variety of qualifications, and the earliest apprenticeship, is the military. The military profession serves on both the land and the sea, in armies and navies; and while both the land and the sea branches are exacting in their demands, the sea or naval branch is the more exacting of the two; by reason of the fact that the naval profession is the more esoteric, the more apart from the others, the more peculiar. In all the naval countries, suitable youths are taken in hand by their governments and initiated into the "mysteries" of the naval profession—mysteries that would always remain mysteries to them, if their initiation were begun too late in life. Many instances are known of men who obtained great excellence in professions which they entered late in life; but not one instance in the case of a man who entered the naval profession late in life. And though some civilian heads of navies have shown great mental capacity, and after—say three years'—incumbency have shown a comprehension of naval matters greater than might have been expected, none has made a record of performance like those of the naval ministers of Germany and Japan; or of Admiral Barham, as first lord of the admiralty, or Sir John Fisher as first sea lord, in England.[35]

35. This excessive scorn of the military late-comer can be attributed to Fiske's frustration under Secretary Daniels, whom he regarded as a naval

A navy is so evidently a machine that the expression "naval machine" has often been applied to it. It is a machine that, both in peace and in war, must be handled by one man, no matter how many assistants he may have. If a machine cannot be made to obey the will of one man, it is not one machine. If two men are needed, at least two machines are to be operated; if three men are needed there are at least three machines, etc. One fleet is handled by one man, called the commander-in-chief. If there are two commanders-in-chief, there are two fleets; and these two fleets may act in conjunction, in opposition, or without reference to each other.

The fact of a machine being operated by one man does not, however, prevent the machine from comprising several machines, operated by several men. A vessel of war, for instance, is operated as a unit by one man; the words "vessel of war," meaning not only the inert hull, but all the parts of personnel and material that make a vessel of war. The captain does not handle each individual machine or man; but he operates the mechanism and the personnel, by means of which all the machines and men are made to perform their tasks.

Now the naval machine is composed of many machines, but the machines that have to be "operated" in war, using the word "operated" in the usual military sense, are only the active fleet, the bureaus and offices and the bases; including in the bases any navy-yards within them. Using the word "operated" still more technically, the only thing to be operated in

---

amateur. This observer was once taken to task for expressing a viewpoint parallel with Fiske's by a friend who pointed out that the Combat Information Center as we now know it was the World War II creation of Naval Reserve officers, in only for the duration. Some had an interest in electronics absent among regulars, along with a certain detachment that permitted them to see how to blend radar, radio communications, and displays into a vital, nearly invisible component of air combat effectiveness. There are other examples of successful amateurs, especially in the fields of strategy, logistics, and technology, who learned very quickly on the job.

war is the fleet: but the head of the Navy Department must also so direct the logistical efforts of the bureaus and offices and bases, that the fleet shall be given the material in fuel, supplies, and ammunition with which to conduct those operations. Like the chief engineer of a ship, he must both operate and maintain the machine.[36]

The fleet itself is a complex machine, even in time of peace. In war time it is more so, for the reason that many additions are made to the fleet when war breaks out; and these additions, being largely of craft and men held in reserve, or brought in hurriedly from civil life, cannot be so efficient or so reliable as are the parts of the fleet that existed in time of peace.

The active fleet consists of battleships, battle cruisers, cruisers of various speeds and sizes, destroyers, submarines, and aircraft. The fleet is under the immediate command of its commander-in-chief, just as the New York naval station is under the command of its commandant; but the commander-in-chief of the fleet is just as strictly under the command of the head of the admiralty or Navy Department as is the commandant. The commander-in-chief is the principal part of the naval machine that is operated in war; and the ultimate success of the naval machine in war depends largely on the amount and degree of understanding that exists between the commander-in-chief and the head of the Navy Department. That goodwill and kindly feeling should exist between them may be assumed, since both have the same object in view; but that real understanding should exist between them is more difficult to assume, especially if they have been trained in different schools and have not known each other until late in life. In the latter case, misunderstandings are apt to arise, as time goes on; and if they do, the most cordial good feeling

36. In this paragraph Fiske all but defines naval "operational art." His analogy of the navy as a coherent fighting machine helps to cut through the complexity and see the tasks at their essence.

may change into mutual distrust and suspicion, and even hatred. To see that such things have happened in the past, we do not have to look further back in history than the records of our own Civil War, especially the records of the mutual relations of the head of the War Department and some generals. That a situation equally grave did not exist between the head of the Navy Department and any of the admirals may be attributed to the fact that the number of naval defeats was less than the number of defeats on land, to the lesser number of persons in the navy, and to the smaller number of operations. Perhaps a still greater reason was the greater confidence shown by civilians in their ability to handle troops, compared with their confidence in their ability to handle fleets.

Even between the Navy Department and the officers, however, mutual respect and understanding can hardly be said to have existed. This did not prevent the ultimate triumph of the Union navy; but that could hardly have been prevented by any means, since the Union navy was so much superior to the Confederate.[37]

Co-operation between the Navy Department and the Fleet.—In any war with a powerful navy, into which the U.S. navy may enter, the question of co-operation between the department and the fleet will be the most important factor in the portentous situation that will face us. We shall be confronted with the necessity of handling the most complex and powerful machine known to man with the utmost possible skill; and any lack of understanding between the fleet and the department, and any slowness of apprehension or of action by the department, may cause a national disaster. One of the

37. Fiske exposes his, and his navy's, fundamental blindness to joint operations in this paragraph: the War Department and the army generals are creatures apart from the Navy Department and its admirals. The U.S. Navy is still in the process of thinking out defense problems as an interrelated whole.

most important dangers to be guarded against will be loss of time. In naval operations the speed of movement of the forces is so great that crises develop and pass with a rapidity unexampled formerly; so that delays of any kind, or due to any causes, must be prevented if that be possible. If a swordsman directs a thrust at the heart, the thrust must be parried—*in time.*[38]

38. It is fitting that Fiske ends with words on time and timeliness.

APPENDIX A

FLEET TACTICS

When鲁 rear admiral fiske was in command at sea in 1915, the U.S. Navy's tactics for operating the fleet as a unit were sketchy. Attached is Fiske's approach to fleet combat doctrine. He was concerned with three elements of tactics: first, what to do; second, organizing to do it; and third, training to do it quickly and efficiently. His fighting instructions were a model of clarity, precision, and conciseness for their time. It is worth considering whether a similarly clear, precise, and concise basis for a modern set of fighting instructions is possible for the fleet today.

The original document is contained in the Naval War College Archives, RG 8, Box 107, XTAG.

UNITED STATES ATLANTIC FLEET
First Division

No. 729.   U.S.S. "FLORIDA", Flagship,
                            Charleston, S.C.,
                            November 19, 1912.

From: Rear Admiral B. A. Fiske, U.S.N., (Senior Member,
      Tactical Board)
To: Fleet Tactical Board.

Subject: Fleet Tactics

GENERAL CONSIDERATIONS.

1. Inasmuch as the work outlined for the Board is of a very general character, and it will probably be difficult to hold many meetings, I beg leave to present the following general considerations to the Board, in order to start the work.

2. The fact that none of us can be said to have had very much experience in fleet tactics, or even in tactical drills, seems to make it impossible for the Board to state any opinions dogmatically, or to make any recommendations except tentatively, and modestly.

3. In making the following suggestions to the Board, I wish it to be clearly understood that I have not myself, personally, come to any decided views. The present status of our system of fleet tactics seems to me to have some defects; and I take this opportunity to bring them to the attention of the Board, with the idea that the Board may determine whether, in their opinion, they are defects, and, if so, if any means can be suggested for remedying them; or whether it would be better, before formulating opinions, to undertake some systematic investigations as to the relative advantages and disadvantages of certain formations and evolutions.

4. As a starting point, it seems desirable to come to an understanding as to the scope of "fleet tactics." Before doing this we must first agree as to what is a "fleet."

5. Probably there will be little disagreement as to the proposition that a fleet is a unit made up of a number of vessels of different classes, that unit being subdivided into as many parts as there are classes, and those classes being again subdivided into squadrons, divisions and groups.

6. Our Atlantic Fleet is divided into battleships, cruisers, torpedo vessels, submarines and auxiliaries; and these classes of vessels are subdivided into squadrons, divisions and groups.

7. These classes are wholly distinct from each other. They are so distinct that they must be handled according to different principles; and though they may act in conjunction with each other, there are very few conditions under which they would act absolutely together. It is easy to realize battleships acting together, destroyers acting together, submarines acting together and auxiliaries acting together; but it is impossible to imagine a battleship, a destroyer, a submarine and an auxiliary acting together in the same sense as that in which four battleships are said to act together.

8. In order to have a system of fleet tactics which may be of the maximum value in a war, it seems clear that it should be designed for use against a fleet of a strength about equal to ours. It would seem idle to attempt to devise a system of tactics for use against a fleet much more powerful, and foolish to devise a system for use against a fleet decidedly inferior; and not only because this is the natural basis to work on, but because a real war with a fleet practically equal to ours would be not only more important and more critical but more probable.

9. It is also suggested, for the consideration of the Board, that the fleet tactics used by the United States Navy in peace should be those which the United States Navy would use if we should go to war in the near future. If this idea be correct, then our fleet tactics should be designed for the ships which we have now, and will have in the next two or three years; and should not be designed for any ships, or any kinds of ships, which we do not have now or expect to have in the very near future. That is, we should not in our fleet exercises, assume, as we sometimes have done, that a cruiser is a battleship, or an armored cruiser is a scout, or that a destroyer is anything except a destroyer; but we should exercise on the basis that the various ships are exactly what they are. Of course, this does not mean that we might not oppose to our fleet in an assumed battle, some vessels, say destroyers, representing say the fast battleship wing of an en-

emy; but it does mean that the ships which we are using as United States ships should be distinctly the United States ships which we have or expect to have very soon.

10. It is also suggested, that our tactics and war games should represent conditions which probably may occur within the next two or three years. This would mean, for instance, that we should not engage our fleet against submarines near the coast, or anchor our battleships in the vicinity of destroyers; because these are things which we would probably not do in any war in the near future. There is unquestionably in the Service a widespread doubt as to the practical value of many of our formations and evolutions; a feeling that our System of Tactics is not a system of tactics at all, but merely a collection of drills, in which officers are exercised at grouping and regrouping ships in arbitrary formations, many of which have no military value.

Cruising Tactics, Approach Tactics and Battle Tactics.

11. Tactics may be divided into three parts, Cruising Tactics, Approach Tactics, and Battle Tactics.

Cruising Tactics

12. Cruising Tactics may be divided into two parts: Peace Cruising Tactics and War Cruising Tactics. Peace Cruising Tactics would naturally govern simply the going of a naval fleet from one place to another in time of peace; War Cruising Tactics would govern the formations, maneuvers and general disposition of the fleet, including the train while making speed at sea in time of war.

13. Peace Cruising Tactics, so far as absolute necessity is concerned, do not seem to need any other formation than the column. It is evident that a fleet can go all over the ocean, enter and leave all ports, without using any other formation. With a great number of ships, however, it would probably be convenient, though not necessary, to put the fleet into more columns.

14. War Cruising Tactics do not seem to require complicated formations; but if there be a train to be protected, scouts to be handled, and destroyers to be maneuvered, it would seem that some simple formations should be adopted in which the various units could be handled by their own commanders largely at their own discretion,

though in obedience to the instructions from the Commander-in-Chief. The speed in the case of the scouts would be that of the slowest in the formation, and the formation need not, probably, be deviated from materially until battle became imminent.

APPROACH TACTICS

15. Approach Tactics would include the handling of an actual fighting force in the immediate presence of the enemy, but beyond the reach of the enemy's gun fire.

16. Approach Tactics seem to be those which comprise the greater part of the tactics prescribed in our Signal Book. As these tactics are to be carried on while not under gun fire, it seems obvious that every formation and maneuver should be used which the Commander-in-Chief might need in the vicinity of the enemy. Inasmuch, however, as we know from long experience that we get very little time for tactical drills, and as it is highly important that in time of war we should make no mistakes in handling our vessels and fleets, it is suggested that no formation or maneuver should be included in our scheme of proposed tactics whose usefulness cannot be explicitly stated and described, in order that our efforts may be concentrated in getting the utmost skill in making the maneuvers we would actually use in war. Inasmuch as every Commander-in-Chief will realize when near the enemy, that he must not be brought to a serious battle when not in column, or with his divisions and squadrons separated, we seem led to question the necessity for having many formations, and therefore the necessity for having many evolutions or maneuvers. Is there any necessity, for instance, for any compound formation whatever? If there be no necessity for any compound formation, then there is no necessity for changing from a simple to a compound formation, or from a compound to a simple formation. If we could eliminate all compound formations, we could cut down our tactical work by more than a half; and this would give us whatever time we can spend on tactical drills for drilling at handling our vessels under conditions such as we would handle them in battle, or in the approach to battle.

17. If we have any compound formations such as line of divisions then we must have also column of divisions; because just as soon as we go ships right or left from line of divisions we find ourselves in column of divisions. And the handling of these separate units as one unit (fleet), wherein all the divisions, squadrons and ships are com-

pelled to devote a great deal of attention to keeping exact bearings and distances, is not an easy matter, even in peace times and in good weather. If we have such a formation as line of divisions, and try to direct the whole fleet as a unit, (as we do now), then we must have also many signals and maneuvers whereby this collection of many units can be turned in any direction; and the formation changed to column and vice versa; and this necessitates most of the difficult maneuvers which are found in the Signal Book.

18. It need not be supposed that, even if such formations as line of divisions or line of squadrons were eliminated, the Commander-in-Chief would be debarred from sending any division or any squadron in any direction that he wished, or to any place; but if he did so detach any division, squadron or ship, that squadron, division or ship would be sent for a specific purpose, and would be handled directly by its commander, who would devote his energies to carrying out the object intended, and not to keeping at a certain distance and direction from the flagship, prescribed in the Signal Book. If, for instance, the Second Squadron of our present fleet should be sent off, say to the eastward, for any purposes, the purpose itself would indicate the proper bearing and distance of the squadron from the fleet flagship; and the commander of the squadron would maneuver it accordingly. In other words, it may be suggested that whatever reason there would be for having the fleet divided up into separate columns or detachments would carry with it the idea that those separate columns or detachments would, by the very intention, be separate, and not simply a part of a solid fleet, and would not be required to keep, a fixed geometrical relation to the rest of the fleet.

19. Cruising Tactics and Approach Tactics would not seem to require that the personnel should occupy battle stations; but approach tactics would seem to require that the personnel should be able to take up their battle stations very quickly before gun fire should begin.

BATTLE TACTICS

20. Battle Tactics would include the handling of a fighting force while actually under gun fire.

21. In a war with a fleet practically equal to ours, it seems logical to suppose that both fleets would be kept concentrated as much as possible. This does not mean that circumstances might not make it

advisable, or even necessary, to send parts of our fleets on detached service at times; but it does mean that when the critical battle occurs, we must have all our fleet at the place of battle, and fitted in the best possible way to fight it.

22. It seems plain that we should keep clearly before our eyes the fact that the most important duty that our fleet will have to do in the next war will be not so much to "conduct operations," not so much to "scout," or "to convoy," or to move across the ocean, as to fight a stand-up, pitched battle, just as brutal as any battles that have ever occurred in the past, which will be decided in the same way as that in which battles have always been decided, simply by ability to inflict injury, and ability to withstand injury.

23. Of course this does not mean that we should neglect schemes for scouting and receiving information, or ignore questions of logistics and supplies, but it does mean that these questions must not be allowed to cloud our minds to the fact that the principal thing that our fleet will have to do will be to fight a battle like the Battle of Tsushima; and the question with us will be simply whether in that battle we shall play the role of the Japanese or the role of the Russians. A great many reasons have been given why the Russians were whipped so quickly, and a great deal of fault has been found with the Russians for what they did preliminary to the battle, and a great deal of praise has been given to the Japanese for what they did preliminary to the battle; but the real thing which decided that battle was the fact that the Japanese hit the Russians with their projectiles more often than the Russians hit the Japanese. The Russian ships may have been dirty, may have been undisciplined, may have had too much coal on, and the Russian Commander-in-Chief may not have conducted his fleet to Asia as wisely as he might; but if, when he came to the actual battle, he had hit the Japanese with his projectiles more often than the Japanese had hit him, the Russians would have been the victors and not the Japanese.

24. There seems to be no reason why a similar battle would not be reenacted between two fleets in any naval war of the near future. It is true that we can imagine cruisers, destroyers and auxiliaries merged in the organization of the various divisions and squadrons of the fleet in such a way that when any squadron or division was acting singly the cruisers and destroyers would be maneuvered by the Division or Squadron Commander. But even if the various vessels were so merged, we can hardly imagine them remaining with their divisions in an actual hotly contested battle, without doing

more harm than good; and there has no plan yet been devised, so far as is known, which breaks up the battle column of the battleships. In other words, even if the smaller vessels of a fleet should be so assigned to the divisions, that each division would contain all the various kinds of vessels in the fleet; yet nevertheless, in an actual big battle at sea, it seems that the battleships would have to be maneuvered separately as one force, the destroyers as another, the submarines as another, and the auxiliaries as another.

25. If it be realized that the whole endeavor of a commander of any fighting force is to deliver the greatest possible blow at a given point, or points, and if it be further realized that at the present time, and in the near future, the gun will be the controlling weapon in any probable sea battle, then we seem forced to the conclusion that the most important part of fleet tactics is the tactics of the battleship column, or columns. The problem of the individual tactics of destroyers, submarines and auxiliaries, and the problem of the handling of those arms (considered as units in themselves) by the Commander-in-Chief of the fleet may also be taken up; but, inasmuch as the actual result of the battle will almost certainly depend upon the success of the battleships, it would seem that the first and most urgent thing to consider is the best system of fleet tactics for bringing a large number of battleships into battle and fighting them with the maximum effect.

26. Probably we all agree that the best form in which to fight battleships on the open sea, is column; though we will probably also agree the column must be modified from time to time by being made into line of bearing and line.

27. This being the case, one might ask why should we not always drill our fleet in this simple formation? Why drill at a lot of complicated evolutions in compound formations? The answer might be that there would be nothing to drill at, that anybody can steam in column, and that it is such a simple formation that there is no special skill to be derived, and therefore no practice is needed.

28. But maybe this idea is erroneous. There are many things which it is easy to do, but there are few of these which it is easy to do well. It is easy to play billiards, but it takes years of persistent practice to enable one to play well. The same thing is true of any art; and if we should attempt to carry out the handling of a column of twenty ships, and attempt, at the same time, to keep an active "enemy" on a certain bearing, to guard against quick changes of rudder and speed, and to provide for the casualties that would

probably occur under gunfire, we might find that we had a good deal to learn.

29. I, personally have never seen a column being drilled at changing course very gradually, as a column would have to do under battle plan No. 1; and yet it is obvious that it must be rather difficult to do it, especially if everybody is at his battle station.

30. We have not devoted much thought to this maneuver. We are quite convinced of the necessity of having an accurate sight-bar range, of keeping up a uniform speed, and of changing the relative bearing of the enemy both from our column and from each ship as little as possible; also of maintaining control of the fleet by the Commander-in-Chief, and of each ship by her captain as long as possible in the battle. And yet we propose fighting at a high speed, regardless of the fact that the very first 12-inch shot that lets water into any one of the rapidly moving ships, (maybe the ship of the Commander-in-Chief itself) is going to cause that ship to slow down immediately. This would disarrange the plan at once, because that ship would either have to be left behind, thus reducing the number of ships, or else the entire column would have to slow down. As this would probably be impracticable, and would produce confusion in the entire column if it were attempted, because no one would know how much to slow down and signals would be difficult, the ship would probably be left behind, and also the next ship that received a similar injury. Our system of tactics has taken no account whatever of this contingency; and yet it is one of the very first contingencies that would occur in battle. Besides, we have no means by which the Commander-in-Chief will be kept informed of every happening in his long column, or by which the slowing down of any ship can be made known to other ships, except by the sheering out of column of that ship. Our tactics even include such disaster producing maneuvers as changing line of bearing as much as *four* points in battle, with all the changes of speed and course produced thereby throughout the entire fleet!

31. In considering whether the one formation, column, (including line and line of bearing), be sufficient for time of war, it must be borne in mind that at the present time destroyers, submarines and mines have become such a menace to battleships, that battleships will have to keep pretty well away from land, at least from land in possession of the enemy. But if one fleet keeps away from the land, the other fleet will have to keep away from the land also, if it is to fight the first fleet. This seems to mean that in any probable battle

359

between large fleets, the fleets will be out on the open ocean, with plenty of sea-room. A probable "objective," or cause of battle, will be the attempt of one fleet to drive off another, which is attacking a trade route, or perhaps is supporting "commerce destroyers" that are cruising on a trade route.

32. It is true that history does not bear out this statement; but it would seem that fleets are now in a different category from any that they have ever been in before. Fleets have never before been under the necessity of keeping away from the land, but they are now under that necessity. It may seem at first glance that this necessity of keeping away from the land impairs a great deal the efficiency of an attack of a fleet upon the enemy's coast. Doubtless this is true in a measure; in other words, destroyers, submarines and mines have brought about such a condition that the enemy's fleet must keep away from the coast. But nevertheless, under the conditions of sea trade now prevailing, a fleet even far off the coast, may blockade that coast very effectively, by cruising on the trade routes of steamers from its principal ports. A foreign fleet could almost obliterate the entire foreign trade of New York, without going within a hundred miles of the port.

33. If it be true that in the near future, fleet battles will be fought out on the ocean far away from land, it would then seem that, for purposes either of preparation for battle or battle itself, there is no reason why the fleet should not be always in a simple formation. For a fleet, column is what in the Army is called "line of battle." It is the formation in which the guns can be used with the most effect. If a fleet is in column, then it is in "line of battle," and ready for battle, so far as its formation is concerned.

34. But even if the circumstances of war require a fleet to maneuver near a coast, the advantages of keeping in a simple formation seem to remain. In fact, the advantages of keeping in a simple formation seem to be even greater than if there be plenty of sea-room, because the difficulty of handling a large number of ships in compound formation near the shoals and headlands and in the crooked passages that exist in most navigable waters near a coast is exceedingly great—much greater than that of handling them in simple formation. As has been said before, this does not mean that different parts of a fleet may not be sent to different places, or in different directions, for specific purposes; it merely means that if the fleet is to remain in any regular formation wherein the parts maintain fixed relations to each other, the formation in which it is the most easily

handled is column; and next to column come the derivatives of column,—line of bearing, and line.

35. It may be considered that the head or rear of a very long column would be exposed to attack from two sides; that if we had our fleet in one long column and the enemy had his in two columns, the enemy would get the head of our column between his two columns and crush it. But it can hardly be imagined that our Commander-in-Chief would not so maneuver the head of his column as to keep it outside of the enemy's column, so that he could attack one column or the other, or at least threaten it:—either of which maneuvers would compel the enemy to go into column.

36. It may be held that we should continue to have evolutions in compound formations, because they give us excellent drill in handling ships. To this it may be replied that this reason is not, in itself, sufficient, unless there is no other means by which we can get skill in handling ships. It is plain that we need skill in handling ships for two purposes, one is for handling them under the conditions of battle, and the other for handling them under the conditions of peace. If the conditions of war and peace were the same, and if handling ships in compound formations would give us skill for the conditions of both war and peace, then we ought to continue drilling in compound formations. But if the thing which we want to learn to do in battle is to handle one long column, with the utmost skill; and if the things which we want to learn to do in peace are to keep our ships clear of each other and of other vessels, while making passages at sea, and going in and out of port, then clearly, we should have two different exercises for these two different kinds of conditions. Furthermore, when we are having any exercise we should hold clearly in mind the object of that exercise and carry it out in such a way as to achieve that definite object. If we do not do this,—if we have exercise with merely a vague idea of learning to handle ships,—then our tactical exercises will have the same relation to the purposes of tactics that the setting up drill has to the daily life of the men; and will partake more of the nature of what might be called "tactical gymnastics" than of tactical exercises.

37. Our exercises in compound formations do not seem, if carefully analyzed, to be good training for either war or peace. The only training they give is in handling ships in compound formations. They do not train for battle; they do not train for avoiding vessels on the high sea under ordinary conditions, and they do not train for handling ships when going in or out of port, except very indirectly.

If we wish to train the fleet for battle, let us train the fleet in the formation and under the conditions that would prevail in battle; if we wish to train the ships, and the fleet itself, for going in and out of port, let us go in and out of port as often as necessary in order to get the necessary training.

38. Inasmuch as we have never trained our fleet to maneuver in one long column against an enemy going at an unknown speed and in an unknown direction, and since according to Battle Plan No. 1, this is exactly the thing we shall do in battle, why not hold a few exercises with the entire available fleet in one long column, and with some destroyers representing an enemy? In case the two columns go ahead at exactly the same speed, and in exactly the same direction with the various ships abeam of each other, then no special skill will be required, and no training will be had. But, if the two forces meet on the ocean without either knowing the direction in which to expect the other one, the chances are extremely small that those relative formations will be taken up immediately. As both "fleets" will be assumed to want to fight, they will maneuver to bring on a fight, and each one will try to get the advantageous position, relative to the sun and the wind. Approach Tactics will be employed here; and the exercise will clear up our ideas on this matter. After a time, however, perhaps a long time, perhaps a short time, the fleets will line up in columns approximately parallel.

39. After the columns are lined up, the obvious drill for our fleet would seem to be to maneuver so as to keep the enemy's column abeam of our column; and, as far as possible, for each ship to keep her opposite approximately abeam of herself. If the enemy is going at considerably greater speed than we, (say, for instance, if our fleet were going five knots, and the enemy were going fifteen knots), this would result after a while in our fleet being drawn up on an arc of about 90°, steaming around a circle whose radius was 5,000 yards; and the enemy on an arc about 30°, of a circle whose radius was about 15,000 yards. Of course, such relative positions would be very unfavorable to our fleet, and therefore we ought not to allow them to be assumed, unless the time required to take up such positions would prove to be so great that the enemy's force would long before have lost its speed, and therefore be unable to take her position. If our fleet were going five knots and the enemy's fifteen, at the beginning of the gun fire, it is obvious that our fleet would be much less handicapped as regards speed by injuries than the enemy's fleet would; and that it might be that the enemy would be defeated be-

fore he could obtain any position of tactical advantage. In other words, we might find that, under certain conditions, we would more than offset the tactical disadvantage of a lower speed by the greater permanency of conditions and consequent superiority of our gun fire; or, to put the matter in other words, we might make the enemy pay more for his tactical advantage than the tactical advantage would prove to be worth. Exactly what would happen, of course, we do not know, but it does seem that it is exactly what we ought to find out. Instead of wasting the small amount of time that we have to spend on tactical drills, in charging around the ocean, making utterly futile and meaningless maneuvers, why not spend time on finding out something definite? What we want to know is what would happen if two columns of opposing battleships should meet on the ocean, and what to do in consequence. Personally I am under the impression that we would find that there is a good deal to learn, and also a good deal which we could learn, and that we ought to investigate this matter first, and put arbitrary "maneuvers" into a secondary place.

SPEED

40. If a fleet be in column, and if it meets an enemy's fleet, the fleets are bound to line up in columns approximately parallel, and fight.

41. So long as the two fleets are lined up side by side, neither fleet has any tactical advantage over the other. In order to gain a tactical advantage on the open sea, almost the only thing that can be done is to cap the enemy or T him, or approximate that position; and usually this can be done only by the fleet that has the superior speed. The idea of capping or T'ing seems to have taken possession of naval tacticians to such an extent that it is no great exaggeration to state that almost the entire underlying idea of naval tactics now is to cap.

42. In order that we shall be able to cap the enemy as quickly as practicable, our ships must go as fast as practicable. It may be admitted at once that it would be very advantageous if we could cap the enemy; but it was very forcibly imprinted on my mind last August, west of Block Island, when the BLUE force capped the RED force, that although this took place under absolutely ideal conditions, yet, nevertheless, it took a long time to get to that capping position, during which time all our ships were under gun-fire from

all the RED ships; and also that after the capping position had been attained, it could not be maintained long.

43. Under the conditions prevailing on that occasion, BLUE was able to cap RED without going at high speed, by reason of the directions from which RED came relatively to BLUE; and it then occurred to me that we had gained whatever advantage there was in capping, without having to sacrifice anything to attain it; but that under most conditions, such a position would have cost a great deal.

44. I mean that we would have had to pay for it by high speed; and this suggested the question whether we may not have exaggerated the advantages to be gained by high speed and underestimated its various disadvantages.

45. To make plain the meaning of this idea, it may be pointed out that what really decides and always has decided every modern naval battle, with the possible exception of the Battle of Lissa, is *gunfire,* or rather *hits;* and that we ought to determine first what are the best conditions for securing hits, then determine the best tactical plan for obtaining those conditions and preserving them as long as possible in a battle, and then ascertain whether or not high speed is favorable to carrying out that plan.

46. Now there can be no doubt that conditions are favorable to securing hits in proportion as the ship is steady, as everything is quiet, as the change of bearing and distance are small, and as there is an absence of haste in our operations;—also in proportion to the clearness with which we can see the target.

47. Battle will have to be carried on, of course, with the personnel at battle stations; but, clearly, our Battle Tactics should not ignore the fact that these battle stations are not invulnerable and neither are the ships; therefore, our Battle Tactics should be such that favorable conditions will be impaired as little as possible by any damage received. This seems to mean that our formations and maneuvers should be as simple as possible, and as "fool proof" as possible;—also that the speed should be as low as practicable under the circumstances.

48. This does not mean that ships need not be provided with means for going fast, because there is a strategical use for speed, which has nothing whatever to do with its tactical use; and furthermore, all ships, even when going at slow speed in battle, must have a great deal of reserve power, in order to maintain speed in case an injury increases the resistance of the under water body, in order to

back hard if necessary, and in order to take up a high speed, if circumstances should require it.

49. Neither does it mean that there may not be a necessity in battle, for a fleet to go at high speed; but it does mean that we should recognize that this high speed carries with it several distinct disadvantages. Some of these disadvantages are as follows:

(a) A high speed causes greater vibration to a ship, not so much from the engines as from the way the bow meets the waves, thus making it more difficult to use range finders and spotting instruments accurately;

(b) It tends to throw more water over the guns and telescope sights;

(c) It makes more smoke;

(d) In case a smoke pipe is hit, it causes greater and quicker change of speed; and in some cases, a greater amount of smoke between decks;

(e) In case a ship is struck near the water line in such a way as to let in water, the speed of a ship is more reduced. If enough water is let in to reduce the speed of the ship below that of the rest of the fleet, the fleet will either have to slow down, which could not be done without confusion and loss of accuracy of gun fire, or else the ship would have to be left behind, and the size of the fleet reduced;

(f) It reduces the number of ships that could fight in column, because some of the older ships would not be able to keep up;

(g) Under most circumstances, it increases the disturbing influences of the wind.

50. It may seem at a first glance, that one item mentioned above, that of the effect of high speed on the range finders, is hardly worthy of consideration; but it is believed that a more careful consideration of this matter would show that this is very important. Of all the factors that go to make up the accuracy of gun fire, the most important single factor is the determination of the sight-bar range. This matter has not received the consideration that its importance deserves; but a very simple calculation will show that, say at 10,000 yards, a 12-inch gun of 2,700 f.s. whose sight-bar range was given it with an error of only 50 yards would hit its target twelve and one-half times as often as it would if its sight-bar range were in error one hundred fifty yards. The enormous advantage which could thus be obtained, which would put twelve ships on an equality with one hundred fifty ships is many times greater than any advantage attainable by any tactical maneuver or disposition of forces, and can be

gotten under average conditions, by taking the proper measures. It is a matter of fact that a fifteen-foot range finder, used under good conditions of quietness, can determine a range of 10,000 yards with an average error much less than fifty yards; but the disturbing effects of wind and vibration are so great that this error can be very easily increased to one hundred fifty yards, and even much more. Not only is the error increased by unfavorable conditions of wind and vibration, but the rapidity of the observations is very much lessened; so that there are frequent long intervals, when no range whatever can be obtained. It is true that range clocks, and other apparatus, are in use; but these apparatus all require knowledge of the movements of the enemy which we might not be able to obtain in a battle, and probably could not, except approximately.

51. The reason why a seemingly small change in the conditions under which guns are fired makes a great deal of difference in the percentage of hits may not seem clear at first. But it may become clear if we realize how small a change in the way in which a gun is pointed will make the difference between a miss or hit, when the target is small and the probability of hitting also small. Of course, the smaller the percentage of probability, the greater the change in probability which is produced by any error. For instance, if the probability of hitting under given conditions were 1%, and the probability of missing 99%, then any improvement in the conditions under which the guns were fired, by which the chance of missing was decreased from 99% to 98%—(about 1%)—would double the chance of hitting! Similarly, if the chance of hitting were 10% and the chance of missing 90% (which may be assumed as, roughly, service condition), then any improvement which, by lessening the errors, reduced the chance of missing from 90% to 80%, would increase the chance of hitting from 10% to 20%. That is, if by care in avoiding sources of error we reduce the chance of missing by about 11%, we *double* the chance of hitting. In other words, we double the h.p.g.p.m. [hits per guns per minute].

RUDDER ANGLE

52. While large angles of rudder are undoubtedly necessary at times, and while it is clear that the present ability of ships to turn in small circles must not be surrendered, nevertheless, it would seem that *for tactical purposes* it might be better to use small angles.

53. At present it seems to be the idea that, in making the ap-

proach for a battle, ships should approach at quite a sharp angle, and then make a sudden turn, just previous to opening gun-fire. This is the plan used in target practice for the last few years; but it is suggested that this is exactly what a fleet ought not to do. In the First Division, when firing under Plan "B", we found that, if a ten-degree angle was used, the guns could be kept on the target with great success; but that this could not be done if standard rudder of about 17° were used.

54. Clearly every means should be employed which will increase the h.p.g.p.m., and all things avoided [which] will decrease them.

55. This seems to mean that we should approach at a small angle, and make gradual turns.

Night Maneuvers

56. We have been exercising at night maneuvers for several years, with little if any, definite result. We know little more than we did twenty years ago in regard to the best way to repel destroyers at night, and everybody seems to feel that about the only thing to do is to extinguish all lights, spread a "screen" out at least five miles away, and realize that if a destroyer gets within torpedo range we cannot prevent her from firing her torpedo at us.

57. This being the case, would it not be better to drop these highly picturesque and laborious maneuvers for a while, and devote our time and our energies and our mental faculties to solving the practical and urgent problem of how to fight a column of battle-ships in the daytime?

58. This will not prevent our putting out lights whenever we wish to do so, while cruising at night, and making whatever observations we wish as to visibility under different states of the weather, handling screens, etc. Apparently this is about all we can do, until some genius invents what may be called a "megaphote," that will enable us to see in the night-time. Such an invention, by the way, does not seem theoretically impossible.

(Signed) B. A. FISKE

APPENDIX B

THE TORPEDO PLANE

B RADLEY FISKE WAS AN early enthusiast of naval aviation. Moreover, he immediately went beyond the obvious potential of aircraft for scouting (reconnaissance and spotting of the fall of shots) and strove to develop aircraft that could strike crippling blows. Destroyer-delivered torpedoes being a potentially devastating weapon at the time, it was natural that his fertile mind saw the possibility of marrying the speed and range of aircraft with the wallop of the torpedo to create a decisive weapon. The accompanying lecture, delivered to the students at the U.S. Naval War College on 11 September 1919, exhibits the rhetorical skill, technological knowledge, and strategic breadth that Fiske was able to combine into a tight little half-hour sermon on one aspect of naval warfare.

The original document is contained in the Naval War College Archives, Naval Historical Collection, Lectures, RG 15, Box 3.

THE TORPEDO-PLANE

On page 9 of the Monthly Information Bulletin issued by the Office of Naval Intelligence July 15, 1919, is the declaration, "A ship of the FURIOUS or ARGUS type with 12 to 15 torpedo-planes, should be a match for a whole Battleship Division." While regarding this as an exaggerated declaration, I believe the subject of the torpedo-plane to be nevertheless of sufficient importance to warrant my asking your attention as strategists to its possibilities, and to the desirability of not being too slow in studying the degree and direction of its correct employment.

Before starting on the subject of the Torpedo-plane, I wish to ask your attention to the fact that the whole art of war consists in directing the employment of weapons. Even when the only weapons of warfare were the fists of the human body, the art of war consisted in handling weapons; and now when the art of war consists in handling weapons and instruments and methods of the highest possible complexity and power, the art of war still consists in handling weapons. The more numerous and complicated and powerful the weapons, the more numerous and complicated and complete must be the plans which strategy must devise and carry into effect. The difficulties have become so great, and the plans have become so complicated, that some strategists seem to have lost sight of the fact that the art of war is merely the art of fighting, and to concern themselves wholly with plans, with an apparent forgetfulness of the objects of the plans. They seem to devote their attention so much to the means to the end as to forget the end itself.

To such an extreme has this idea of strategy advanced, that one may often hear the declaration that strategy should not concern itself with the material appliances of war, but only with the plans by which the weapons and the ships and men carrying those weapons can be brought to the field of battle. Any army or navy is not restricted, of course, to adopting any conception of strategy that it may choose; but it may be pointed out that if two nations contend in war, and if one nation limits its view of strategy and the efforts of its strategists to the mere planning of how to use the appliances which it already possesses, while its enemy directs the efforts of its strategists first to obtaining the most effective weapons and second to using them, the second nation will enter war much better prepared than the other.

Let us not forget that weapons precede the methods formulated to employ them, and that therefore the first effort of strategy must be to get the best weapons, and the second effort must be to employ them skillfully. Writers on strategy are too prone, it seems to me, to belittle the value of the mechanician in war, and to exalt the man who employs the weapons that the mechanician furnishes.

It is not necessary to go into a detailed account of the influence of weapons on war; for you doubtless remember that the success of

Alexander in Asia, and still more of Caesar in Gaul, were due in great measure to the superiority of their weapons and appliances over the weapons and appliances of their antagonists. You remember, too, that the superiority of the English archers over the French armored knights at the Battle of Cressy in 1346, not only achieved a victory, but wholly obliterated the knight in armor from warfare, and put an end to the feudal system. You doubtless remember the effect of the needle-gun in the war between Prussia and Austria, and realize that supplying the Prussian army with that needle-gun was the most effective single part of all the Prussian strategic preparation. You also know that the building of the MONITOR and her subsequent victory over the MERRIMAC, was the real cause of the victory of the North over the South; that the most important cause of the Japanese victory over the Russians was the superiority of the Japanese gunnery appliances that were used at the Battle of Tsushima; and that the most important single factor in whatever measure of success the Germans achieved in the last Great War was the submarine. Instances might of course be multiplied; but enough instances have probably been mentioned to justify the declaration that strategy should concern itself with the weapons of war, as well as with the methods of using them.

Of course, this does not mean that strategy should concern itself with the details of the weapons or other material appliances. Those things, of course, come within the province of logistics,—which is an assistant of strategy.

Coming now to the subject of the Torpedo-plane, I beg leave to point out that the vessels which are used in the Navy, and which are sent hither and thither in your strategic and tactical games, are of no value in themselves for purposes of war, except in that they carry guns and torpedoes. Let us remember that the value of any vessel for the purposes of national defense or offense is proportional to the destructive power which she can exert at a point, and the speed with which she can get to that point. The ideal vessel of war would be one which could carry an infinite amount of destructive power with infinite speed. Such vessels are unobtainable; but this fact should not blind us to the further fact that our aim should be to come as close to them as practicable, and secure appliances which convey the most destructive weapons at the greatest speed. In military operations these appliances would seem to be bombing aeroplanes, and in naval operations—torpedo-planes. At the present time, the radius of action of the aeroplanes is so comparatively small, that, for distant operations, it is necessary to use seaplane ships to carry the aeroplanes till within a short distance of the enemy. I believe the first instance of doing this on an extensive scale in war was in the latter part of December, 1914, when the British sent a seaplane ship to the vicinity of Cuxhaven, and there liberated aeroplanes that bombed the base there and its vicinity. This was nearly five years ago. The Monthly Information Bulletin states that the ARGUS of 15,750 tons displacement and 20 knots speed, is fitted to carry 20 torpedo-planes; that the EAGLE of 23,000 tons and 24 knots speed, is to carry 23 torpedo-planes; and that every endeavor has been made to get the ARGUS to the fleet as soon as possible.

Let me now ask your attention to the application of these ideas and facts to your studies here. Your problems here are divided into strategic and tactical problems, and in each of those problems both the offensive and the defensive are considered. Imagine that you are studying the problem of sending our fleet offensively to the coasts of some European country or Japan. The last war has shown you that our battleships cannot get very near those coasts, because of submarines, mines, torpedoes, forts, and aeroplanes. What would the fleet do there? Doubtless you answer, "blockade." Doubtless we could blockade; but it may be pointed out that the blockading would have to be done at a considerable distance from the shore, far away from a United States naval base or a drydock, and in constant danger from attack by torpedoes, launched from submarines and aeroplanes. If we sent, however, a large number of swift seaplane carriers, like the ARGUS and EAGLE, each carrying twenty torpedo-planes, and other seaplane carriers equipped with reconnaissance and bombing planes, they could avoid the enemy's battleships, and not only attack all surface craft, but also do very effective work against land defenses; not being deterred by such obstacles as shoals, mines, submarines and forts.

Please consider also the case of preventing a blockade of our own coast by a foreign fleet. That fleet could easily be located by our aeroplanes; but the task of attacking it would be one of great difficulty, unless we had a fleet considerably superior. If we had two or three hundred torpedo-planes, however, distributed along our coast, those torpedo-planes could be concentrated on the enemy fleet within a very few hours. If an enemy fleet, for instance, was sixty miles from Newport, any torpedo-planes here could attack that enemy fleet in an hour, and come back for more torpedoes.

In this connection, it is important to realize that the torpedo is a weapon that is rapidly improving. I was recently told in confidence at the Torpedo Station, and of course, I am justified in repeating it to you, that we have a torpedo which has gone 16,700 yards, and that a range of 20,000 yards will soon be easily attained. I was also told that they have been getting good results with the plan that you of course have heard of, by which a torpedo may be set to run a certain distance in a given direction, then turn to the right, then to the left, and so forth. This enables us to shoot into a harbor, and have the torpedo hunt around the harbor until it hits something, or exhausts its fuel. It also enables us to fire at a column of battleships from either ahead or on the flank and have several chances of hitting, even if the ship first aimed at is missed. I was also told that a plan that I went to the Torpedo Station to suggest had been undergoing experimental work for nearly two years, and that success was now practically certain. This plan is to explode a torpedo *under* a ship, where it is the weakest, by utilizing the magnetic force of the ship itself. As you may know, the Germans used this plan with some measure of success.

These improvements in the torpedo and the great things that we were about to do with novel appliances when the war closed, impel me to suggest that the War College endeavor to forsee and to forecast the use of novel appliances, so that when the next war breaks out, we shall have those appliances and the methods for employing them instantly available. To me the appliances that seem to promise the greatest usefulness are aeroplanes, because they can carry the most destructive instrumentalities at the greatest speed. *It may be that the ARGUS and the EAGLE are the prototypes of the battleship of the future.*

APPENDIX C

Lieutenant J. V. Chase's Force-on-Force Effectiveness Model for Battle Lines

I N A FOOTNOTE on page 240 of *The Navy as a Fighting Machine* Fiske alludes to a development similar to his own by Rear Admiral Jehu Valentine Chase using "an application of the calculus" done in 1902. Chase wrote his equations three years before Fiske first published his salvo method in "American Naval Policy" (1905), and thirteen years before F. W. Lanchester in England and M. Osipov in Russia published their mathematical force-on-force equations. As far as is known, Chase produced the first mathematics exhibiting the square law effect of concentration of force. This is the first publication of his development. His paper was not declassified until 1972, and is a classic example of secret science becoming lost science. It was located in April 1988 by Professor John B. Hattendorf, the co-editor of the Classics of Sea Power series, in the Naval War College Archives, RG 8, Box 109, XTAV (1902).

Chase's short 1902 paper consists of a cover sheet, a page of introductory text, and two pages of mathematical development. Chase was on duty at the Naval War College at the time and directed the paper to Lieutenant W. McCarty Little, who was in charge of war-gaming then. In the War College Archives are also eight pages of handwritten notes and ten typed pages written later in 1921 when Chase was a captain. Some of Chase's later comments found in the file indicate that he understood the utility of his equations much as F. W. Lanchester did:

Some years ago (1902) when I was a member of the War College Staff, there was considerable discussion among the members of the staff as to the value of concentration of fire. Most of the statements, pro and con, I noticed, were couched in vague general terms and partook of the nature of statements commonly termed "glittering generalities." I was not satisfied to deal in these generalities and sought some more tangible expression of the advantages to be derived from concentration.

. . . the term "unit of destruction" is a quantity that does not admit of exact definition but it is readily seen that it serves as a measure of both the offensive and defensive qualities of a ship. By "units of destruction delivered" by a ship is not meant the units leaving the muzzles of the battery of that ship but the "units delivered" . . . in this way the relative marksmanship of the contending forces may be taken into account.

For example, let there be eight ships originally on each side and let one ship on one side be masked so that $m = 8$ and $n = 7$. Then the eight ships will destroy the seven ships and will have the equivalent of $\sqrt{15}$ (nearly four) intact ships with which to engage the remaining one intact ship . . . it will be seen that after destroying this one intact ship there will remain $\sqrt{14}$. In other words by blanking one ship until the other seven have been destroyed and then destroying this remaining ship, the eight ships have destroyed an exactly equal force and have remaining the equivalent of 3.74 ships, that is, the annihilation of an equal hostile force has cost them [only] about 53% of their force.

. . . if there be twice as many units on one side as there are on the other, each unit of the force having the smaller number of units must be *twice* as strong *offensively and* twice as strong *defensively* as one of the hostile units.

This has a bearing upon the question of large or small ships.

Inasmuch as the displacement of a ship represents the total weights of the materials composing the ship and borne by her, the various materials could be segregated and transformed into separate masses of such material.

Having certain definite quantities of the various materials the question of ship design [is], . . . in the simplest form: "Shall we construct from these materials *one* ship or *two* ships?" . . . if we decide to build *one* ship instead of *two*, this *single* ship must be twice as strong offensively *and twice* as strong *defensively as one* of the two ships.

It seems to me that while it may be possible to make a ship carry twice as many guns as one of half the displacement it is, at least, debatable if she can be made twice as strong defensively. The chances of hitting her certainly are much greater and she certainly is not twice as strong defensively against underwater attack.

It is perhaps worth outlining how Lanchester, or a modern writer, might have derived Chase's basic equation:

Define m, n, D, a_1, a_2, b_1, and b_2 as Chase does on page 380.

The collective capacity of all units on a side to absorb hits and continue fighting is $(a_1 m)$ and $(a_2 n)$ respectively, where m and n are now variables in time. Refer to these values as total remaining *staying power*.

The associated capacity of all units on a side to deliver hits against the enemy is $b_1 m$ and $b_2 n$. This is under the key assumption (acknowledged by Chase) that hitting power is directly proportional to $(a_1 m)$ or $(a_2 n)$.

The coupled differential equations corresponding to Lanchester's form of the equations are therefore:

$$\frac{d(a_1 m)}{dt} = -b_2 n \quad \text{and} \quad \frac{d(a_2 n)}{dt} = -b_1 m$$

Divide the first equation by the second and separate the variables:

$$\frac{d(a_1m)}{d(a_2n)} = \frac{b_2n}{b_1m}$$

$$b_1m \, d(a_1m) = b_2n \, d(a_2n)$$

Integrate both sides over the time it takes, t, to eliminate the smaller force:

$$\frac{b_1}{a_1} \int_0^t (a_1m) d(a_1m) = \frac{b_2}{a_2} \int_0^t (a_2n) d(a_2n)$$

$$\frac{b_1}{a_1} \left[\frac{(a_1m)^2}{2} \right]_0^t = \frac{b_2}{a_2} \left[\frac{(a_2n)^2}{2} \right]_0^t$$

Denote the initial force status with subscript 0, and with subscript t at time t. Since at time t, $a_2n = 0$, we have:

$$\frac{b_1}{a_1} \left[\left(a_1m \right)_0^2 - \left(a_1m \right)_t^2 \right] = \frac{b_2}{a_2} \left(a_2n \right)_0^2$$

The winner's total staying power remaining when the loser is eliminated is:

$$(a_1m_t) = \left[\left(a_1m \right)_0^2 - \frac{b_2a_1}{b_1a_2} \left(a_2n \right)_0^2 \right]^{1/2}$$

If we regard a_1 and a_2 as constants and degrade the number of ships we have:

$$a_1m_t = a_1 \left[m_0^2 - \frac{b_2a_2}{b_1a_1} n_0^2 \right]^{1/2} = a_1S^{1/2}$$

Winner's total staying power lost is:

$$a_1m_0 - a_1m_t = a_1m_0 - a_1S^{1/2}$$

Next we write the ratio of winner's staying power lost to loser's staying power lost (all of it), which is the final form in which Chase expresses his results:

$$\frac{mD_m}{nD_n} = \frac{a_1 m_0 - a_1 S^{1/2}}{a_2 n_0} = \frac{a_1}{a_2}\left(\frac{m_0 - S^{1/2}}{n_0}\right)$$

Lanchester's solution was more parsimonious and elegant than Chase's. Chase undertook a more difficult problem, however. Unlike Lanchester, who assumed that fighting units on both sides were equally survivable, Chase represented the staying power, or "life" as he called it, of a warship with a separate coefficient of survivability. A well-known design problem of his day was the relative value of guns and armor, and the survivability of ships varied sufficiently that Chase felt he must treat it explicitly.

J. V. Chase's original 1902 paper, reprinted in its entirety, follows.

A MATHEMATICAL INVESTIGATION OF THE EFFECT OF SUPERIORITY OF FORCE IN COMBATS UPON THE SEA

The following investigation is based upon the assumption that in a naval combat the unit ships will be subjected to a continuous gradual process of destruction—an ebbing away of their destructive power, which destructive power is assumed always to be proportional to the remaining life of the vessel concerned.

Naturally such an investigation does not include those cases wherein a vessel meets *sudden* destruction and so passes in an instant from being a more or less powerful engine of war to a mere hulk, possessing no destructive power whatsoever. Such *sudden* destruction may be brought about by a successful ramming blow, a successful torpedo shot or by a lucky shell entering the magazine and causing the explosion of its contents. Such disasters may be also caused by collision between friendly vessels or by striking rocks or shoals, should the engagement take place near the coast.

As sudden destruction, caused by collision with friendly vessels or by grounding, should be rare if the vessels be skillfully handled and as the chance of a shell entering the magazine of a properly constructed vessel is very small, it will be noted that there remain only those cases where *sudden* destruction is caused by the ram or the torpedo.

379

The investigation, therefore, applies only to the effect of gunfire.

It is to be remarked, however, that *sudden* destruction arising from any cause whatsoever will have least effect upon the accuracy of the results of this investigation if it take place near the end of the engagement.

It would, therefore, seem logical that the force inferior in gunfire should use the ram or torpedo as early as possible.

Let m ships each having a life of a_1 units and each capable of delivering in a unit of time b_1 units of destruction be pitted against n ships each having a life of a_2 units and each capable of delivering in a unit of time b_2 units of destruction.

Let Dm be the damage received by each m ship.

Let Dn be the damage received by each n ship.

Let x be any instant of time (reckoned from the beginning of the action).

Let y be the destructive power of each m ship at the time x.

Let z be the destructive power of each n ship at the time x.

Then by assumption we have

$$\frac{y}{b_1} = \frac{a_1 - Dm}{a_1} \tag{1}$$

$$\frac{z}{b_2} = \frac{a_2 - Dn}{a_2} \tag{2}$$

or $\quad \dfrac{a_1}{b_1} (b_1 - y) = Dm \tag{3}$

and $\quad \dfrac{a_2}{b_2} (b_2 - z) = Dn \tag{4}$

but $\quad Dm = \dfrac{n}{m} \displaystyle\int_0^x z \, dx \tag{5}$

and $\quad Dn = \dfrac{m}{n} \displaystyle\int_0^x y \, dx \tag{6}$

Therefore $\quad \dfrac{a_1}{b_1} (b_1 - y) = \dfrac{n}{m} \displaystyle\int_0^x z \, dx \tag{7}$

$$\frac{a_2}{b_2} (b_2 - z) = \frac{m}{n} \int_0^x y \, dx \tag{8}$$

380

Therefore $\quad \dfrac{-a_1}{b_1}\, dy = \dfrac{n}{m}\, z\, dx$ (9)

$$\dfrac{-a_2}{b_2}\, dz = \dfrac{m}{n}\, y\, dx \tag{10}$$

$$\dfrac{a_1 b_2}{a_2 b_1}\, \dfrac{dy}{dz} = \dfrac{n^2}{m^2}\, \dfrac{z}{y} \tag{11}$$

$$\dfrac{a_1 b_2}{a_2 b_1}\, y^2 = \dfrac{n^2}{m^2}\, z^2 + C \tag{12}$$

When $\quad y = b_1, \quad z = b_2$ (13)

Therefore $\quad C = (b_2)^2 \left(\dfrac{a_1 b_1}{a_2 b_2} - \dfrac{n^2}{m^2} \right)$ (14)

Which gives $\quad \dfrac{a_1 b_2}{a_2 b_1}\, y^2 = \dfrac{n^2}{m^2}\, z^2 + (b_2)^2 \left(\dfrac{a_1 b_1}{a_2 b_2} - \dfrac{n^2}{m^2} \right)$ (15)

Now if the m ships destroy the n ships, $z = 0$; therefore

$$y^2 = \dfrac{b_1}{a_1} \left(\dfrac{m^2 a_1 b_1 - n^2 a_2 b_2}{m^2} \right) \tag{16}$$

$$y = \pm \dfrac{b_1}{a_1} \dfrac{(m^2 a_1 b_1 - n^2 a_2 b_2)^{1/2}}{m} \tag{17}$$

$$Dm = \dfrac{a_1}{b_1} (b_1 - y) = a_1 \left(1 - \dfrac{y}{b_1} \right) \tag{18}$$

$$Dm = a_1 \left\{ 1 - \dfrac{\left[\dfrac{b_1}{a_1} (m^2 a_1 b_1 - n^2 a_2 b_2) \right]^{1/2}}{b_1 m} \right\} \tag{19}$$

$$Dm = a_1 - \dfrac{\left[\dfrac{a_1}{b_1} (m^2 a_1 b_1 - n^2 a_2 b_2) \right]^{1/2}}{m} \tag{20}$$

$$Dn = a_2 \tag{21}$$

Therefore $\quad \dfrac{mDm}{nDn} = \dfrac{ma_1 - \left[\dfrac{a_1}{b_1} (m^2 a_1 b_1 - n^2 a_2 b_2) \right]^{1/2}}{na_2}$ (22)

$$\frac{mDm}{nDn} = \frac{a_1}{a_2} \left\{ \frac{m - \left(m^2 - \frac{a_2 b_2}{a_1 b_1} n^2\right)^{1/2}}{n} \right\} \qquad (23)$$

Now in order that there shall be equality of force, y and z must vanish together. Therefore from (15) we have

$$\frac{n^2}{m^2} = \frac{a_1 b_1}{a_2 b_2} \qquad (24)$$

$$\frac{n}{m} = \left(\frac{a_1 b_1}{a_2 b_2}\right)^{1/2} \qquad (25)$$

When the opposing ships are similar, $a_1 = a_2$ and $b_1 = b_2$, and (23) and (25) become

$$\frac{mDm}{nDn} = \frac{m - \sqrt{m^2 - n^2}}{n} \qquad (26)$$

$$\frac{n}{m} = 1 \qquad (27)$$

RESULTS

$$\left. \begin{array}{l} \dfrac{mDm}{nDn} = \dfrac{a_1}{a_2} \left[\dfrac{m - \left(m^2 - \dfrac{a_2 b_2}{a_1 b_1} n^2\right)^{1/2}}{n} \right] \\[3em] \dfrac{n}{m} = \left(\dfrac{a_1 b_1}{a_2 b_2}\right)^{1/2} \end{array} \right\} \quad \begin{array}{l} \text{Dissimilar} \\ \text{Ships} \end{array}$$

$$\left. \begin{array}{l} \dfrac{mDm}{nDn} = \dfrac{m - \sqrt{m^2 - n^2}}{n} \\[2em] n = m \end{array} \right\} \quad \begin{array}{l} \text{Similar} \\ \text{Ships} \end{array}$$

INDEX

ABOUT THE EDITOR

Wayne Hughes is co-editor of the Classics of Sea Power series, in which this is the second book. He is author of the Naval Institute Press book *Fleet Tactics: Theory and Practice* and of two prize-winning essays in the U.S. Naval Institute *Proceedings*. He has edited or contributed chapters to four other books and written over twenty articles on naval warfare.

During thirty-one years of active duty his commands included two ships and one major training complex ashore. He served three tours in the Korean and Vietnam war zones. Shore duty included three tours in the Pentagon, one of which was as naval aide and executive assistant to the Under Secretary of the Navy.

Hughes is currently on the faculty of the Naval Postgraduate School, Monterey, where he has held two research chairs, including the Chair of Tactical Analysis. He resides with his wife in Pacific Grove, California.